Mind-Body, Birth®
Your Guide to Fearless Childbirth

Sam Vaive, Ph.D.

ISBN: 979-8-9917635-2-3

Library of Congress Control Number: 2024921676

Published by Bad Ass Books LLC
Cover design by Samantha Vaive
Edited by Derek Vaive

Printed in the United States of America
First Edition: January, 2025

For permissions requests, write to the publisher at:
contact@sound-birthing.com

Mind-Body, Birth® is a registered trademark of Samantha Vaive

For anyone who has ever been robbed of the joy that can be found in their body

Table of Contents

LIST OF ACTIVITIES

Welcome

I overheard a conversation between two women. It was an older woman and a younger woman. The younger woman was saying, "I don't know if I want to have kids. I don't think I do, but everybody says once you hold that baby for the first time, everything changes." The older woman got really quiet and said in a soft tone, "Yeah...that didn't happen for me." The way she said it...

I turned around and said, "I'm sorry to interrupt, but did I hear you say you had a c-section?" She said, "Yes, I had an emergency c-section." Me—with my PhD, research-focused, writing my dissertation mindset—said, "OH! The medications that they give you during a c-section block the oxytocin receptors in your brain, so even though your body is flooding with bonding chemicals, you might not be able to feel it." She stared at me. For a long time.

Then she said, "For twenty years, I've thought something was wrong with me. Why didn't anybody ever tell me?"

My heart broke. All I could say was, "Yeah, there's a lot of stuff they don't tell you."

She didn't have any more kids. She thought there was something fundamentally wrong with her as a mother. But she wasn't broken. And she wasn't a bad mom. She just didn't have all the information.

As I continued my work, I heard so many birth stories. It seemed everyone wanted to tell me their story or the story of someone close to them. Eventually, I realized people needed me to bear witness. The trauma of birth, be it their own or vicarious, needed to be heard. As trauma often does. This troubled me, as I think it would anyone. This glorious, beautiful thing we have literally been doing since the dawn of humans was crushing the people around me. Birth should not be devastating, yet it was. The more I heard, the more I learned it wasn't always the horror story you might expect that stuck out.

Instead, it was the married 20-year-old who was immediately dismissed as some knocked-up teen. She was strong and bold and knew exactly how to understand her body. She told the nurses she needed to walk, and they dismissed her. She told the nurses she wanted a shower, and they fought her. She told the nurses the baby was coming, and they told her not to be ridiculous.

"You haven't labored long enough," they informed her as if her body was supposed to follow some predetermined schedule. When she demanded an exam, those nurses discovered it was, in fact, time for her to push. She had known. It was, after all, her body. And yet she had to fight to be heard. Her childbirth was fast and uneventful. Yet this free, easy birth was still tarnished by the belittling of her experience and how hard she had to demand to be supported in listening to her body.

It was the woman who had an ecstatic birth. She felt she had left her body, traveled to another plane of existence, and learned fundamental truths about the universe. Her birth was likely the pinnacle of what birth can be. And yet, she, too, carried trauma, not because of the birth itself, but because no one understood her experience. She felt completely isolated. It is not uncommon that when people suffer, they want to hear that other people have suffered as well. So, when someone has a traumatic birth—which most people in this country do—they don't know how to respond when someone says their birth was joyous and positively life-changing.

I understand. Trauma doesn't just want to be heard. It wants to be shared. It wants to be soothed through commonality. And when you can't share it, you illuminate that someone didn't have to experience the trauma they did, which frankly feels terrible. To know there was another way, that it could not only have been better but great, yet it wasn't. That hurts. There is grief there. Grief over the loss of something positive. Grief over carrying the trauma. Grief that comes with self-doubt. When a person has an awful experience and someone else doesn't, it's so common to think, "What did I do wrong? What's wrong with me?"

The thing is, it can feel that way even when the experience is great, which is what happened to her. Not only did no one else support her in her experience. She didn't understand what had happened or why it happened to her and no one else. Not understanding—even something so positive—can be quite difficult. It wasn't until about thirty years later, when she was reading a book about birth stories, that she discovered ecstatic childbirth. She learned that other people had had similar experiences. As she told me this story, she said, "Sam, when I discovered that I was not alone, I broke down. I cried and cried." This is what isolation does. It spoils even the most positive experience.

What I have found is an overwhelming sense of loneliness in pregnancy and birth. They say it takes a village to raise a child. But what about to create one and bring it into the world? Sure, you have a doctor. If you are truly lucky, you have a doula and a person who loves you holding your hand. But while you may be sharing your experience with them, that isn't the same as a shared experience. It is not the same as being surrounded by people going through what you are going through. And it isn't the same as information. Information combats isolation.

Without having all the information, we are at the whims of other people's stories and what our minds create. When we don't know that the medications given during cesarean sections can impact bonding, we cannot calmly say, "This is a natural reaction that is common to experience, and it will pass."

Instead, we say, "There is something wrong with me," and we live our lives believing we are broken. You are not broken. *You* are not broken. You are part of a broken system, yes, but you are not broken. You are magnificent, beautiful, wonderful, and doing your very best in a very difficult situation. You are not broken.

And it is a difficult situation. Giving birth in the United States today is dangerous, especially for people of color. I'm not saying that birth was always easy and has suddenly become hard. Overall, maternal mortality rates are improving.[1] But in the United States, they are nowhere near what they are in countries with the best maternal mortality rates.[2] Which means birth is scary.

Prior to the global pandemic of 2020, it was estimated that 10-15% of women in the United States had a fear of childbirth so strong that it impacted their daily functioning.[3] During the pandemic, that number rose to 62%.[4] As I write this, some of the stressors of birth during COVID have dissipated. However, the impact of them is not fully gone. It may never be.

Either way, we learn early on that birth is terrible. That it is the worst pain a person can experience. *Can.* "Can" is an important distinction because I am not going to lie to you. Childbirth *can* be the worst pain a person experiences. It doesn't *have* to be. Which is why I am writing this book.

I don't just want you to have a great experience. I want you not to feel alone when you do. And you know what? If you read this book and you don't have a great experience, I don't want you to feel alone then, either. No matter what your experience is, I do not want isolation to tell you how good or bad it was. You get to decide that. Not a comparison to others.

This book is backed by science and research. I will do my best to give you all the tools you need to take control and birth better. But at the end of the day, you are a totally unique person with your own background, experiences, and beliefs. Research only tells us what we can say on average about the group of people we are looking at based on the information we have at the time. Which is a long-winded way of saying that what the research says might not be true for you. That's okay. It's just information. Information we can use to make the best possible choices for our personal circumstances at that moment.

Circumstances which, by the way, change. That means you get to change too. You can change your mind. Whether that is because you learned something new, or your life shifted. There is no *should* here. I am not going to tell you there is a right way or a wrong way. There is only your way at this particular point in time. When you have all the information and make a decision based on you, your life, and that information, well, *that* is the best way.

We all have desires. We all make plans. Both are great to have. As long as we understand that they won't always come to fruition. That is why I am going to give you all kinds of information. I encourage you to take it all in, even if it doesn't fit with what you want.

We cannot know what is going to happen. Information is the best way we can prepare ourselves to weather unpredictability. That being said, if there are decisions that you have already made, feel free to skip sections that don't apply to you. For example, if you know 100% you are going to formula feed, don't read the sections on BBC feeding. I'm sure you have better things to do with your time.

This book is here to support you. To help you have your best birth. Not to tell you how you should be. There is too much pressure and too much judgment as it is. So, use this book however it most benefits you. If you want to do every activity as you go and then do them again when you get to the end, great! If you want to use this book as a coaster to hold your morning latte, then I am happy to help.

Let's talk a little bit more about this book and its format before we jump into *The Big Lie*. I recommend you read this book as early in pregnancy as possible. It will give you more time to process and integrate the information. But if you are giving birth this week, I still encourage you to read this book. Each section finishes with a Support Report. These are bullet points that you can share with the people in your life who will be helping you through pregnancy, birth, and beyond. If you are short on time, I recommend you read through each Support Report first and use that to guide you to the parts of this book that will be most beneficial for you.

As you move through this book there will be various activities and journaling prompts. You can head to my website, mindbodybirthbook.com, to get printouts of the activity sheets. Or you can make your own. I encourage you to do the activities as you move through the book, but if you prefer to read first, then you do you.

These activities and prompts are important as they will help integrate the information in this book and personalize it, so you are getting what is right for you. Not the generic stuff that is for everyone. When you get to the end of the book, you will use all the work you've done to create your birth toolkit. Your birth toolkit is a hard copy document that helps you organize all the information you've learned so you can have your best birth. You will be able to reference your birth toolkit, so you don't have to think or remember when you've got other stuff going on, like birthing a human. I have put a lot into creating these activities. I hope you find them not only valuable but also fun.

I also want to take a moment to talk about language. It is very important to me that everyone feels welcome and included in Mind-Body, Birth. For this reason, I may use some language that is confusing. You've already seen it with my mention of BBC feeding. This stands for Breast/Body/Chest Feeding. I started using the term because it was more inclusive and because some terms do not make people feel good. I have had people ask me why I say body, or why this, or why that. I used to work really hard to try to make people understand. I don't do that anymore. If someone tells me something makes them uncomfortable, it's not my place to question it. I respect it. So, at this point, BBC is the best term I have come up with. But I reserve the right to use a different term in the future if and when I learn more. If this term or any other term doesn't work for you, I encourage you to reach out to me so that I can work to be better.

Additionally, along those lines, I understand that not everyone has a spouse or a partner. Not everyone giving birth identifies as female. Not everyone giving birth plans to be a parent. So, I do my best to stay away from terms that assume any of these. I will frequently use the acronym AFAB—which means assigned female at birth. I know that it can sometimes make the writing a little clunky. But the path to inclusion and equity is often bumpy. Until the assumptions of gender and nuclear families are a thing of the past, we all have to get a little creative. I hope you bear with me.

And finally, I want to reiterate my disclaimer about research. Research, while extremely valuable, is not always inclusive. Unfortunately, we can't make assumptions about any population the research doesn't specifically look at. For example, if I conducted a study on Asian elephants at the San Diego Zoo and their preferred treats, I could not use the results of that study to draw conclusions about African elephants in the wild. Are there likely similarities? Maybe. But we can't make that assumption.

The same is true for populations of people. And unfortunately, the research tends to exclude trans individuals and people of color, as well as people below a certain socioeconomic level. So, the conclusions they are drawing, aren't really about everyone. They are about specific populations.

This also means, that if the research says "women," I can't say pregnant people because they looked specifically at women. It would be incorrect for me to assume the results encompass people other than women. While inclusive language is extremely important to me, I need to be consistent with the research. If I am using gendered terms, it is because I am referring to the research, as all the research that is available on this topic is gendered at the time of this writing.

The research has a long way to go. After all, we still conduct most clinical trials on men, and we didn't use menstrual blood to test menstrual product absorbency until 2023.[5] But even if it was somehow perfect, it still wouldn't be true for everyone all the time. Whether it is something I cite or something I say, I encourage you to be skeptical. If it doesn't sound right for you, it may not be right for you. You are the only person living in your body. Which means you have the best ability to understand and know what your body needs. Trust your gut first. It is, after all, full of neurons and considered to be your second brain.[6]

Support Report

- C-section medications can affect bonding.

- Pregnancy and birth can be isolating.

- 10-15% of women felt fear of childbirth impacted their daily lives. That number rose to 62% during the pandemic of 2020.

- Research shows us what is mostly true for specific populations and is not always true for individuals. Research tends to exclude people of color, the trans community, and people with a low socioeconomic status.

- This book works to use inclusive language, which may be new to you.
- The book contains journaling prompts and activities to help you build your birth toolkit.

Journaling Prompts

- What led you to read this book? How have you been feeling about giving birth? What are your hopes? What are your fears around birth?

Before Birth

Fear

The summer of 2024, Michigan got hit by the tail of Hurricane Beryl. The lightning was unlike anything I'd ever experienced, and I lived on the coast of North Carolina during Hurricane Irene. It felt like being at an EDM show with the near-constant flashing of light. It had been a rough summer for my two rescue dogs. One utterly petrified of fireworks had struggled to go outside after 5 pm for more than two weeks. The other was terrified of storms, despite her name being Rain.

We'd only had Rain for a year. She had lived a tragic life before being picked up by animal control, then sent to foster care, then finally to her home with us. The chaotic nature of her existence had made housebreaking quite difficult. Whenever there were changes to her schedule or periods of stress, she would regress. It was extremely frustrating. When the storm woke her at 3 am, and she couldn't be coaxed back to sleep, I knew it was going to be an issue. So, shaking house be damned, I dragged myself out of bed and took her downstairs.

She was eager until I opened the door. Her little face was so scared as she curled her tail between her legs and hunched away. That wasn't what surprised me though. I was expecting that. What surprised me was the way my own body recoiled at the sound, light, pressure, heat, and feel of the gumball-sized raindrops. I hadn't felt afraid before I opened the door. Tired. Irritated. Slightly awe-struck. But not afraid. Yet, at the prospect of going outside in what was clearly dangerous weather, my body reacted. My first thought was, "Fear is so annoying!" My second thought was, "Our bodies are unbelievably cool."

We are such intellectual beings. We distance ourselves from animals by focusing on our mental acuity. We think—because we think—that we can control not only the world around us but also what's happening inside of us. And yes, to some degree, you can. That is more or less the purpose of this book. To teach you to hack your body systems to change your experience of childbirth. But the only reason you need to do that in the first place is because your body has its own intelligence. Intelligence that may seem misguided and misplaced in a world of gene splicing and self-driving cars.

When that door to the storm opened, my PhD didn't matter. All the books I've read and hours I've spent writing papers didn't matter. Whether or not I could code didn't matter. My body reacted just the same as my dog's body. Fear is fascinating because—like pain—it protects us. You will find book after book and podcast after podcast on conquering your fears. You probably picked up this book because it offered you a path to fearless birth. But fear isn't something to be conquered any more than sexual yearning or the desire to eat. It is a part of being alive. A part that has been honed over millennia to keep us safe.

So yes, in this book, we are going to talk about putting a stop to fear and not letting it control you, through understanding the how's and whys of both the modern and ancient acts of giving birth. Still, I would be remiss if I didn't start this book in awe of fear. Fear protects. Fear motivates. Fear inspires. Fear is a profound piece of the human experience even if it is something that ties us to the "less human" parts of ourselves.

In this book, you will hear me say, "Nothing is ever always good 100% of the time. Nothing is ever always bad 100% of the time." Yes, of course, there are very specific instances where that isn't true. We could fight about it. Or we could acknowledge that nothing is ever always good 100% of the time, including the statement that nothing is ever always good 100% of the time. Though, the statement is helpful for conveying an idea. We will journey through this book towards fearless birth, but you need to know that fear is not the enemy.

To make fear the enemy is to make your body the enemy. Your body is not the enemy. Not when it is afraid. Not when it wants chocolate cake. Or a nap. Or a good schtup. Fear isn't inherently bad. Not only does it protect us, it also makes life more exciting. Horror movies, jump scares, roller coasters. Even reaching over to touch someone's hand for the first time. Applying for a new job. Trying a cuisine you've never sampled before. Anticipation and excitement are tied to fear.

Fear can also make us better. Imagine that you genuinely had no fear of what happens to this baby. You might not try very hard. You might make sloppy or dangerous choices. Now, imagine that you're consumed with fear. You might make overprotective, stunting choices that instill a sense of fear in others. Neither is good. Just like no chocolate ever is bad. Only chocolate always, is also bad.

It's about finding the place where fear—like all other systems and aspects of the body—can be appreciated and respected. Be in awe always. Of your body. Of pregnancy. Of life. Of chocolate. Getting to fearless birth is not about controlling the body or disconnecting from the body. It is about understanding the body and its relationship with the mind. It is about embracing the body in all of its slimy, sticky, sexy, painful, glorious, beautiful ways of being.

We get, we *get*, this opportunity to exist on earth in a human body with an overwhelming capacity to feel. Good, bad, painful, pleasurable, sad, ecstatic, chocolate, fluffy kitties with sharp claws, turbulent airplanes to exotic locations, muddy boots, and hot showers. We get all of it. As we move through this book, I encourage you to lean in and not away. Parts of this book are hard. Terrible even. By going down and into your experience, you will learn so much more than if you turn away. Now, to end this section with a combined thought from Emily Nagoski and Twenty One Pilots—which is something I can do because the human mind is incredible— "there's no 'above, 'or 'under, 'or 'around 'it"[1] we can only move through fear and come out the other side.[7,8]

---

[1]I know that Tyler is talking about death here. But what is death if not the epitome of human fear? To say we can't get around death is to say we can't get around fear. We must meet both death and fear. Avoiding them will only lead to them controlling us. After all, "Death isn't cruel, merely, terribly, terribly, good at his job." [Pratchett, T. (1988). *Sourcery*. Corgi Books. (p. 78).]

The Big Lie

When I was 12, I really liked the show, *Dharma and Greg*. If you aren't familiar with the show, it was about a very hippy-flowery sort of woman and a very wealthy old money lawyer falling in love. The show explored how their different lifestyles were at odds and how they came together to be their authentic selves even when they struggled to understand each other.

At one point in the series, there is a pregnant woman who goes into labor in their living room. The running joke throughout the episode is people from Greg's family keep saying, "We have to get her to the hospital." And people from Dharma's family respond with, "Why? She's not sick." In the end, the woman has a healthy baby in the bathtub.

This blew my mind. Do you remember when you were a little kid, and you realized something new? The doors are blown off, and suddenly, the world seems bigger. Like when you learn that 4 out of 5 dentists aren't really recommending a specific toothpaste. It's just advertising. People could birth a baby outside of a hospital. And not because their cab got stuck in New York City traffic. Mind. Blown.

Now, here I am, 20-some-odd years later, educating pregnant people on medicalized birth and the choices they get to make. Would I be here today without that episode? Maybe? Probably? I honestly don't know. But I can tell you I come back to the memory over and over in my life. I've only seen the episode once. It isn't a show I have binged obsessively throughout my life like *New Girl*, *Parks and Rec*, or *Community*. I saw it once. Yet, I can picture it so clearly in my mind.

I learned something new that fundamentally changed my perception of reality. All because of something I saw on television. One time. The media can have a primal impact on us. It can change our views and our understanding. With that in mind, I'd like you to take a moment and picture the way you've seen childbirth depicted—on television or in films—or described by others.

Okay. What did it look like? Sound like? When I present on Mind-Body, Birth, I ask the audience if it looks happy? Fun? Enjoyable? I get laughter, heads shaking, and usually people shouting, "No!" When I ask what they did picture, I get: *screaming*. Screaming and pain. Painful screaming. Fear. Does this sound familiar? How many times have you seen something like the scene I described from *Dharma and Greg*? And how many times have you seen someone giving birth while screaming?

So, without any more delay, I want to let you in on a secret. I call it *The Big Lie*. If you don't read any other part of this book, read this. This information can change your birth experience, your outcomes, and the outcomes for the baby. This, right here, is the key to everything. Ready to change the course of your birth?

Okay. Here's the truth about *The Big Lie*. Childbirth does not have to be awful. It does not have to be brutally painful. It does not have to be something you just get through to get to the good part. Childbirth can *be* the good part.

Have I lost you already? Stick with me. I will explain why that's true and why it hasn't been true in the stories you've heard or the experiences you've had. But I need you to know right now before we go any further that: **the inherent suffering of childbirth is a lie.**

We have a general tendency to tell women and people assigned female at birth that their pain isn't real or that their pain doesn't matter. This is even more true for people of color. And frankly, it's bullshit. Pain is real. Pain is disruptive. And pain is not something you should just accept and grit through in any part of your life.

Honestly, I understand the jump to medicated birth, no questions asked. Estrogen-based body pain is ignored all the time, so someone straight up offering to dull that pain seems like an incredible thing. There are definitely positives to it. But it is a bigger story than that, which we will get into so that you can make the best decision for you.

The thing is, offering pain medication is not the same as acknowledging that childbirth doesn't have to be painful in the first place. It doesn't. To some degree, I find the pushing of pain medications infantilizing and disempowering. Not the medications themselves but the idea that, as a society, we can dismiss estrogen-based body pain all the time, then take birth—something humans have been doing since the dawn of time—and imply that pregnant people are too weak to do it. When you think about it like that, it's all a bit ludicrous.

Which brings me back to **it shouldn't be that painful in the first place.** So, if you are ready to understand what makes childbirth painful and how to prevent your birth from being awful, let's get into the mind-body connection.

The Mind-Body Connection

Okay, to be honest, I said *mind-body connection* because I didn't want to scare you away with *biopsychosocial framework*. Don't be scared off. A framework is just the lens researchers use to focus their research, based on other research that exists. It is the perspective that guides the work. Mine is the biopsychosocial framework. This is the idea that there are three factors that impact health and well-being.[9] Biological, what is physically happening in the body. Psychological, what is happening in the mind. Social, what is happening around the person. All of these factors interact with each other to create a person's experience. This is considered a more holistic view of a person as opposed to just looking at their biology.

Let's look at an example. A person has chest pain, shortness of breath, and changes in their heart's rhythm. They go to the hospital with what appears to be a heart attack. A doctor will check their biological factors like genetics, high blood pressure, and history of smoking. But someone working from a biopsychosocial approach will also look at psychological factors like chronic stress, depression, and anxiety. And they will look at social factors like socioeconomic status—which may limit access to healthcare or nutritious food—and support systems. Socioeconomic status can also contribute to stress, which is the social and the psychological interacting.

Exploring social factors, the doctor might discover that the person recently lost their partner of 30 years. Knowing that *Broken Heart Syndrome* can lead to cardiomyopathy, the doctor may discover that this was not a heart attack but another condition that looks like a heart attack. The loss of a partner—social—can lead to extreme stress—psychological—which can cause cardiomyopathy—biological—a condition that looks very much like a heart attack and requires medical treatment.[10]

It benefits us to look at health from the biopsychosocial perspective because people are whole beings with lots of stuff going on that can impact health, not just sacks of blood and bones. We might miss important information if we don't. As individuals, it benefits us to look at our experiences from the biopsychosocial perspective because science shows us that the mind and the body are connected. If what is happening psychologically can impact what is happening biologically, there is a relationship between the mind and body that we cannot ignore.

It might be easiest to accept that the biological can impact the psychological. One common way to think about this is PMS. It is a physical process that occurs in the body—biological. It can impact mood—psychological. Although, this is not my favorite example. PMS, while very real, can be used to make estrogen-based bodies into a joke. How many deeming, condescending or dismissive jokes have you heard about PMS? The answer is too many. It also normalizes pain and suffering in estrogen-based bodies. Still, it is an example most people understand. Most people have experienced it or know someone who has.

Another example is clinical depression. The serotonin imbalance in the brain is biological, but symptoms can be psychological, such as extreme sadness. When we agree that biological factors can impact psychological factors, it can be easier to accept that the reverse is true. The mind can impact the functioning of the body. This is very powerful because the mind doesn't just impact the body in negative ways. The mind can impact the body in positive ways, improving health, wellness, and childbirth outcomes.

Now that we've explored the relationship between the mind, the body, and the society that surrounds them, let's look at how this connection impacts childbirth. I asked you to picture childbirth at the beginning of this section. If you're like the majority of people I interact with, you pictured someone screaming. This depiction of someone screaming while giving birth is so common that it actually has a name. It's called *The Screaming Birth* trope. You might be thinking, "Okay, so what's the big deal?" Here's the thing. Seeing screaming birth depicted over and over can actually lead you to have a screaming birth experience yourself.

Research shows that expectations of childbirth are based on what is learned.[11] It makes sense. How else can we have expectations? We are social learners. We needed to be. Back when we were living in small groups, we depended on each other for survival. If someone ate poisonous berries and got very ill, it was in your best interest to believe them. If you didn't, you would eat the berries and become sick or possibly die. Evolution was kind to those who learned to trust the experiences of others like their life depended on it. Back then, it did.

There are many ways our brains have not learned to adapt to the times. This is one of them. We no longer need to take to heart everyone else's experience. Especially because many of the experiences we see aren't real, making the information they provide meaningless. However, our very evolutionarily old brains aren't thinking about that. They are thinking, "survive or die," and the best way to do that is to believe what you see.

Screaming birth, be it on television, witnessed, or heard secondhand, signals to your brain that screaming is the correct reaction to birth. Screaming can be a fun thing. We've seen the fan footage from a Taylor Swift concert. We all scream for ice cream. Screaming can be good. But the term *Screaming Birth* trope doesn't fully encompass the negativity that is displayed in those scenes. It isn't just screaming. It's screaming in pain.

The media complicates birth expectations by portraying inaccurate, highly medicalized, and dramatic births.[12] These scenes are designed for entertainment, leading to something going wrong to create drama, or something going awry to create humor. Like in *Friends* when Rachel and Ross bump heads in the delivery room and Ross falls to the floor. Entertainment is not designed to depict reality. It's designed to be entertaining. Reality tends to be boring.

Imagine you spent your whole life watching movies about murders that occurred at night in corn mazes. What do you think would happen if someone left you in a corn maze at night? You'd probably be terrified. Your heart would start racing. You'd begin to panic. Deep within you, your body would start responding to a threat. One that likely does not exist. But for you—in that moment—the fear is as real as anything.

Now imagine you spent your whole life watching movies about wonderful things that happen in corn mazes. Family fun. Proposals. Magic pumpkins that grant wishes. Pie eating contests. How do you think your body would respond to being left in a corn maze? Quite differently than in the other scenario. Your heart might race but with excitement, not fear. The same is true for childbirth. Our expectations influence our experience. Which means you get to be in control.

There is a story commonly told to help people understand concepts in the Yoga Sutras. The story goes like this: a person goes outside at night and sees a large snake in the grass. They are overcome with fear. Their body—reacting to the looming threat—causes them to run away. They come back the next morning, only to discover it was not a snake at all but a large coil of rope.

We can all remember a time we reacted with bad information or only part of the information, and it concretely affected us, even though what caused the reaction was not real. Childbirth is no different. You've been given partial information and bad information. But now you are getting more information, different information. You get to decide if childbirth is the worst thing a person can experience or a life-affirming magical experience. Or something else entirely.

There is a reason this sort of "hippy-dippy" idea of people giving birth in ponds and having a transcendent experience exists. It isn't that they are different than other people giving birth. It is the belief that birth will be positive that makes it positive. I know that might feel hard to believe, but the science supports it.

When we are afraid, pain feels worse. Fundamentally, fear is a belief. It is the belief that something harmful is happening or going to happen. You can change that belief. You can outgrow it. In the same way that as a child, you may have needed to check under the bed for monsters but stopped when you got older.

Ultimately, there is no universal experience of pain, and the same is true for childbirth. Childbirth is described as "an individual life event, incorporating interrelated subjective psychological and physiological processes, which in turn are influenced by social, environmental, organizational and policy contexts."[13] How you experience childbirth is influenced by so many factors. You can't change your age, or your genetics. But you can change your frame of mind and in doing so, change your experience.

I'm guessing me telling you to just believe probably feels a lot like telling you to wish on a star. And I'm guessing your life is not a Disney movie, so you might be feeling frustrated with that advice. Don't worry. We are going to talk about ways to make your childbirth experience better. Real ways that are data-driven and backed by research. But before we get into that, it is important that you understand the weight that beliefs carry.

Your thoughts really do impact the way your body functions. If you start to visualize something stressful. Really stressful. The thing that stresses you out the most. Physical changes will occur in your body. You might feel heart palpitations or changes to your breathing. You may notice your muscles clenching. All because of your thoughts.

So, for the rest of this book, the rest of your pregnancy, and the rest of your life, I want you to remember that your thoughts have power. They have the power to affect you physiologically, which means you may interact with the world differently. You may be more open or closed to opportunities. You may be short with another person because your heart rate is now increased. That person may then become stressed out and snap at another person. We could speculate on all the ways in which your thoughts have the power to shape the world around you. But most importantly, they shape you. And you get to control them—for better or worse.

Our belief that childbirth is extremely painful creates a self-fulfilling prophecy. The fear-pain cycle takes over and creates extremely painful childbirth. Now you know. We snap our fingers, and your birth is easy peasy, right? Unfortunately, no. I wish it were. Maybe, someday, with your help, it will be that easy. But we aren't there yet.

Cortisol

You might be thinking, "Okay, but what about all of the people I know who've had horrible screaming births?" That's a great question. It is also the critical link here. To understand this, we need to talk about cortisol and the fear-pain cycle.

Cortisol is commonly referred to as the stress hormone. Cortisol tends to increase as stress levels increase, and it plays an important role in the body's stress response. Before what I am about to say turns cortisol into enemy number one, you need to know that cortisol *is* important. Cortisol does many good, vital things. Cortisol is needed for birth and to lactate. Cortisol can combat loneliness. Cortisol is not the enemy. Like ice cream or kale, or anything else, *too much* is the enemy.

The right amount of cortisol is necessary. Too much cortisol causes problems. The biggest problem? Cortisol makes pain feel more painful. Let's imagine we can measure pain as a consistent unit. You have one gumball's worth of pain and one grain of rice's worth of cortisol. Your pain would be a 3 on a scale of 10. Now you have that same gumball of pain, but you have a golf ball's worth of cortisol. Your pain would be a 6 on a scale of 10. If your cortisol is the size of a watermelon? Your pain is off the chart.
Of course, all of this is arbitrary. These aren't real units of measurement. My point is that the same amount of pain feels like more pain as cortisol increases.

Cortisol increases with fear. Imagine you didn't pick up this book, and no one ever told you about *The Big Lie*. You have witnessed only displays of painful, screaming birth— sometimes where things go horribly wrong (drama!). As your birth starts, you become afraid. Why wouldn't you? You've only seen these scary depictions of birth, and your brain believes you have to trust them as fact if you want to survive.

Your fear starts increasing. Now, the pain starts. You think, "Everyone and everything was right. This is painful!" Those thoughts cause more fear, which causes more cortisol. Because your cortisol increases, so does your experience of pain. Now you think, "This is getting worse. How much worse will it get?" More fear. Then more cortisol. More pain and around and around in a loop you go. Until you create what you were afraid of, horrifically painful childbirth.

The fear of pain makes pain worse.

In this way, childbirth pain becomes a self-fulfilling prophecy. A person thinks it will be terrible, so it becomes terrible. Then they tell other people how terrible it was, and they have terrible births because fear gets the better of them. That doesn't have to be your story. We are stopping the cycle. You now know why this is happening. This book will help you prevent fear from becoming the driver in your birth room.

Bears

I mentioned that parts of your brain are very old and not designed for today's way of life. In order to understand our brains, let's talk about bears. Think back to our berry scenario. Imagine that someone you know gets sick from eating bad berries. You, however, are evolutionarily very smart, so you don't eat the berries. Instead, you go out looking for a new patch of berries. While you are out exploring, you come across a bear. The sight of the bear activates the sympathetic nervous system. We often call this reaction the *fight or flight* response. Really, it is the fight, flight, freeze, fawn, or "finding yourself in a romantic situation" response. *I'm going to refer to this as the F's response.

Your brain—at lightning speed—takes in all of the available information and makes a decision. You fight the bear, flee the bear, or freeze and hope the bear doesn't see you. You are evolutionarily smart, so your brain picks from one of those three. Your brain does not try to seduce the bear. It saves that particular f for non-bear scenarios.

---

*Fawn is a newer addition to the F's system. It has gained a lot of focus in trauma work to explain why someone might be appeasing or submissive rather than fighting back or fleeing. Fawning is seen as a protective strategy to avoid triggering aggression. Evolutionarily speaking, the idea is the behavior is rooted in dominance/submissiveness systems for survival [Öhman, A. (1986). Face the beast and fear the face: animal and social fears as prototypes for evolutionary analyses of emotion. *Psychophysiology, 23*, 123-145.] Imagine a young male gorilla that comes across the silverback—the leader of the group. If the silverback determines the young male is a threat the silverback may attack. Since the young gorilla knows it cannot win that fight, it is in his best interest to act submissive—or fawn—to prevent conflict.

You fight, flee, or freeze, and one of two things happens. You survive the bear, or you don't. Either way, the scenario ends. Full stop. Over. It might take until you are safely back with your community or even until your community has put together a hunting party and killed the bear, but the fear of the bear goes away. When this happens, the sympathetic nervous system shuts off and the parasympathetic nervous system turns on.

The parasympathetic nervous system is usually referred to as the *rest and digest* system. When the sympathetic nervous system is done *doing the thing*, the parasympathetic system comes in and *recovers from the thing*. It returns you to a state of normalcy and allows the body to repair. This is how the system is designed. Scary situation—the brain adapts, changing the standard function of the body into survival function. Scary situation ends—the brain reverts and goes back to standard functioning. Perfect.

Here's the problem. Today, most things that give us fear or anxiety don't really end. Or when they do, something else is waiting in the wings to take over. Passed that test you were terrified of failing? Great! Now there's another one. Nervous about your performance review? There's another one is 6 months. Phone, email, social media, the 24-hour news cycle. Our brains never get a break. Not really. Unless we actively seek one out. Meditating, painting, hiking. Whatever it may be. We need to break away from sympathetic activation. Otherwise, it dominates a system designed for balance.

You go about your life hearing terrible stories about birth. Stories that scare you. Your brain doesn't know those stories aren't actual bears. Your brain is supposed to believe the stories you hear to keep you safe—just like with the poisonous berries. Then you walk into your birthing room, and your body does what it is designed to do when there is a big scary threat. It responds as if there is a real live bear in there. A hungry one. Which brings up another problem.

You can't fight, flee, or freeze childbirth. You just can't. So, you kind of have to say, fuck it. And face it head-on. And you can do that! Together, we are going to face your birth head-on. We are going to say "no more" to *The Big Lie* and stop the fear-pain cycle so you can have an awesome birth.

Not Always Bad

We talked about how cortisol is not always bad. Sometimes, it is very important. This is true for so many things. In general, I like to say nothing is always good 100% of the time always and nothing is always bad 100% of the time always. Of course, there will be things that don't fit that. But generally speaking, I think it is a good rule. Especially, when we look at something like birth and parenting.

People have very strong opinions on what you absolutely should and should not do. Things are rarely ever that simple. There are very real reasons not to have a cesarean section, and there are very real reasons to have one. We can say that all of the data says formula pales in comparison to human milk, but if you've had a radical mastectomy due to breast cancer and you don't live somewhere where donor milk is available, people telling you formula isn't as good for your baby is wildly unhelpful. We cannot ever fully understand what it is like to be in someone else's position. Most often times people are doing the best they can. So, something that may seem bad might actually be really good in their situation. Just because we can't understand it, or it isn't a choice we would make, doesn't mean it's a bad choice.

I said that I have found an overwhelming sense of loneliness in pregnancy and birth. This intense sort of tribalism around how someone *should* birth and parent is a major contributor to this loneliness. People need to feel supported by people who make different choices than they do. It is a different kind of support than being supported by people who believe exactly what you believe. That support is easy.

We need to support each other even when it is hard. Or else we all become siloed into factions in a culture war. It is completely okay to have beliefs and preferences. It's even okay to not be open to changing them. The problem is when we decide that what's best for us is best for everyone without respect for their circumstances or their autonomy as people.

The sympathetic nervous system is another example of "not always bad." In fact, it has a pretty incredible impact on birth. Sympathetic nervous system activation during birth strengthens the muscles and boosts energy. There is an increase in the amount of oxygen supplied to the body, which reduces stress and the experience of pain. The mind becomes more focused and alert.

Additionally, adrenaline is released, which does numerous things to help the baby breathe after birth. It helps to clear fluid from the baby's lungs. It stimulates the production of surfactant, which reduces and ensures the baby's lungs do not collapse and are capable of filling with air. It strengthens the baby's respiratory muscles and increases blood flow to vital organs, including the lungs.

There's one more thing the sympathetic nervous system does during birth. It triggers the release of endorphins and anandamide. These are the feel-good pain-relieving chemicals. They are naturally occurring in the body and work the same way as opioids and cannabis. Your body makes these to help ensure childbirth isn't awful.

The sympathetic nervous system is not bad for birth. Just like cortisol, it is only bad when it takes over everything else. The sympathetic and parasympathetic nervous systems need to work in harmony during birth for the body to do what it is designed to do. When fear takes over, the sympathetic nervous system dominates, cortisol increases, and pain becomes the defining experience. But we can activate the sympathetic nervous system without cortisol and pain taking over.

Think of a runner's high. If you run or know anyone who loves to talk about running, you are probably familiar with this concept. Runner's high refers to the intense feel-good experience that happens while running. When someone runs a good distance, or for a length of time, the sympathetic nervous system activates, releasing endorphins and anandamide and reducing stress. This might seem counterintuitive. We are activating the "BEAR!" response and doing one of the things the brain wants us to do when there is a real bear—fleeing. Yet, pain is reduced.

That's because it is not sympathetic nervous system activation in and of itself that is the problem. It's too much cortisol and the length of the experience. When people run for fun, they know they aren't actually fleeing a bear. They are in control of the situation. They aren't afraid, so they can run for a long time without cortisol making their body feel more painful.

It may help to remember that while childbirth is a time-contained event, meaning it has a start point and an endpoint, it isn't a short experience. Unlike running from a bear or cutting your hand, which has a relatively brief and immediate sympathetic nervous system response, birth is considered chronic stress. Birth lasts long enough that cortisol levels have time to build up in the body. This is what leads to the increased perception of pain. Add to this that birth stress doesn't start the moment a person starts birthing—it starts days if not months before—creating an opportunity for cortisol to already be building up before the first contraction.

Low-stress pregnancies are important for many reasons, but this is a big one. Stress prior to birth keeps the body suspended in the F's system. When stuck in the F's system, there isn't a good opportunity for the body to rest and repair or clear all of that extra cortisol out of the system. Of course, all of this is easier said than done. We live in a highly stressful time when it can be difficult to break away from the round-the-clock pressures of just being alive.

I told you childbirth can be wonderful, joyful, and even feel good. Did you believe me? Like really? But like, do you really in your bones, believe me? Probably not. Not because you don't think I'm awesome and smart, and trustworthy, and a great source of wisdom. But because it's a foreign idea. An idea that is rare.

It is odd that the idea is rare because people have been giving birth since…well, since the dawn of people. They do it a lot. As I was doing my research, I was so frustrated that we fear something that has been happening for so long. I wanted something else to compare it to, to try to understand why we are here. I turned to something else we have been doing pretty much since the dawn of people: hunting.

Both childbirth and hunting used to be required for survival. Hunting no longer is, though childbirth technically still is. Rates of both, interestingly, are declining.[14] Both have evolved with technology. Some people choose the traditional way, and some people choose the modern way. In hunting, this would be bow and arrow hunting versus automatic weapons hunting. In childbirth, this might be a "natural" home birth versus a scheduled cesarean section. Both used to be extremely life-threatening. Both are depicted in media. Here's where I noticed a difference.

In media, modern-day hunting is often depicted as a fun activity. Today, hunting is primarily for fun. Imagine for a second that childbirth was just for fun. It wasn't about having a baby. It was just something people chose to do for the fun of it. It's a pretty ludicrous thought, right? Why would someone go through the ordeal of birth for fun? Honestly, why would someone go through the ordeal of hunting for fun? If you are a hunter, I'm sure you have a great answer! And you probably know other people who have great answers or who feel the same way you do.

The problem is that we don't have a great answer for why someone would go through the ordeal of childbirth for the fun of it. Though there are answers out there. People have transcendent experiences during birth. Transformative experiences. Orgasmic experiences (we will talk about this later, and even when we do, I agree there are easier ways to orgasm than by giving birth). There is something powerful and validating, even reparative, about giving birth. If you don't believe me, ask someone who really really wants to give birth and is unable to. There are good answers as to why someone would give birth for fun. We don't talk about them, though. And we certainly don't see them depicted in the media.

No matter what kind of birth you want or will have, I encourage you to find someone on Instagram (or whatever social) who posts videos of home births and water births. Typically, doulas and midwives post them. I follow a few and repost good ones if you want to follow me. Watch some of these videos. Let the expression on these people's faces sink in. It will change something for you. I can tell you birth can be wonderful and without grueling pain. But I am battling every depiction of screaming birth you've ever seen. And it isn't a fair fight. Here's why...

Negativity Bias

Negativity bias is the concept that our brains prioritize negative information. This goes back to that evolutionarily old part of the brain—the part of the brain we share with other animals. The saying goes, "When a rabbit remembers where the carrot is, it gets to eat. When a rabbit remembers where the snare is, it gets to live."[15] It's nice to remember good things. It's vital to remember bad things. Over time, the brains that hyper-focused on the negative survived.

These are the brains that occupy our minds today. Ones that are primed to remember and focus on the negative. Have you ever had a performance review where your supervisor said five positive things and one negative thing, but all you could think about was the negative thing? Or have you ever scrolled through the comments on your post and found yourself obsessing over the one negative comment, no matter how many positive ones there were? That's negativity bias in action. Our minds think they are protecting us when really, they are dooming us to sleepless nights and anxiety. I wasn't kidding when I said our brains are not designed for the world we currently live in.

Out of negativity bias comes the positivity ratio—the idea that we need to hear something positive more frequently than something negative for it to have an impact. There is debate over how many times you need to hear the positive thing to counteract the negative thing. I frequently see three. I was taught eight. I imagine it is different for every person. For example, if someone says, "You look ugly." You might need to hear, "You look beautiful, you look beautiful, you look beautiful, you look beautiful, you look beautiful, you look beautiful, you look beautiful, you look beautiful," just for your brain to stop focusing on the negative comment.

Let's put it all together. You have been inundated with negative birth stories and depictions. You haven't been surrounded by good answers to why someone would give birth for fun. Your brain is primed to cling to the negative over the positive. So, I can tell you about *The Big Lie*, but it won't magically change everything. What it does do is open the door for change. Not just for you, but for everyone.

I said that with your help, someday joyful birth will be as easy as snapping our fingers. When you have a great birth, and you tell other people about your great birth, you are changing our collective narrative. You are fighting back against the negative birth stronghold in our society. There will be a tipping point when joyful birth overtakes screaming birth. Together, over time, we can make fearless birth the dominant idea. Stopping *The Big Lie* from taking root in your birth not only helps you but also helps change the world for every birth that comes after yours.

Since we aren't there yet, we still have to actively work against negativity bias and *The Big Lie*. We are going to talk about ways to hack your brain so you can activate the parasympathetic nervous system and take advantage of all the wonderful chemicals your brain can produce. But…there is still *a lot* to talk about before we get there.

For right now, I want you to remind yourself every time you hear something negative about birth, every time you remember something negative about a previous birth, or just every hour of every day until you've finished giving birth: *That story is not you, not this baby, not this birth.*
Not you, not this baby, not this birth.
Not you, not this baby, not this birth.

Support Report

- *The Big Lie* is that childbirth has to be terrible, but it isn't true. Your pain is real, but that doesn't mean childbirth has to be painful.

- The biopsychosocial framework is the idea that there are three factors that impact health and well-being. Biological, what is physically happening in the body. Psychological, what is happening in the mind. Social, what is happening around the person. All three interact to create a person's experience.

- Seeing birth portrayed as terrible changes our perceptions and expectations.

- Cortisol is commonly called the stress hormone. Cortisol is not always bad. Too much cortisol for too long makes pain feel more painful.

- Childbirth pain becomes a self-fulfilling prophecy because fear of childbirth increases cortisol levels, making pain feel more painful, which leads to more fear, which leads to more cortisol and more pain. On and on in the fear-pain cycle. **We can stop this cycle.**

- Our brains are evolutionarily very old, and they are not designed for today's modern lifestyle. We sometimes have to trick the mind to stop the F's system and start the *rest and digest* system.

- Our brains prioritize negative information to keep us safe, but this is not necessarily helpful.

- We may need to hear a positive thing 3 or more times to counteract hearing a negative thing 1 time.

Journaling Prompts

- What has your experience been with the mind-body connection? Can you think of a time when your physical experience impacted your psychological experience? Or vice versa? What about your social experiences? Have they ever impacted how you felt physically or mentally?

- What has been your experience of *The Big Lie*? How does it feel to learn that childbirth doesn't have to be painful?

Pain

We have a tendency to assume pain is a bad thing. But you've come this far, so you already know that nothing is ever always bad 100% of the time. Pain, cortisol, and the sympathetic nervous system each serve a purpose. Our bodies are very good at protecting us. They had to learn to be, or we wouldn't be here today. It just happens to be that we don't always understand what our bodies are doing or why.

Pain is vital to survival. There is a condition called *Congenital Insensitivity to Pain*—caused by a genetic mutation—where people do not feel pain. You might think that sounds amazing. If you ask someone who has it, you will hear a different story. Pain keeps us safe. Without it, we risk serious injury.

Imagine you go to touch a hot pan—or if you'd rather, you bite into a very hot microwave burrito—you feel pain, and you jerk your hand away, or spit the burrito out. You're burned, which is painful and probably pretty annoying. But if you didn't feel that pain, you would have continued to touch the pan/eat the burrito. You would have continued to burn yourself. Without pain, you could end up with third-degree burns requiring hospitalization and skin grafts. Compared with that outcome, the pain doesn't seem so bad, does it? We need pain to let us know when we are putting ourselves at risk.

How we experience pain is based on different factors. You're well aware now that cortisol will impact how you experience pain. Culture, age, gender, and even religion can all impact how painful pain feels.[16] Even the amount of emotional support received during birth can impact how we perceive pain.[17] Pain is a complex human experience.

When looking at childbirth pain, researchers found that when women giving birth believed the pain had a purpose, the intensity of it was not very severe. When women did not think the pain had a purpose, the intensity of it was overwhelming.[18] Like any other pain, childbirth pain is transmitting information. Imagine there was no childbirth pain at all. You'd be walking through a store, or you would be at the dentist's office, and all of a sudden, a baby would be smooshed up against your pants. Okay, that isn't exactly what would happen. But it wouldn't be ideal.

No pain whatsoever may sound ideal. Except, no pain means no information. No information means you don't know what's going on inside your body. You don't know what your body or the baby needs. Pain may tell you to switch positions to move the baby into an easier location. Pain may tell you to focus. Pain may even tell you that you need to relax.

Take your hand and ball it into a fist. Tighter. Tighter. Keep going. Squeeze tighter. It starts to hurt. Keep going. Hold it. Now relax your hand. Feels pretty good, right? We only ever hear people talk about contractions when talking about childbirth. It's always about contractions. Birth is a balance of contracting *and* relaxing. If you only ever contract, nothing— especially not a baby—can move through the birth canal. Contracting puts pressure on the baby. Relaxing allows the baby to slide down. Repeated over and over, the baby progresses out of the body.

You've likely been told to practice "Kegels" during pregnancy. If you haven't heard this term, it is used to describe contractions of the pelvic floor muscles and vaginal canal. They are called Kegels after the male doctor who coined the term. They can have a lot of benefits throughout life, not just during pregnancy. Though they aren't always good for everyone. Talk to your healthcare team about pelvic floor strengthening, especially if you have pain.

If you do practice them, don't just focus on the contraction. In our society, we tend to be very focused on the action part of everything. The doing. We ignore the relaxing. We think working out is important but not soaking those strained muscles to relax them. Both parts are necessary, just like during birth. The same is true with pelvic floor exercises. After contracting, don't just release, try to fully relax. Your body needs to learn to do both.

PING PONG BALL BALLOON

If you want to simulate the importance of contract-relax balance, try this activity. No balloons will pop! Get a ping pong ball and a balloon. Stretch the opening of the balloon and pop the ping pong ball inside. You may need help from another set of hands. Once the ball is inside, inflate the balloon. Hold the balloon with the opening pointed towards the ground. The ball will settle, trapping the air inside. Blow it up slightly larger than you want it because you will lose some air as the ball settles. Now, taking both hands, slowly squeeze the top of the balloon. Then release. Repeat this for about a minute. The ball will pop out. Be prepared! The balloon does not tear, even though the ball is much bigger than the balloon opening. Now try again, but this time, just hold and continue to squeeze the balloon without releasing. You can probably guess that nothing will happen. Contracting mean nothing without relaxing.

In Yoga when I teach pelvic floor contracting—called Uddiyana Bandha—we explore both depths. We fully contract and work to fully relax. That's right, relaxing is work too. Then, I instruct participants to contract at about a three on a scale of ten. This is the level of engagement we try to keep during practice. Too much tension will stop the movement of energy. Not enough will release it. If you only learn to contract, you can't learn to find balance.

We are not always aware of when we are contracting in our bodies. We hunch our shoulders or clench our jaw. When we chronically clench, we become numb to the pain. One of the cues I learned as a Yoga teacher is "relax the jaw," because so many people carry tension in their jaws without realizing it.

When I teach Yoga, I can always see the faces in the room change when I give that cue. A handful of people visibly relax their jaw. Some contort their faces while they try to figure out how to relax their jaw. A few more think really hard while they try to determine if they need to relax their jaw. If the pain was in the forefront of their minds, they would know that they needed to relax. It likely was at some point, but we are so used to ignoring pain—because we see pain as "bad."

Rather than treating pain like information that can improve the body's functioning, we numb it away. I get it. Pain prevents us from getting done what we need to get done. No one has time for it. Just because it is a nuisance doesn't mean it isn't also important information. Pain is complex.

Pain becomes even more complex when you realize how closely tied it is to pleasure. Have you ever worked out to the point of your muscles aching, and yet it felt so good? Or had a deep tissue massage where you asked for more, firmer, deeper pressure? Eating spicy food, getting tattoos, spanking, jumping in a freezing lake. These are all examples of pain that is pleasurable.

Pain and pleasure are often seen as two sides of the same coin. This is because they use the same opioid and dopamine systems in the brain. The body is very protective of you. We talked about how cortisol can combat loneliness. That's because when the body notices a spike in cortisol, it produces oxytocin to make you feel better. It's remarkable how hard our bodies work to take care of us. In the same way, pain can stimulate the production of feel-good chemicals in the brain. The body wants you to be aware of pain—and the information it provides—but the body is also designed to protect you from that pain.

I told you that I know childbirth does not have to be extremely painful. Here is how I know that is true. The same chemical and physical responses that occur during childbirth occur during orgasm. How is it possible that this thing that is supposed to be the worst pain a person can feel has the exact same features as the thing that is supposed to be the best pleasure a person can feel? It's because birth isn't supposed to be awful. Our bodies are designed to protect us from it.

People will say, "Oh, you hold the baby, and you forget all about the pain." That is usually because the body is flooding with oxytocin, the bonding hormone which makes you feel good.

1. Feeling good after birth does not mean you have to blindly accept terrible pain during birth.
2. This isn't the whole story.

Yes, you *may* flood with oxytocin, and the mind *may* become so blissed-out that you forget about the birth pain. However, that is temporary.

Any medical intervention or tear will continue to hurt as it heals. This can take a while. Holding the baby and triggering the release of oxytocin will help, but it won't erase what has happened in the body. When someone has a traumatic birth, that experience sits in the body and in the mind. It can last for a long time. Possibly forever, if the person never gets help. It can be triggered by different things, including getting pregnant again. In this way, baby-induced oxytocin almost acts like drugs or alcohol after a traumatic event. It numbs the experience and the bad feelings, but it doesn't really make them go away. I would much rather you do not have a painful traumatic birth that depends on oxytocin to dull the memory. Oxytocin, after the fact, is a way the body protects you. It is not the only way or the best way.

Pleasure

We've talked about the impact of media in a negative way. But media can also have a positive impact on the world. I don't think we can talk about the media as a platform for education and change without talking about Shonda Rhimes. She has repeatedly used her influence to shed light on important concepts like police violence, inequity, addiction, and abortion as healthcare. Of course, my favorite of her bold moves occurs in season 14 of *Grey's Anatomy*. In this episode, a pregnant patient is encouraged to masturbate to stimulate oxytocin production to progress childbirth, rather than using synthetic oxytocin. I could practically hear the gasp of the world watching that episode. Yet, I, along with sex-positive birth workers everywhere, exhaled, "Yes!"

With that in mind, let's talk more about pleasure and pain. But first, we need to talk about orgasms. Or rather, lack of orgasms. The term anorgasmia refers to people with delayed, infrequent, or absent orgasms.[19] It's not a great term. It's medicalized, disempowering, and not very sex positive. Pre-orgasmic is now the preferred term. Because many of these women—unfortunately, the research is just on "women"—can and will orgasm. The rates vary, but an estimated 5-15% of women are pre-orgasmic.[20]

If you haven't experienced an orgasm and you want to, if you aren't sure if you have, or if you just want to learn more, there are resources available. Being the mind-body-focused person I am, I highly recommend the book *Come as You Are*, by Emily Nagoski. If you are looking for a more practical hands-on approach, the website OMGYes.com is research-backed and technique-focused with demonstration videos. All of this is there for you to access. Of course, that's only if you want to. Not everyone wants to have orgasms, and that is totally okay and healthy too. Healthy sexuality is whatever feels right to you.

During an orgasm, the body produces oxytocin, beta-endorphin, adrenaline, noradrenaline, prostaglandins, and prolactin. Can you guess what the body produces during childbirth? Oxytocin, beta-endorphin, adrenalin, noradrenaline, prostaglandins and prolactin. During orgasm, there are changes to the breathing pattern, uterine contractions, and abdominal contractions. The mouth opens, the face contorts, and the eyes turn glassy. During childbirth? It is exactly the same.[21] So why isn't everyone having orgasmic childbirth?

You've probably guessed fear and cortisol. And you'd be right, but also stigma. There is a stigma associated with sexuality. Researchers believe this stigma impacts the childbirth experience and leads to pain. Not only because childbirth includes looking at and touching sexual organs but also because there is an extreme taboo around sexual pleasure.

If I said, "Birthing a baby gave that person sexual pleasure." How would you feel? Would it make you uncomfortable? It makes perfect sense if it does. We are collectively uncomfortable with sexual pleasure and birth on their own, let alone together.

We see this same strong desire to desexualize the breast from human milk feeding. *The Badass Breastfeeding Podcast* has a great episode where they talk about how kissing your partner is different than kissing your baby. Even kissing your partner at different times will have different degrees of sexuality to it. Yet, we lump intimacy, affection, and sexuality together. It's confusing. I've heard women say, "Oh, I could never breastfeed, my breasts are sexual." Or "I'm not going to breastfeed. My breasts are for my husband." Your hands are for eating. They are also for wiping your butt. Our body parts can do many different things.

It isn't about the actual evolutionary purpose. If it was, human milk feeding would always take priority over sexuality, as that is the evolutionary purpose for mammary glands and nipples. Instead, sexuality is the driving force. Can this be sexy? If the answer is yes, then it's sexy first, everything else second. I mean, we had a whole culture war over the green M&M's shoes not being sexy enough.

There are all kinds of pleasure. Pleasure is not inherently sexual. Though we tend to act like it is. We take someone moaning in pleasure after biting into a chocolate cake, and we make it sexual. It doesn't have to be sexual. Pleasure is simply satisfaction and enjoyment. Pleasure can come from a walk on a sunny day. Pleasure can be petting a cat or watching a funny movie. Yet we treat the word almost like it's dirty.

We are caught in a sex-negative, fear-based culture where the idea of birthing a baby causing sexual stimulation or being pleasurable makes people tense and think of perverts or pedophiles. If you have an orgasm during birth or any pleasurable feelings, you are not a pedophile. You are not inherently sexually attracted to babies. I hate that I have to write that, but the fear and the shame are so deeply ingrained that it needs to be said.

Out of fear and shame, we shut it all down. We don't make any space for intimacy or to feel good. We hyper-medicalize and desensitize birth, squeezing out anything that isn't orderly. We become so disassociated from the natural process occurring in our bodies that the only thing we are allowed to feel is pain. Pain is seen as pure and noble. So, pain becomes the dominant experience.

I'm not saying your only two choices are pain or sexual pleasure. I am saying our collective fear of sexual pleasure contributes to pain. Shame becomes anxiety becomes cortisol becomes pain. When we are stripped of emotion and connection, the only thing we are allowed to feel is pain. Bodies are quite literally designed to feel pleasure. To deny that denies you a fundamental part of the human experience.

I'd like to share the story of how I came to be writing this book with a PhD that focused on the psychology of childbirth. It wasn't my intention to study childbirth at all. I had planned to study what I called, "the three cognitive splits of female sexuality." A cognitive split or cognitive dissonance is when a person experiences contradictory beliefs, which lead to mental discomfort and compartmentalizing to relieve the discomfort.

The first split is triggered by normal bodily exploration. If you are going to be raising a child, you should know that very young children masturbate. Babies even masturbate in utero. It's not sexual. Not in the traditional sense. They have no concept of sexuality or sexual attraction or even of sex. It's just bodily pleasure. Touching here feels good. It is a common form of self-soothing, like thumb-sucking. Thumb-sucking isn't inherently sexual, though it can be sexual when used in sexual situations. Young childhood masturbation is like this.

Babies are constantly learning about their bodies. *My fingers can open and close, which I can use to hold things. My foot can go in my mouth. I can chew on my tongue. Some hot feels good. Too much hot feels bad. I like this. I don't like that.* In this process, it makes perfect sense a baby's hands will find their genitals. They do not have any preconceived ideas related to genitals. Genitals are just body parts like toes and ears. Except it can feel really good when they touch them—which can also be true for toes and ears.

The first cognitive split occurs when a child touches their genitals, it feels good, and an adult they love and trust says, "No, don't do that," or continually moves their hand away. The child learns *what feels good in my body is bad.* Very young children want to please their caretakers. Their literal survival depends on their caretakers wanting to take care of them. So, very young children defer to the rules of those caretakers even if it contradicts their experience.

The second split occurs in young girls and preteen girls. A 2015 study by Sense Media found that 80% of 10-year-old girls had been on a diet.[*] A 2006 study found that a significant number of the girls in the study wanted thinner bodies by the age of 6.[*] Six! That can be before they reach the first grade. Food tastes good. Being satiated by food feels good. Here, girls learn again that *what feels good in my body is bad.*

The third split occurs during the teenage years with slut-shaming. Bodies with penises are the focus of pleasure, and bodies raised as females are supposed to suppress or deny a desire for pleasure or risk being labeled a "slut." I hope this is decreasing in frequency, as younger generations are leaning toward sex positivity and sexual equality for everyone. However, for those that experience slut shaming, it can be emotionally devasting, confusing, and cause what I thought was the final cognitive split.

Then you have all of these people reaching young adulthood, where there is an expectation that they will be sexy, sexual beings. How does that make any sense? Their whole lives they have been taught to shut down pleasure in their bodies. Then, suddenly, they are supposed to just be oozing in pleasure—usually for the pleasure of others.

When I was preparing to go back to school to study this, I realized that there is another split that happens. This one occurs in bodies that decide to human milk feed babies. When we get to the BBC section—if you choose to read it—we will discuss, in further detail, the hyper-sexualization of breasts and how it impacts feeding human milk.

Human milk feeding creates a rigid Madonna-Whore complex. Where people are supposed to be good, virtuous "mothers." Ones who attend to all the needs of their babies, including feeding them. At the same time, they are supposed to be sexual, sexy beings with a focus on their partner's pleasure. How is someone supposed to balance that, especially when they've experienced such an extreme separation from their bodies since early childhood?

It is a difficult question. One that goes beyond the scope of this book, I recommend the book *Come as You Are* by Emily Nagoski. If you were born with a vagina, AFAB, are attracted to people with vaginas, are attracted to people who were AFAB, or want to understand more about how the female/vagina experience impacts sexuality, then I suggest you read it. [Common Sense Media. (2015). Children, teens, media, and body image. Common Sense Media.]

Another factor that may contribute to childbirth leaning towards painful despite the similarities to orgasm is how people breathe during birth. According to Barbara Carrellas, author of *Urban Tantra*, "childbirth classes, including Lamaze, teach a breath that encourages a 'hold it...push...shoot' style of giving birth that is more like the way men ejaculate than the way women orgasm."[22] She goes on to say that childbirth breathing should mimic orgasmic breathing, in particular for bodies that are multiorgasmic, as the peaks of contraction and orgasm will feel similar, as will the spaces in between. She goes as far as to encourage those who are not multiorgasmic to learn to be before giving birth. Easier said than done, of course, but possibly more fun than some of the other stuff you may do to prepare for birth…

PELVIC BREATH ORGASMS

This activity is not for everyone. But if it sounds intriguing to you, I encourage you to try it. It can take a lot of practice, so try not to become frustrated. Frustration can cause tension in the body, making it hard to relax. This process depends on the ability to find a balance between contracting and relaxing. This can be a great practice for anyone at any time in life, but it can be particularly nice if more "traditional" methods of sexual release are not accessible due to pregnancy or having recently given birth. This technique is adapted from *Urban Tantra* by Barbara Carrella. If you are interested in more techniques or a deeper exploration of sexuality, I recommend you read her book. It's quite fascinating.

Find a comfortable location where you will not be disturbed. You may want to sit up, lie down, be propped at an angle or you may like to try being in the bath. This tantric practice combines breath movement with pelvic floor movement to build awareness and sensitivity, which can lead to orgasm without physical touch.

First, tune into your body. Just notice what you feel. Notice the support of the bed, chair, or floor underneath you. Notice the temperature of the water if you are in the bath. Take a moment to give yourself conscious permission. Permission to prioritize time in your body and your pleasure. In my Sound Therapist training, I learned to start each session with an opening monologue that included, "There is nowhere you need to be. There is nothing you need to do. Right now, in this moment, you are perfect just as you are. You are perfect just as you are." It may feel helpful to tell yourself those words, or something similar. Whatever to-do list may be drifting into your mind, it will still be there when you are done. And you may approach it with renewed vigor and calm because you took time for yourself.

After you have become aware of your body. Notice how it feels. Are any places stiff or stuck? Do any places feel really good? It's all okay. You're just noticing, like waving at someone walking by your window. You acknowledge them and let them keep walking.

Next, focus on your breath. Notice where you feel your breath. Is there movement in your shoulders or your belly? Do your nostrils flare? One side more than the other? Once you have a good grasp of what your breath is doing naturally, start to take control of it.

Guide the breath low into your belly, keeping your shoulders still. Your belly will expand as it fills with air. You can place a hand on your belly or look at your belly to confirm it is expanding. When you have reached the top of your inhale, and your belly has fully expanded, hold for a count of three.*

Then, release all the air. This exhale can be through the nose or sighed out the mouth if that feels better. Repeat this process of breathing until you feel a sense of ease.

When you are ready for the next step, as you inhale, clench the vaginal walls. It can take practice to localize where you are squeezing. If clenching the vaginal walls is not there for you today, imagine you need to hold your pee on a long car ride or stop the flow of urine. That action includes additional muscles but is a great place to start. You might find that clenching more muscles works well for you, and you want to continue in that way. You do not need to clench as hard as you possibly can. Aim

---

* Three is a suggestion. You can always hold for longer or shorter. Do what feels good in your body.

for 60%. Of course, experiment to see if more or less strength feels better for you.

Clench for the length of your inhale and your hold. When you exhale, relax any muscles you were clenching. Repeat this inhaling clench, exhaling release pattern until you do not want to do it anymore. This could be before an orgasm happens, after one, or after many. Orgasm does not need to be the goal. Feeling good is the goal. Spending time with your body is the goal.

If you want another variation, you can swap the clench, so you inhale relaxed and exhale clench. Sometimes this can feel more intuitive because the stomach is contracting with the exhale, and the vaginal canal/pelvic floor is lifting with the clench. You can almost imagine the cervix rising up to meet the belly button. You get to play around. This is play. Find what works for you and throw out what doesn't. There's no right or wrong as long as you are having a good time.

Cortisol...Again...

By now, you are very familiar with the way cortisol impacts the experience of pain. Let's look at some of the other ways high cortisol levels impact birth and what comes after. Remember that some cortisol is good. It's too much cortisol that becomes a problem.

Cortisol is linked to longer childbirth durations. In general, shorter birth is better. For one, even though I keep telling you that childbirth can be amazing, it is still exhausting, and you don't want to have to do it for longer than necessary. When you think about it, that's true for all amazing things. The body sees childbirth as chronic stress because of how long it lasts, allowing cortisol to build up in the body. This build-up of cortisol is why long childbirth doesn't benefit from the immediate pain relief someone feels from the quick stimulation of the sympathetic nervous system.

Stress during birth causes a chain reaction. The sympathetic nervous system is stimulated, which causes the release of a hormone called the corticotropin-releasing hormone. This hormone stimulates the pituitary gland—the part of the brain responsible for growth, metabolism, reproduction, responding to stress and trauma, and lactation—to release another hormone called the adrenocorticotropic hormone. This causes the production of glucocorticoids, which decreases the frequency and strength of contractions.[23]

Less frequent and less strong contractions might seem like a good thing, but that's *The Big Lie* talking. Strong, frequent contractions are how you get the baby out quickly. They are what you want. When contractions are weak and infrequent, childbirth lasts longer. This increases the stress on the body and can lead to medical interventions, including cesarean sections. The body turns glucocorticoids into cortisol, making pain feel more painful. Too much cortisol can also interfere with the production of oxytocin. This explains why high cortisol levels are correlated with low maternal attachment—meaning moms with high cortisol levels felt less attached to their babies.[24] Not only is oxytocin important for bonding, but it is also required to regulate the milk ejection response.[25]

A small amount of cortisol is actually required to induce lactogenesis—the start of milk letdown.[26] Cortisol is not inherently bad. It is necessary. Too much cortisol, however, can lead to low LATCH scores and difficulty suckling.[27]

LATCH scores are a five-point assessment given to newborns to determine how successful the baby is at breastfeeding. Each item is given a score of zero to two. LATCH is an acronym for each of the items.

L—latch—how well the baby latches.

A—audible—swallowing, the amount of audible swallowing during a feeding.

T—type of nipple—this assesses the type and texture of the nipple.

C—comfort—how comfortable the feeding person feels during feeding.

H—help with hold—the amount of help the feeding person needs to hold the baby.

[Jensen, D., Wallace, S., & Kelsay, P. (1994). LATCH: A breastfeeding charting system and documentation tool. *Journal of Obstetric, Gynecologic, & Neonatal Nursing, 23*(1), 27–32.]

Higher cortisol levels increase negative feelings towards childbirth and rates of post-traumatic stress.[28] High cortisol levels during pregnancy increase the risk of low birth weight and preterm birth.[29]

It isn't just stress and fear that increases cortisol levels. Fasting has been shown to increase cortisol levels.[30] When giving birth in the hospital, they reduce or completely stop any food intake, as food in the stomach is a safety risk should you end up needing emergency surgery. If you are in the hospital, the longer your childbirth, the longer you go without eating. The body can then go into fasting mode increasing cortisol levels. Fasting is one reason that the duration of childbirth matters, though it isn't one that's often talked about. Maybe it's only high up on my list because of how much I love food. So, let's explore the other reasons why childbirth duration matters.

A longer length of childbirth means an increase in pain thanks to cortisol, which increases the likelihood of asking for an epidural. Epidurals slow down childbirth—specifically the second stage—creating a cycle of trying to balance pain and duration.[31]

Birth is exhausting, physically and mentally. The longer you spend birthing the baby, the more fatigued you can become. Fatigue is linked to assisted birth, either by forceps or cesarean section.[32] Longer second stage of birth is linked to anal and sphincter injuries and the need for episiotomies.[33] Both of these can cause discomfort, leading to difficulties postpartum. There are also higher incidences of postpartum hemorrhage with a longer duration of childbirth.[34] Postpartum hemorrhage can be very serious. It is not always, but it can be.

For the baby, a longer duration of childbirth can lead to stress on the baby. This prolonged stress can cause respiratory issues.[35] Other risks include hypoglycemia, low five-minute Apgar score, and admission to the Neonatal Intensive Care Units.[36] These are all very real health-related reasons that long childbirth is a problem.

There is one other less health-related reason that long childbirth is a "problem." That's money. Hospitals are businesses that need to make money.[37] Hospitals also provide much-needed services that take up space. Hospitals have a limited amount of space. There are only so many rooms for people to give birth in. The longer a person spends birthing a baby, the longer they occupy a room. This means that someone else who might need that room—maybe even more seriously than the person occupying it needs it—can't use it.

It also means that only one person is paying to use that room. Just like a person waiting tables needs their tables to turn over so they can make more tip money, the hospital needs the birthing rooms to turn over so they can bill more than one insurance. Doctors may face pressure from hospital administrators, who in turn face pressure from hospital boards and CEOs, to get more people in and out in a shorter timeframe. This can lead to measures to speed up childbirth, such as giving synthetic oxytocin. We talked about a great many reasons why long childbirth can be problematic. However, rushing birth for the sake of shareholders is not good for anyone—except the shareholders. Before you accept any intervention to speed up childbirth, make sure you are clear on your specific risks. If you are working with a doula, they will likely be able to advise you on whether or not speed increasing measures are required.

Finally, a longer length of childbirth is associated with an increased risk of maternal mortality. It is a very low percentage, 2.8%.[38] But nonetheless, it is a good reason to try to avoid long births. Fortunately, we will talk about ways— backed by research—to shorten childbirth duration without increasing medical interventions when we get to Complementary Alternative Medicine.

Pre-Traumatic Stress Disorder

You may be familiar with the term "post-traumatic stress disorder" or PTSD. We hear it a lot in terms of veterans returning from war and people who have experienced sexual assault. Post-traumatic stress disorder is a clinical diagnosis where a mental health condition is triggered by a traumatic event. The key here is that the mental health concern arises *after* the triggering event.

A new traumatic stress disorder is starting to gain attention in the research community. It's called pre-traumatic stress disorder or PreTSD. This occurs when the mental health concern arises before—and in anticipation of—a traumatic event. Does this sound familiar?

Researchers Goutaudier et al. believe that women can develop pre-traumatic stress disorder related to childbirth due to the fear of childbirth.[39] I mentioned at the beginning of the book the estimated rates of tokophobia—the diagnosable fear of childbirth. You'll recall that prior to the COVID-19 pandemic, it was estimated that 10-15% of women experienced tokophobia, and that rate rose to 62% during the pandemic. Some of these people had experienced previous traumatic births, so their fear of birth falls more into the post-traumatic stress disorder category because their fear stems from a triggering experience.

For those who have never given birth or been pregnant before, the fear of childbirth can be seen as a pre-traumatic stress disorder.* Right now, this concept is pretty

---

*Miscarriages can be awful and traumatic. Although, I know a wonderful woman who had a miscarriage her first time being pregnant, and she found that the experience gave her hope. Everyone responds differently. But in the case of a traumatic

new, and we don't have a good grasp on how much of childbirth-related post-traumatic stress disorder is actually pre-traumatic stress disorder. When we talk about post-traumatic stress disorder, as it relates to childbirth, we need to remember that we don't know if the trigger is occurring before or after, as fear of childbirth is so common.

It is also important to remember that having a traumatic birth doesn't mean that the next birth will automatically be traumatic. I worked with a woman who had had a very traumatic first birth. As she neared the third trimester of her second pregnancy, she found herself becoming increasingly anxious about giving birth again. She didn't want to feel that way, so she learned about how the mind can impact the birth experience. She changed her perspective and her process. The birth of her second child was smooth and fast. She felt empowered during her birth. She changed her story. If you have experienced a traumatic birth in the past, you can change your story too. In fact, you've already started.

---

miscarriage, that can act as a triggering event even if the person "technically didn't give birth." Whatever your feelings: sad, angry, hopeful, numb, or otherwise, they are right, and they are valid. You get to feel however you feel, no matter when the miscarriage occurred, whether you knew you were pregnant or not. Your feelings are right. Your feelings are valid.

Lean In

We've talked a lot about cortisol. By now, you know that some cortisol is important to bodily functioning and survival. You know that too much cortisol makes pain feel more painful. You know that cortisol is often called the stress hormone. Cortisol isn't always bad, but what about stress? *Stress* is so common now we use it on a daily basis. The word gained widespread use in the 1960s, yet it is hard to imagine a time when people didn't feel stressed out regularly.[40] As a society, we are overworked and overtired.

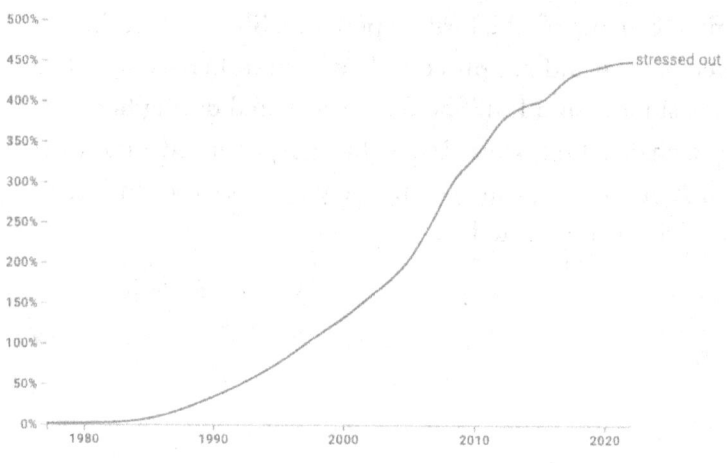

Usage of the Term "Stressed Out" in the United States Over Time

According to Brené Brown, "We are the most in-debt, obese, addicted, and medicated adult cohort in U.S. history," because we are trying to numb vulnerability instead of embracing it.[41] As a vulnerability researcher, she has done a lot of work to help people embrace this uncomfortable emotional space. Her work centers on a key point that vulnerability—when embraced—makes life better. Vulnerability is not a weakness but a source of strength.

We are all the things Brené Brown suggests. All because our lives are stressful. They are. Being alive today is stressful. But if cortisol is the stress hormone, and cortisol isn't always bad, can't the same be true for stress? It's true that stress can be terrible for both our mental and physical health. And…think of all the ways we go out of our way to intentionally put stress on our bodies. High-Intensity Interval Training. Cryotherapy. Sky diving.

In the futurist dystopian book *A Brave New World,* everyone is highly medicated on a drug called soma, and they live a virtually stress-free existence.[42] They weren't better off because of it. In fact, they had to participate in various rituals designed to put stress on the body. Of course, this is a work of fiction. Still, I like the message behind it. If everything was completely stress-free and comfy and cozy, we'd never get off the couch. We'd never make art or express ourselves. We wouldn't need to.

The day my great uncle Julian turned 90, he went skydiving. He was terrified. And…he loved it. It put an immense amount of stress on his body. How could it not? He was jumping out of a plane. But the stress, the fear, were also the anticipation. It is because of the "negative" that the positive existed. I like to tell kids—and sometimes adults—if you're never afraid, you can never be brave. Brave doesn't exist without fear. You can be blindly bold. To me, that isn't as impressive as being afraid and not letting it hold you back.

I say nothing is ever always 100% good, and nothing is ever always 100% bad. But there is also a Yogic idea that nothing good can be good without bad. The opposite is also true. If you have only ever eaten flaxseed oil, you wouldn't know that it tastes worse than ice cream. If you only ever ate ice cream, you wouldn't be able to appreciate how much sweeter it tastes than lemons. It's quite hard to miss someone if you've never found joy in their company. At the same time that missing someone feels bad, it can also feel good. It means you are connected to another person. That you have felt connection.

When we stop looking at everything as binary and grouped, "This is good. This is bad," and instead look at how relationships and context impact our feelings about things we would have labeled good or bad, we free ourselves. Think about the first time you tried a food you thought would taste bad that ended up being delicious. If you've never done this, I suggest you try it. Your mind had you locked in a state of "this is bad." You moved through that state to discover your mind was wrong. You opened yourself up to more.

Melissa Spamer, an expert on Yoga, mental health, and Ayurveda, whom I have the privilege of calling my teacher, says that when we face challenges, we expand our capacity. I remember a time I spent with her somewhere that was exceedingly hot. So hot that my hands and feet swelled. I couldn't sleep. I struggled to function. When it was over and I left, not only did the cool air feel that much sweeter, but I was overwhelmingly proud of myself. I could have left early, but I stayed and faced the difficulty, coming out stronger on the other side. I expanded my capacity.

Birth is hard. Amazing, joyful, awesome things can be hard. They can be scary. That doesn't make them less amazing, joyful, or awesome. It may make them more so. I encourage you not to pull away from the fear or to numb the vulnerability. Let them make you brave. Let them make your joy that much more joyful. If it was easy, it wouldn't be impressive.

Now, why did my great uncle Julian wait until 90? According to him, if something went wrong, well he had lived a good 90 years, so no big deal. He didn't charge blindly and recklessly into fear and danger. He made conscious choices based on the information available to him to decide what was right for him. Prior to 90, skydiving was not right for him. At 90, it was exactly what he needed. I hope we can all learn from Brené Brown, Melissa Spamer, and Uncle Julian as we embrace the unknown, the scary, and the hard to become better, braver, stronger versions of ourselves.

Fear, pain, and stress are all complex. In and of themselves, they are neither good nor bad. They serve a purpose and provide information we can use to make the best choices. However, when fear, pain, or stress take center stage and overwhelm everything else, then they become a problem.

This fear of birth. This overwhelming fear is valid. It's what we've been taught. It's what we've witnessed in the media and overheard from friends. Maybe you've even experienced it firsthand. But it doesn't have to be your story. I hate to break it to Franklin D. Roosevelt, but there's no reason to fear fear.[43] Fear is just a protective mechanism in the body. Sometimes, it is overactive. Sometimes, it is unhelpful. It might not feel pleasant. Although, sometimes, it can. When we remember that fear of birth is the same mechanism as fear of starting a new job, a new relationship, watching a scary movie, or traveling somewhere new, we realize it's really a combination of fear and excitement. Hope and anticipation. Loss of control and letting control go. Then, we can see fear for what it is. Part of the glorious human experience. Being fearless isn't being without fear, not really. It's giving fear less control. It's giving fear less power. It is fearing fear less. This is how we become fearless.

Support Report

- Pain serves a purpose and keeps us safe. How we perceive pain is influenced by many factors, including our beliefs about pain.

- We tend to focus on contracting during birth, but relaxing is just as important. Birth requires a balance of contracting and relaxing. When practicing pelvic floor strengthening, care should be taken to fully relax after each contraction.

- Chronic tension or pain in the body can desensitize us, leading us to ignore what the body is trying to tell us.

- Pain and pleasure are two sides of the same coin. They both use the opioid and dopamine systems in the brain.

- Birth and orgasm have similar physical and chemical responses showing us that birth doesn't have to be awful.

- Cultural stigma around sexuality and pleasure impacts childbirth and can make it more painful.

- High cortisol levels make pain feel more painful and increase the length of birth. Longer birth can lead to complications and interventions. Fasting can raise cortisol levels and contribute to longer birth.

- PreTSD is a traumatic response that occurs before an event due to fear of the event. Childbirth can cause PreTSD due to the horror stories people hear. If you've had a traumatic birth in the past, PTSD can impact this birth. Remember that you have the power to change your thoughts and by doing so change your body's physical reactions.

- Stress is not always bad. It can be a motivator. Fear of birth is the same mechanism as fear of a new relationship or traveling somewhere new. Fear and excitement can go hand in hand. We must give fear less control and focus on the good anticipation that feels like fear.

Journaling Prompts

- What are your thoughts on pain during childbirth? What has your experience with pain been throughout your life? How has your pain been treated by others? By you? What do you do when you are in physical pain? What about mental or emotional pain? Have you had an experience of pain being positive?

- What is your relationship with sexuality? How was it different before pregnancy compared to now? What were you taught or not taught about your body and sexuality?

Birth

Ways to Birth

There are a lot of different ways to give birth. Although we tend to talk about birth in two categories: "natural birth" and everything that isn't considered natural birth. This can be confusing because what exactly does natural birth mean? Does it mean you have to use a midwife? Give birth at home? Have no medical interventions? Or does it just mean no pain medications? If we can't clearly define what natural birth is, how are we supposed to define what natural birth isn't? We can't.

Frankly, it's not particularly helpful to force people who are giving birth into two categories. It creates a sense of tribalism or in-group/out-group where people feel judged or excluded. It also doesn't mean much, as things are rarely that black and white. Even if they were, people are making the best decisions that they can with the information that they have and their current circumstances.

Our culture doesn't give birthing people enough support in general. It doesn't make anything better when birthing people stop supporting each other because of different choices. Of course, we all have our opinions and beliefs. I certainly have my own. I just don't think it is helpful for me to share them. They are just my beliefs.

Instead, I am going to give you information. Information on all kinds of ways that birth happens. It is up to you to use that information to make decisions about what kind of birth you want. But no matter what you choose, try to be kind to the people who choose differently. And remember that no matter what you choose, sometimes—though I wish it weren't true—we don't get what we choose. Then we have to live with that. The trauma of birth can follow a person around for a very long time. It is hard enough knowing you didn't get what you wanted, without people making you feel bad for actions and outcomes that were forced on you.

You may think, "I know exactly what my plan is, and I don't need to read this section." That's cool. Feel free to skip it. But before you do, I want to remind you that things really can change regardless of the best-laid plans. In those cases, it can be useful to know the information presented in this section. This information can prepare you for what to expect during a medical intervention and what outcomes you might want to be on the lookout for.

Support People and Advocates

No matter how you plan to give birth, there are two types of people that are beneficial to have with you. A support person(s) and an advocate. It is important to have both. They have distinct roles.

A support person is someone you love. The person or people who are there for the whole pregnancy and beyond. The person who rubs your feet or brings you ice cream. The person you want holding your hand. You can have as many support people as you want—although hospitals may limit the number of people you can have in the room.

A support person is with you while you give birth. They have two jobs. The first is to take care of you. The second is to handle their own stuff so that it doesn't become your stuff. That means if you are hot, but they are cold, they quietly and subtly put on a sweater. It means if they are scared, they keep it to themselves. You have no responsibility to take care of anyone else emotionally or otherwise while you are giving birth.

A support person may not realize that they have a tendency to put things on you, so it is important that they start preparing long before you start giving birth. When you have decided on a support person(s)—and you are allowed to change your mind—let them know their two jobs: take care of you and make sure that their problems don't become your problems. Then, expect them to practice. If they can't do it outside the birth room, they may struggle to do it in the birth room. Which is just information for you to have so you can make the best decisions for you. You get to decide who is a support person and who isn't. Sometimes, it can be really hard telling someone you don't want them to be a support person. It can help to consider it a step into post-birth life. Like with pregnancy, after birth, there will be all kinds of people telling you all kinds of "shoulds." It's vital to tune them out or shut it down. You know what's best for you, for your body, and for your birth.

I have named these people, support people because that is what they should be: supportive. If it is a person who makes you second guess or feel bad. If it is a person who steals focus or that you have to take care of, then they are not a good support person. It doesn't mean they are a bad person or that you don't love them. It doesn't mean they won't be vital in all kinds of other ways. It just means they aren't the best support person. An Eco-Map can help you think about who might be good support people. Even if you know exactly who you want, I suggest doing the activity. It never hurts to have more information.

ECO-MAP

An Eco-Map is a visual representation of social and personal relationships. To make one, take a blank sheet of paper and draw a circle in the center. Label this circle "me" or put your name.

Next, draw circles for each of the relationships, positive or negative, in your life. These relationships do not need to be with people. Maybe it's a pet or even an activity. You can cluster people together in a larger circle to help keep things organized.

Next, you will draw relationship lines. A solid line means a strong relationship. A dashed line means a weak relationship. A zigzag line means a stressful relationship. Arrows can be used to indicate if the relationship is giving, taking, or both.

Finally, you can write down characteristics for each person, especially if you are considering them to be on your birth team.

SAMPLE ECO-MAP

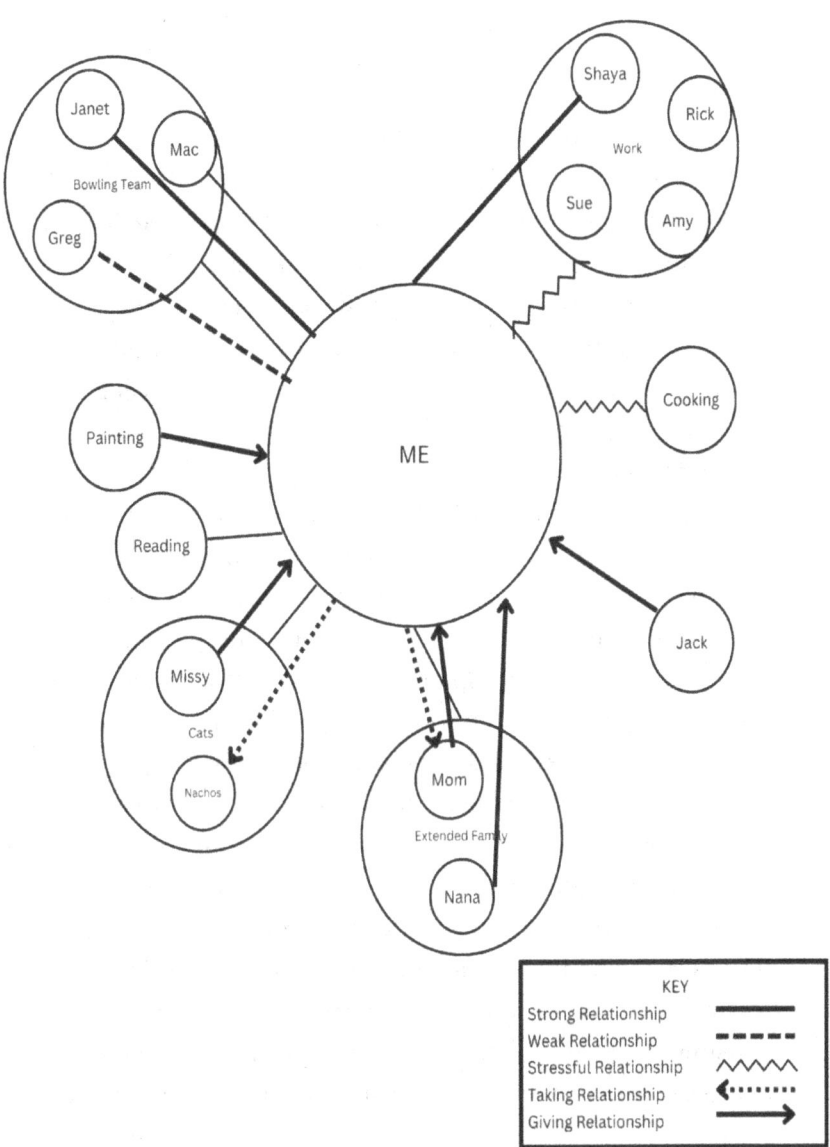

An advocate is different than a support person. Where a support person's focus is on you, an advocate's focus is on anyone trying to interact with you. They act as a sort of bouncer. Their job is to fight for your wishes so that you don't have to.

During birth, it can be really hard to advocate for yourself. It can be hard in any medical setting, let alone when you are dealing with contractions, possibly pain medications, people coming in and out, machines beeping. There may even be a situation where you are physically unable to advocate for yourself. In that situation, you don't necessarily want a support person trying to advocate for you. They will have too much else on their mind. Plus, it takes them away from taking care of you.

I recommend whenever possible people use a doula as their support person. Research consistently shows that birth outcomes are better when there is a doula present[44]. A lot better. They are trained to advocate. They are also trained to watch you and anticipate your needs. If I could wave a magic wand and ensure some things for everyone when they give birth, access to a doula—one you vibe with—would be on that list. So would paid leave one month before birth and a minimum of 6 months after birth. Unfortunately, no one gave me a magic wand. I'm not sure who I should bring this complaint to. If you've got a lead, let me know because I'd do some amazing things with a magic wand. Since I don't have one, know that in some cases, doulas are covered by insurance. Some also work on sliding scales. I strongly suggest you do some research and look into the possibility of having a doula, no matter where you are going to give birth.

If a doula is not possible, or you just don't want one, start thinking about the people you know who would make a good advocate. Let's say you've decided you want to get in the shower, and the nurse tells you that you can't. You don't want to fight with the nurse. That's exhausting, and you need all the physical and mental energy you have focused on birth. Your advocate is the one that says, "why not," and "explain it to me," or "what will happen if," etc. Try to pick the most stoic and unflappable person you know. Someone who always has your back and is good at standing up to authority figures makes a good advocate. It helps if they aren't squeamish. Your eco-map will help you identify relevant people in your life.

Cesarean Sections

To further understand why a support person might be necessary, let's talk about cesarean sections. Cesarean sections are the act of removing the baby through an incision in the abdomen rather than through the birth canal. This is a major surgery. There are several benefits to cesarean sections, including that they save lives. There are also very real negative outcomes associated with cesarean sections. But the main problem with cesarean sections occurs when they are both unnecessary and unwanted, yet they still happen.

If you want a cesarean section and schedule it, great! If you are in a medically necessary situation that requires a cesarean section, we are lucky they exist. Unfortunately, there has been a trend of cesarean sections that are not medically necessary nor are they wanted. There was a drastic increase in cesarean sections starting in the 1970s. That increase rose 500% in 2009.[45] As there are real consequences of cesarean sections, this caught a lot of attention. Investigations were launched to understand the increase. It was discovered that emergency cesarean sections were happening more frequently at times that were most convenient for doctors. Notably there was an increase around 4 and 5pm.[46] Meaning rather than waiting around for someone to give birth, the doctor could push a c-section and be done in time to have dinner with their family.

Birth can last a long time, and it can be unpredictable. Cesarean sections have a pretty consistent timeline, and it's short. So, a doctor who doesn't want to sit around all night or all weekend might be motivated to encourage a cesarean section when it isn't necessary. Sometimes through fear tactics. Awareness of this started to lead to a decrease in cesarean sections rates between 2009 and 2019. Unfortunately, according to the Centers for Disease Control and Prevention, in 2023, cesarean sections had increased four years in a row leading to 32.4% of births resulting in one.[47]

There is another reason that a doctor might push a cesarean section before it is necessary. Fear that it will have been necessary. Hospitals are fundamentally businesses, and lawsuits are expensive.[48] A cesarean section is considered the greatest possible intervention. In the event that the person giving birth, or the baby does not survive the birth, and the doctor has performed a cesarean section, they can say, "We did everything possible. We did the greatest possible intervention. You can't sue us." If they didn't perform the cesarean section, they are at risk because they didn't do "everything." This can make doctors a little preemptive in their encouragement of cesarean sections.

An advocate will interact with the doctor to get more information. If you are strongly opposed to a cesarean section, they will make that clear. The doctor might— intentionally or unintentionally—intimidate the person giving birth. The advocate—remember, is unflappable—and will not be intimated.

This is not a judgment of your character. If you are giving birth and someone says, "If you don't do this, your baby could die!" You are very likely going to say, "Yes, of course." The advocate is not giving birth. So, they have the time and energy to breathe, and ask, "Why?" "What happens if we wait an hour to see if there are any changes?" "What are the other options?" "What are the risks of saying no?" "What are the risks of saying yes?"

You can see where the support person trying to have this conversation takes them away from taking care of you.

This conversation is a time when you need your support
person supporting you, not advocating. That is why it is
important to have both. Now that we have a good grasp on
support people and advocates, we are going to take a more in
depth look at medical interventions. Since we are already
talking about cesarean sections, let's dive into what one
entails, what's good about it, and what's not.

A cesarean section, also called a c-section, is a medical
procedure that involves surgically removing the baby through
incisions in the abdomen. The first step in any medical
procedure should always be consent. After the consent, an
epidural will be given. It is less common, but a person can be
given full anesthesia. The procedure will occur in an
operating room. Unless you are watching a medical drama
like *Grey's Anatomy*, in which case it will occur somewhere like
the dining room of a boat that is docked but also sinking.

Here are some things that may happen when you
reach the surgical area and get on the table. You may have an
oxygen mask placed over your nose and mouth, or an oxygen
cannula placed in the nose. An oxygen cannula is a small
plastic tube with two prongs that rest inside the nostrils. A
light, gauzy surgical cap may be placed on your head to keep
your hair out of the way. Your arms may be temporarily
strapped down. They will likely have a bag stationed near
your head in case you need to vomit. You may hear the
doctors and nurses whispering. You may feel very out of
control and may even experience disassociation from the
body. Disassociation is the feeling of being disconnected
from your body or a feeling that what's happening is not real.

All of this can feel very scary, especially if you are not
prepared. I would say to remember that fear is the enemy of a
pain-free birth, but if you reach the point of needing an

emergency cesarean and someone said that to you, your kindest response would likely be rolling your eyes. Emergency C-sections are scary. There is no way around that. But remember, **they save lives**. You will have a whole medical team there to take care of you and the baby. We are going to talk about all kinds of coping skills that you can use to reduce—or at least distract from—the fear. Reducing the element of surprise is one way to regain control and reduce anxiety, so let's keep talking about the process.

Your abdomen is cleaned with an antiseptic to prevent infection. A sterile drape is used to cover most of the body, and a curtain is placed below the head. This obstructs your view of what is happening. Not being able to see can be scary. However, the mind doesn't react well to seeing the body being cut into. It can lead to passing out. The curtain isn't there to hide anything. It is there to keep you safe.

Incisions are made through seven layers of the body. These incisions can be vertical or horizontal. One is not better than the other. The skin, fat, fascia, and muscle are the first layers. Then, the bladder is moved to the side. The incisions continue through the peritoneum, uterus, and finally, the amniotic sac. The baby is removed through the incision. Most often, the placenta is also removed. In some cases, the placenta may be expelled through the vaginal canal by pushing rather than through the incision.* The umbilical cord is cut. The incisions are closed with stitches and staples.

---

*I have no explanation for why the placenta might be expelled through the vaginal canal. It doesn't appear to be a thing that happens medically speaking. However, individuals have had this experience. So technically it could happen. If it happens to you, ask a lot of questions and then send me an email because I would love to understand.

The whole procedure will likely take less than an hour. Delayed cord clamping can make the procedure a little longer. You should be able to hold your baby as soon as you are in the recovery room. However, they will bring the baby by your face so you can see them. At this point, I recommend having them brush the baby's face against your face. This acts as a little preview before full skin-to-skin happens. We will talk about the benefits of skin-to-skin and the importance of the microbiome later in the book.

Delayed cord clamping is the act of waiting for the umbilical cord to turn white before cutting it. By doing this, all the stem cell-rich blood from the umbilical cord gets a chance to make it into the baby. Umbilical cord blood is very good for the health of the baby. Delayed cord clamping can be done in cesarean births. If you are interested in delayed cord clamping, talk to your healthcare team.

Cesarean sections, although very common, are major medical procedures. Seven layers of the body are cut through and put back together. The body needs to recover from any surgery. If you have a cesarean section, you will likely be given pain medications to help with the recovery. You may also be given iron pills, blood pressure medication, and/or blood thinning medication that may need to be injected. You may experience ankle swelling and need to wear compression socks. They make cute compression socks now. I wear them for EDS, and there are a lot of brands with fun designs, so if you do need compression socks, there are choices out there.

People also experience difficulty moving around and severe pain. The pain can make it difficult to hold the baby or BBC feed. It doesn't mean you can't do either. It just means you might need extra support. I do not tell you this to freak you out. I tell you because a very common complaint with cesarean sections is people not being told ahead of time about what comes after. Especially when it comes to needing to give yourself injections. That is not a great thing to have sprung on you.

There is one more thing I am going to tell you about c-sections. I tell you this because if you go on Reddit or TikTok, or find yourself going down an internet rabbit hole, you will hear about it. Sometimes, the epidural does not work, and people can feel the entire cesarean section procedure. It is rare. However, when it does happen, people tend to talk about it on the internet, making it seem more common than it is. With most trauma, there can be a desire to share it. It can help the person feel better. It can also give a skewed perspective on how often it is actually happening.

Estimations of how frequently this happens vary. When it does happen, it happens for a few reasons. The anesthesia was not administered properly, or enough of it was not given. Enough time may not have passed for it to take effect. Some people are resistant to certain types of anesthesia, making them less effective.

If you feel like you are not going numb with your epidural, talk to your medical team. Talk to your advocate. Steps can very likely be taken to help get you numb, like switching to a different medication. You can do this. You and your body are astoundingly strong and capable. It will be okay.

Now that you have an understanding of the procedure, let's look at the negatives and positives associated with cesarean sections. We will start with the negatives so we can end on a high note. There can be a decrease in oxytocin and prolactin, which are needed for bonding and lactation.[49] Remember the woman from the beginning of the book who struggled to bond with her baby after an emergency c-section? The decrease in oxytocin is why.

There can be difficulties in feeding, both because of the impact on lactation and because it can be difficult to hold the baby.[50] There are delays in skin-to-skin contact. Skin-to-skin contact can still happen, though you may have to ask for it.[51] As with any major surgery, there is post-procedure pain, and pain medications can make people feel fuzzy or groggy. There is possibly a link between cesarean sections and an increased risk of fertility issues and future pregnancy complications.[52] Some research shows cesarean sections lead to higher rates of post-partum depression.[53] This appears to be more common in emergency cesarean sections as opposed to scheduled ones.[54] Likely because emergency cesarean sections are scary and can be traumatic. Now, the good part!

That was a lot of negatives, but there are great parts to a c-section as well. You can schedule them. Scheduling c-sections can get a bad rap, but if you are a caretaker of other children, an elderly family member, or someone with special needs, being able to schedule your birth can be very important. It also increases the likelihood of having the same doctor since it is planned. Cesarean sections can give a person a sense of control. My hope is that through reading this book, you will feel more in control in general and prepared to face spontaneous birth. If you don't, scheduling a cesarean section might give you that sense of control.

Cesarean sections are major surgeries, which means it can be easier to rest and ask for help. Again, I hope that this book will help you prioritize your needs and ask for the necessary help for any birth. But if asking for help and giving yourself time to rest is difficult for you, playing the *I had a major surgery where they cut through seven layers of my body* card might be really helpful. With a cesarean section, you likely won't experience any pain during birth. If you have one, you can have a vaginal birth in the future, though the type of incision you have will affect that. We used to think, "once a c-section, always a c-section." That isn't true anymore. You can even find doulas who specialize in VBAC—vaginal birth after a cesarean.

One last thing on cesarean sections. The most important thing. They save lives. The lives of birthers and the lives of babies. The cesarean section is a vital medical procedure that we are lucky to have access to. Like so many things, it is easy, when you are in the best of circumstances, to dismiss them or put them down, but if you don't have the best of circumstances, you will be grateful they exist. I mentioned that the first step—after consent—for a cesarean section is an epidural. Let's explore epidurals and pain medications next.

Epidurals and Pain Medications

Pain medication is not well-defined in the research and can mean different things in terms of what medications and how much constitutes "pain medication." It is an umbrella term in the research. Here are some basic things to know about pain medication in general.

Pain medications can be administered in several different ways. Oral medication that you swallow, although this is uncommon when it comes to birth. Intravenous (IV) or injections are more common. Patient-Controlled Analgesia Pumps allow the person to control the delivery of their pain medication. In the case of nitrous oxide, the medication is inhaled.

Pain medications serve the purpose of reducing pain. Yay! That's a great purpose for them to serve. However, there are some things to be aware of if you're using pain medications during childbirth. They can have side effects, including nausea and vomiting, itching, dizziness, breathing complications, and feeling groggy.[55] If you've ever taken pain medication for your wisdom teeth removal or back pain, you are probably familiar with the effects of pain medication. The effects will be similar during childbirth. Remember that if you give birth in a hospital, they will likely not allow you to consume any food, which can impact the side effects, especially nausea.

There are more complications when it comes to the baby. These are side effects that *can* happen, not *will* happen. But pain medication use during childbirth is linked to respiratory issues, lack of oxygen to the blood, altered neurological behavior, difficulty regulating body temperature, and changes in fetal heart rate.[56] The doctors may have to administer Naloxone to the baby.[57] If you aren't familiar with the medication—brand name Narcan—it is used to stop opioid overdoses. Pain medication can also delay lactation and decrease the baby's ability to latch and suckle.[58] None of this is to say don't use pain medication. It is here so you can make an informed decision and be prepared to tackle any complications.

If the baby is having trouble regulating their body temperature, provide more skin-to-skin contact. Providing skin-to-skin contact will also help transfer the microbiome that cesarean section babies don't get from birth—more on this later. If your milk doesn't let down right away, don't panic. You may just need to wait for the medication to leave your system.

Epidurals

Epidurals are the most common type of nerve block for childbirth, and the one frequently referred to in research. Technically, there are other kinds, but most often we talk about epidurals. Epidurals are pain medications that are injected directly into the space around the spine using a long needle. They prevent pain signals in the spine from reaching the brain.[*]

Imagine that your pain is inside a delivery truck. Your nerves are the highway and your brain is the drop-off location. In this scenario, the epidural is a roadblock that prevents the truck from getting to the drop-off location. Great! The brain doesn't know about the truck. But...the

---

[*]When we discussed cesarean section, we went over the rare occurrence when epidurals do not provide pain relief.

truck is still on the road, and it is still full of pain. Your body is technically still experiencing pain even if your mind isn't registering it.

An epidural may need to be administered multiple times—remember the cesarean sections that don't go numb. To prevent needing to give multiple injections, a small tube is usually placed to keep the pathway open. Tape will be secured over the spine to prevent infection and to stabilize the tube. Sometimes, the tubes fall out. You may have heard this referred to as "your epidural falling out." If the tube comes out, they will replace it. Make sure your medical team knows if you have any allergies to tape.

Like with a cesarean, there are negatives and positives to an epidural. Epidurals can increase birth length—by slowing down contractions, which increases the need for assisted birth, instrument delivery, and an emergency cesarean.[59] Epidurals numb the body, including the legs. This can make it unsafe to move around, preventing you from using spontaneous movement to help position and encourage the baby. You also likely will not be able to get up to use the bathroom. A catheter may be placed so that you do not need to.

There are also "walking epidurals." This combined spinal-epidural anesthesia uses both a lose dose local anesthetic and a pain medication, like fentanyl.[60] This allows for more movement including the ability to birth in other positions besides supine. They do require significant monitoring for blood pressure, fetal heart rate, and when moving around, as falls do happen. They are less likely to cause the complications associated with traditional pain medications however, there are still some concerns. They can increase labor length. They can cause a drop in blood pressure which can reduce the oxygen supply to the baby. However, they are less likely to impact the baby and latching.

Despite the fact that there is no pain with an epidural, cortisol levels remain high.[61] All of the negatives associated with high cortisol, including disrupting oxytocin production, low maternal attachment, and delayed lactation, can still be an issue. We know that a decrease in oxytocin levels impacts bonding and successful lactation.[62] This takes us back to the blocked highway metaphor. Even though the truck can't get to the drop-off location, i.e., you can't feel the pain. The truck is still on the road, meaning your body is responding to pain even if you can't feel it.

The research is conflicting on the relationship between epidurals and postpartum depression. However, a review of ten studies, including two meta-analyses, found some evidence that epidurals reduced the risk of postpartum depression, and some evidence that they do not.[63] Currently, we do not know if epidurals are beneficial when it comes to postpartum depression. Epidurals do have positives to consider over traditional pain medication. There are no feelings of being high or groggy. The baby is less likely to need Naloxone when compared to traditional pain medication because very little of the pain medication enters the bloodstream.[64] And most importantly, epidurals can prevent pain.

A meta-analysis is when researchers analyze multiple previous studies to explore consistencies and patterns.

The last form of medical intervention for pain relief we are going to look at is nitrous gas. You may be familiar with nitrous gas from the dentist's office. Or from the play *Little Shop of Horrors*. Nitrous gas is commonly referred to as laughing gas because it makes people feel silly, and they tend to laugh a lot while on it. Unlike the other forms of pain relief that we discussed, this one is inhaled either through a mouthpiece or a mask.

This method of pain relief is common for childbirth pain in countries like the United Kingdom, Australia, Canada, Finland, Sweden, New Zealand, and Norway.[65] I could tell you what the research says about nitrous gas, but it is really outdated and feels unhelpful. Instead, I am going to tell you that all those countries I just mentioned—which regularly use nitrous gas for pain relief during childbirth—are considered to have very good infant and maternal mortality ratings. It is unlikely that they would have such good infant and maternal mortality ratings if the pain relief method they were using was dangerous.

In the past, the United States used nitrous gas more frequently, though not as often as other countries. The rates of nitrous gas declined in favor of narcotics and anesthetics, including epidurals. When rates of nitrous gas declined, maternal mortality rates increased. Now, this is a casual relationship. We don't have the data to say that the decline in nitrous gas led to an increase in maternal mortality. We don't want to make assumptions.

In the statistics world, we say correlation is not causation. There are so many other unknowns that could be happening. I remember in my first stats class, to illustrate this point, my professor Anne O'Dwyer, put a graph on the board with the rates of ice cream consumption and rates of violent crimes for each month of the year. As ice cream sales increase, so do rates of violent crimes. If you were to assume causation, it would mean that ice cream makes people commit violent crimes. That is not true. What is true is the other unseen variable. Heat. When it gets hotter, people eat more ice cream. When it gets hotter, people are more likely to commit violent crimes. Ice cream and violent crimes themselves are unrelated.

This is important to understand as you go out and do your own research after you finish this book. Just because there is a relationship between two (or more) things doesn't mean we understand what that relationship means. I'm not saying that nitrous gas reduced maternal mortality. I am saying that it's interesting information that we don't fully understand right now, and we should not underestimate it.

I feel confident it is a safe form of pain relief for those who are interested. Use started increasing in the United States in 2010, making it more accessible. In the past, you might not have had the option, but now it's more likely you will. If you think you might want to use nitrous oxide, check with your birthing location right away to find out if nitrous oxide will be accessible.

Monitoring

Now, let's talk about some medical interventions that are not related to pain relief. These are interventions that can occur either for monitoring or to assist childbirth. First, we will explore monitors. Monitors are used for two purposes: to gather information about the baby's heart rate and to measure the strength and frequency of uterine contractions.

Fetal Heart Rate Monitors can be internal or external. An external monitor, called a tocodynamometer, sits on the belly and is secured by a strap worn around the belly. Fetal Scalp Electrodes, or FSE for short, are used for internal monitoring. For this procedure, a small electrode is threaded through the cervix and attached directly to the baby's head. To have a Fetal Scalp Electrode, the cervix must be dilated, and the amniotic sac cannot be intact. If the sac has not ruptured naturally and an FSE needs to be placed, the sac will be ruptured by a member of the healthcare team.

FSEs provide more accurate data about the baby's heart rate compared to external monitors. External monitors can be affected by movement and contractions. FSEs provide consistent information, which can be vital in high-risk pregnancies.[66] The downside is that they can be uncomfortable, they are invasive, they limit mobility, and generally, they can give a sort of creepy heebie-jeebies feeling.

Intrauterine Pressure Catheters, or IUPC for short, monitor the strength and frequency of uterine contractions. Again, the device is threaded through the cervix, although, it is not attached directly to the baby. The cervix must be dilated, and the amniotic sac cannot be intact. The IUPC gives information on contractions in real time.[67] These would be used when your own awareness of your body does not provide sufficient information for everyone's safety. The downsides are the same as with FSEs: they are invasive, can cause discomfort, limit mobility, and it might feel icky to some people knowing there is something going through their cervix and then out into the world connected to monitors. If your healthcare team thinks you might need internal monitoring, then you can start preparing yourself now if you find it a little creepy.

When it comes to internal monitoring there is contradicting research about the risk of infection. One study found that internal monitoring did not increase the risk of infection. This study looked at 188 women who gave birth.[68] Another study looking at 8,482 women who gave birth found that there was an increased risk of maternal infection.[69] That study also found that obesity increased the likelihood of internal monitoring, and that internal monitoring increased the likelihood of cesarean sections.

This could be another example of correlation, not causation. For example, obesity increases the likelihood of needing a cesarean section, so maybe the internal monitoring and the cesarean section were a result of the pregnant person's weight. Internal monitoring is used in high-risk pregnancies, which may result in cesarean sections more often. I don't want to assume that internal monitors cause cesarean sections. I don't think that would be accurate. Another possibility is that internal monitors are part of the *Cascade of Interventions,* which we will talk more about now in relation to synthetic oxytocin.

Synthetic Oxytocin

Synthetic oxytocin is another medical intervention you may come across. Synthetic oxytocin is often referred to as Pitocin. Pitocin is a brand name. In the same way, we say Band-Aid instead of adhesive bandage or Kleenex instead of tissue; Pitocin is the commonly used term.

Oxytocin naturally occurs in the body. It can occur after childbirth, during breastfeeding, or during sexual activity. It can also be stimulated by touch—which does not have to be sexual, exercise, or music.[70] Synthetic oxytocin is created in a lab. Synthetic oxytocin is used to stimulate contractions and speed up birth or to prevent postpartum hemorrhaging. The body, however, does not respond the same way to synthetic oxytocin as it does to naturally occurring oxytocin.

Synthetic oxytocin can lead to hyperstimulation, which can lead to fetal distress and an increase in emergency cesarean sections.[71] Synthetic oxytocin leading to a cesarean section is an example of the "Cascade of Interventions." The Cascade of Interventions is the term used to describe how one intervention can lead to multiple interventions and even end in an emergency cesarean section.

It is important to be aware of the Cascade of Interventions when making a decision about interventions, as a seemingly small decision may cause additional interventions to be forced on you. Synthetic oxytocin is often used to explain the Cascade of Interventions.

A person is at the hospital, and birth is slow to progress. Contractions are infrequent and may be weak. Synthetic oxytocin is administered. This speeds up contractions and makes them very, very strong. So strong that the pain becomes unbearable, and an epidural is needed. Except, the epidural slows down contractions and makes them weaker, bringing us back to the starting point. More synthetic oxytocin is administered to speed the contractions back up. Then, the pain increases, leading to more epidural medications, which leads to more synthetic oxytocin. This cycle continues, which can lead to fetal distress. Fetal distress means there is an emergency, which leads to an emergency cesarean section.

Does this happen every time? Absolutely not. I was a synthetic oxytocin baby that was not delivered by cesarean section. But it happens enough that there is a name for it, so it is important to be aware of the Cascade of Interventions.

Synthetic oxytocin can also increase the likelihood of needing an Intrauterine Pressure Catheter to check for hyperstimulation.[72] If synthetic oxytocin is going to be administered, it is a good time for your advocate to step in and start asking questions. In addition to the Cascade of Interventions, synthetic oxytocin can also lead to allergic reactions.[73] In one study, women who had synthetic oxytocin during childbirth had higher rates of depression and anxiety two months postpartum.[74] It is important to balance the risks and benefits of any intervention, but this is especially true with synthetic oxytocin.

Instrument Deliveries

Instrument deliveries are a type of assisted birth. There are two types of instrument deliveries: forceps delivery and vacuum extraction. Forceps are medical "tongs" that surround the baby's head. While the birthing person pushes down, the forceps are used to pull the baby out of the birth canal.

They are used when the baby's positioning is problematic, birth is not progressing, or when the baby needs to be delivered quickly. An epidural or local anesthetic is used to prevent pain. Forceps can lead to tearing. To prevent tearing—sometimes not always—an episiotomy will be performed. An episiotomy is when a surgical cut is made in the area between the vulva and the anus—called the perineum. This creates more space in the vaginal opening.

Other things to be aware of are that forceps delivery can damage the body, leading to urinary incontinence or bladder/urethra injuries. These injuries can be repaired. If you have a forceps delivery, you will want to watch for any issues that arise so you can speak to your healthcare team about them.

Forceps delivery can lead to minor facial injuries or facial weakness in the baby. You may notice bruising or marks on their head. Their head may be slightly misshapen but will return to normal shape. Very rarely, there can be skull fractures or damage to the cranial molding that requires medical intervention.

Vacuum extraction is similar in a lot of ways to forceps delivery. But rather than medical tongs a vacuum pump with a suction cap is attached to the baby's head. The birthing person pushes, and the suction is used to pull the baby out of the birth canal.

Vacuum extraction is used when birth is not progressing or when the baby needs to be delivered quickly. An epidural or local anesthetic is used to prevent pain. Vacuum extraction requires less space than forceps, so an episiotomy is less likely. There is still a risk of tearing, though. There is also a risk of urinary incontinence. The risks to the baby include minor scalp wounds and jaundice.[75]

It might seem odd that a birth intervention can lead to jaundice, so let's break that down. Remember, this is something that can happen, not something that will happen. The suction from the vacuum can cause substantial bruising on the baby's head. Blood collects between the baby's skin and skull bone, causing a cephalohematoma, which is a fancy way of saying the blood is clotting around the scalp. When red blood cells break down—which is what happens with bruising—they produce bilirubin. Bilirubin gives the skin a yellow pigment. You've seen it if you've had a bruise go from purple to yellow.

In adults and older children, the liver processes the bilirubin and excretes it in the bile. The livers of newborns aren't fully developed, preventing them from completely processing the bilirubin. When bilirubin accumulates faster than the body can process it, the skin and eyes can yellow, which is what we call jaundice. Jaundice is commonly treated with phototherapy, where a blue spectrum light is used to break down the bilirubin. However, skin-to-skin contact and human milk are also supportive in treating jaundice.

A holistic approach uses all three to treat jaundice. Phototherapy can be important, but so is skin-to-skin— which we will talk more about when we get to what happens after birth. If phototherapy is necessary, you or your advocate should talk to your healthcare team about your skin-to-skin plan.

A final note on vacuum extraction: very rarely, it can lead to skull fractures or internal bleeding. Again, this is rare, but you always want to balance risk with reward when making any medical decision. You get to determine the value of those risks and rewards. Get all the information about your specific situation so you can make an informed decision that is right for you and your circumstances.

Membrane Sweeping

We are now going to talk about our last medical intervention. I am going to let you know upfront this section can be difficult. After we discuss the intervention itself, we are going to go straight into talking about consent and medical consent. I know that these conversations can be upsetting, scary, and enraging. But I am not here to sugarcoat the truth. I am here to give you information that, frankly, you have every right to have.

In her TedTalk, "The Lies We Tell Pregnant Women," Dr. Jawed-Wessel talks about our tendency in to infantilize pregnant women.[76] We reduce them to cute entities that need to be protected. Protection, however, tends to go hand in hand with a lack of autonomy. Society strips pregnant people of their autonomy every time a pregnant belly is touched without permission, or even when a stranger asks. It's weird. You wouldn't ask a random person if you could touch their hair.

I personally believe the inherent desire to touch a pregnant person's belly comes from the evolutionarily old part of our brain that understands that communities survive better than individuals on their own. When we lived in small groups, a baby was the community's baby. Everyone was responsible for the well-being of the baby and, thus, felt a part of the pregnancy. Of course, that isn't true for how we live anymore, and a random person in the supermarket should not ask to touch your belly.

We ask pregnant people for personal details about their medical plans. That's weird. If you wouldn't ask someone about their most recent pap smear, don't ask them about their birth plan. These are personal medical decisions.

And as much as I talk about "non-medicalized birth," birth is inherently medical in our society, making a birth plan private. It is protected by HIPPA like all other medical information and medical procedure plans.

We also strip pregnant people of their autonomy by withholding information. Society acts as though pregnant women are not smart enough or strong enough to be trusted with the truth about pregnancy. It's bizarre. They are literally the ones making the baby. It all feels very *Handmaid's Tale* when you really think about it.

A very classic example of this is alcohol consumption. How often have you heard that pregnant people cannot consume alcohol? How many signs in bathrooms have you seen about fetal alcohol syndrome? If you have ordered alcohol while visibly pregnant, did someone refuse to serve you—as though they know more about your well-being than you do? Now, how often has someone offered you an alcoholic drink while pregnant?

The consumption of any amount of alcohol is not automatically dangerous. It is the amount of alcohol, the rate at which it is consumed, and other factors that impact when alcohol consumption becomes dangerous.[77] Pregnant people are literally creating life, carrying life around, and releasing it from their bodies so that an entirely new person can exist. I think pregnant people are strong enough to handle all the information. Even when the information sucks. With that, let's get into membrane stripping.

> If you are interested in learning more about alcohol consumption or other myths you've been told, I suggest you check out Emily Oster's book *Expecting Better*. Emily Oster is an economist who is very good at breaking down research studies. She goes through what pregnant women are typically told and whether the research actually supports it.

Membrane sweeping—also called membrane stripping—is the act of detaching the membranes from the lower part of the uterus. This causes the production of hormones that stimulate dilation and speed up childbirth. The procedure consists of two fingers being inserted into the vaginal canal up to the cervix. A sweeping motion is made to detach the membranes.[78] This technique was invented in 1810 to induce birth, long before synthetic oxytocin was invented.[79] Today, it is typically used when synthetic oxytocin has not been successful at speeding up childbirth.[80]

Membrane sweeping is sometimes practiced by midwives. However, I will say there appears to be conflict in the midwife community over whether this is considered best practice. One study found that membrane sweeping is only effective 21% of the time and it introduced bacteria causing infection.[81] Another study found no increased risk of infection. However, in that same study, membrane sweeping did not reduce the need for instrument delivery or cesarean section.[82] So, while it did not increase the risk of infection, it also didn't really do anything of value either.

The reason I started this section with a discussion about autonomy is because of the frequency that membrane sweeping occurs without consent.[83] This looks like a person being told they are going to be checked for their dilation status. A routine exam. Then suddenly, something feels wrong or bad or very painful. They may even feel the insertion of an "amnihook," a long, thin plastic hook that is used to break the amniotic sac. There is less data on amniotomies—the procedure that breaks the amniotic sac—without consent, but it does occur.

Oftentimes, no one tells the person what occurred or why it felt different. They may not know for years until they hear about someone else's experience. Sometimes, they very casually and without concern say, "Oh, I stripped your membranes," as though you shouldn't be bothered by the information. You absolutely should be bothered.

Giving birth is not a blanket consent for the healthcare team to do whatever they want to you, whenever they want, without talking to you. That is a violation of your body. Even if a person doesn't feel pain—not everyone does—the body is aware of being violated. And that a violent action occurred against it without permission.

If you want your childbirth to speed up and synthetic oxytocin didn't do it for you, and you want to try membrane sweeping. Great! Go for it! All the power to you. Membrane sweeping isn't inherently bad. What is bad? Action without consent. So, with that in mind, let's explore consent.

Medical Interventions		
Intervention	**Upside**	**Downside**
C Section	Can schedule Increases the likelihood of having the same doctor Control Makes it easier to rest and ask for help Likely less pain during birth Save lives Can still have a vaginal delivery	Decreases oxytocin and prolactin Needed for bonding and feeding Difficulty BBC Feeding Delays skin to skin contact Post procedure pain Increased risk of fertility issues, pregnancy complications, and asthma in infants Higher rates of PPD
Pain Medication	Can be administered in a variety of ways Relives pain Fentanyl reduced the duration of active labor in one study	Birthing Person: Nausea/vomiting Itching Dizziness Breathing complications Feeling groggy Delated lactation Infant: respiratory issues Altered neurological behaviors difficulty regulating body temperature May need Naloxone Heart rate changes Difficulty latching and sucking
Epidural	No pain (usually) No feeling of groggy or being high infant less likely to need Naloxone than with pain medication More positive feelings, lower rates of PTSD, and earlier first feeding in one study	Cortisol remains high Can increase labor length Increased rate of assisted Birth/instrument delivery Decreases oxytocin levels Can't move around
Synthetic Oxytocin	Stimulates contractions Speeds up labor Prevents hemorrhage	Lab created Hyperstimulation Fetal distress Increased need for C section Allergic reactions Postpartum depression and anxiety Possible increased risk for autism in male infants
Nitrous Gas	Laughing Gas Reduces pain Popular in countries with excellent infant and maternal mortality	Nausea/vomiting Lightheadedness

Birth Better.

For your convenience, I have provided a quick reference breakdown of the medical interventions discussed in this section. A printable version can be found at mindbodybirthbook.com

Medical Interventions

Intervention	About
Forceps Delivery	Medical "tongs" surround the baby's head, and the baby is pulled while the birthing person pushes Used when baby positioning is problematic, labor is not progressing or the baby needs to be delivered quickly Epidural or local anesthetic is used Can lead to tearing, urinary incontinence, bladder/urethra injuries This can lead to minor facial injuries, weakness in facial muscles
Vacuum Delivery	A vacuum pump with a cap is attached to the baby's head, and the suction pulls while the birthing person pushes Labor is not progressing, or the baby needs to be delivered quickly Epidural or local anesthetic is used Can lead to tearing, urinary incontinence Can lead to minor scalp wounds, jaundice, RARELY skull fracture, or internal bleeding
Internal Monitoring	Two Kinds: one for fetal heart rate, one for uterine contractions Both insert a wire through the cervix Amniotic sac is ruptured if intact May increase the risk of maternal infection May increase the likelihood of C-section
Membrane Sweeping	Fingers are inserted to detach the membranes around the cervix Stimulates hormones causing dilation and progressing birth Conflict over whether it helps May cause a risk of infection Occurs without consent

Consent

I come from a psychology and social work background. So, from my experience, there are three types of consent: consent, informed consent, and complete consent. Consent is the idea that someone needs to ask your permission before doing something. It is the most basic form of consent. All parties must agree to an action before it occurs. This definition looks at consent from a legal perspective. "Can I kiss you?" is an example of consent.

Informed consent is a more formal term. It is used in healthcare and in research. Informed consent is the idea that you cannot consent to something without having all of the information, including the right to change your mind. Informed consent often looks like really long forms people sign but do not read. This definition looks at consent from an ethical perspective. "Can I kiss you? I have an active herpes outbreak, and I'm in a monogamous relationship," is informed consent.

You can see the difference. Sure, they are asking for permission in the first example. But asking for permission doesn't really tell you what you are consenting to. Which, in this case, would be exposing yourself to herpes and kissing a person who would be engaging in cheating. If you want to do those things, that is your prerogative. That's the point. It is your prerogative. Your decision. You can't decide to do or not do something if you don't have all the information.

The final type of consent comes from the therapy world. This is full and complete consent. In full and complete consent, the person isn't just given all of the information. Full and complete consent makes sure that the person understands what that information means and that they do not have to consent to every part. If consent is based on legal standards, and informed consent is based on ethical standards, then complete consent is guided by compassion and empathy.

It's great for a person to have the information, but it doesn't mean much if they don't understand it. In our kissing example, if the person didn't know what herpes is or what the risks of herpes are, being informed of a herpes outbreak doesn't mean anything. Another example is if your medical team says, "We want to administer synthetic oxytocin, and there is a potential iatrogenic complication of oxytocin augmentation in labor, which can be delineated as an acute onset of alveolar-capillary barrier dysfunction precipitated by a rapid transudation of fluid into the pulmonary interstitium and alveolar spaces, do you consent?" That is not a super helpful question. They may be doing their due diligence by asking for consent. However, the intent of consent is not being met.

If you do not ensure that a person understands what they are consenting to and the possible implications of that consent, to me, it isn't consent. Of course, we can't always know every possible outcome to every possible scenario. Complete consent asks that, to the best of the person's ability, they are giving all the information and helping to ensure the consenter understands what they are consenting to and the possible outcomes.

Here's one more example. Conversations with licensed therapists are protected. The therapist cannot share the information given to them by a client in a session. However, there are exceptions to this rule including if the client has plans to hurt themselves or someone else. Everyone who goes to therapy fills out a bunch of paperwork, and somewhere in that paperwork, these exceptions are written. When the client signs the papers, they consent to having those exceptions be reported should they come up. If a therapist hears of plans that are not protected and reports them, they have the signed consent, and legally, they are all good. Ethically though…

The person I consider to be a good therapist will have a conversation with the client about the limits of therapist-patient privilege so the client can make an informed decision about what information they want to disclose. It is the client's right to choose not to share information, even if it is information that the therapist—and possibly legal authorities—should have.

Complete consent is hard. All consent can be hard. But it is also vital. When I work with professionals to teach them about Mind-Body, Birth, we talk at length about consent. It can be difficult for someone in the helping profession to set aside their experience and expertise. It can be hard for a therapist to not dig deeper into a safety issue and instead remind a client of the limits of privileged conversation. Even if you're not a professional, it can be hard to watch someone make decisions that you disagree with. But people are autonomous beings. They deserve to be treated as such. We need to let people make their own decisions, by giving them the most accurate information that we can, because they are the ones that live with the outcomes of what they consent to.

There are other ethical considerations when it comes to consent, and these come in the form of power dynamics. If someone has a weapon or is threatening you, is it consent? Of course not. What if the threat is subtle or implied? Perhaps a boss or someone you are trying to get a business contract with hints that if you do not do something they want you to do, you'll be passed over. We heard about that occurring frequently during the *Time's Up* movement in Hollywood. Producers or directors had been pressuring—usually young—actresses in order for them to keep their roles.

What if the person is not a boss but a different type of authority figure? How does that power dynamic change the way people consent? To answer that, we need to travel all the way back to 1961 to Yale University. Stanley Milgram was conducting an experiment to try to understand genocide.[84] Milgram conducted a psychological experiment that included three roles: the experimenter, the teacher, and the learner. The teacher was the only actual participant in the study, although they did not know the learner was part of the experiment. The teacher and learner—a paid actor—arrived together where they met and interacted. They were told they were taking part in a memory and learning study for which they would be compensated $4.00, worth roughly $40 today.

The two "participants" would draw slips of paper to determine who was the teacher and who was the learner. The paid actor who was in on the study would always claim their paper said learner. In reality, both papers said "teacher." With the roles assigned, they were then taken to different rooms.

They could communicate through speakers, but they were unable to see each other. The learner was strapped to an electric chair. The experimenter would inform the teacher that the learner was strapped down, so they could not escape. The teacher received a sample mild electric shock to experience what the learner would be feeling. Then, the experiment would "begin." But not really. It had all been part of the experiment.

The teacher was given a list of word pairs to teach the learner. After reading the list, the teacher would give the learner a word and four possible answers. If the answer was incorrect, the teacher would administer a shock to the learner. Each wrong answer caused the shock voltage to increase. The shock generator was labeled from "Slight Shock" to "Danger: Severe Shock." **No shocks were actually given**.

Prerecorded responses to the shocks, including banging on the wall and audible distress, were played so the teacher believed the learner was being shocked. If the teacher tried to stop, the experimenter—who wore a white coat to visually signal his authority—would give verbal prods in this order:

1.   Please continue, *or* Please go on.
2.   The experiment requires that you continue.
3.   It is absolutely essential that you continue.
4.   You have no other choice; you *must* go on.

What do you think the results were? Did the teachers give shocks up to the danger level? Participants in the study displayed stress and tension. They would sweat, tremble, and dig their fingernails into their skin. Every participant paused the study at least once, but most continued after the experimenter's prods. 14 participants stopped before the highest shock level. 26 administered it.

This study is pretty messed up. Not just because of the results, but also because of the deception and distress caused to the participants, which is something that would not pass an ethics review board today. While there are criticisms of this study—like most well-known experiments—including the ethical component, we learned a lot about how this specific group of people responded to pressure from authority figures. In short, the study concluded that people would go against their own judgment—even to the point of causing themselves physical distress—when an authority figure tells them to.

What does this have to do with you and giving birth? Think about the fact that the experimenter wore a white coat to solidify their air of authority. It is likely that if you give birth in a hospital, people in white coats are going to be asking for your consent. They may not only be wearing a white coat, but they may say pressuring statements. We discussed that it isn't really consent if you are being threatened. What if a doctor says, "If you don't have a c-section right now, your baby might suffer." Consent becomes more grey. Especially if you don't have all the information.

I'm not saying all doctors are bad or immoral or will pressure you to do things you don't want to do. I am saying that some will. It might be a very, very small percentage, but it is more than zero. This may never happen to you—and I really hope that is the case. But if I don't give you the forewarning so that you are prepared to be skeptical and ask for all the information, then I would be failing you just like someone who doesn't offer complete consent.

Look, I know reading this book kind of sucks. I know I started this book explaining that you were going to birth fearlessly, and now I am throwing all kinds of terrifying stuff at you. I get that it is awful. I do.

I am an extremely nervous flyer. I hate it. Yet I travel a lot, both for professional reasons and because I love visiting other cultures and going on adventures. My sister once had to talk me down on a plane from Las Vegas to Michigan because I was so claustrophobic, I was convinced I was going to give myself a heart attack and I would die on the plane. I was trying to get the flight attendant to let me off the plane before they closed the doors. Katie kept me calm, and thankfully, the plane had Wi-Fi, so she could text me the whole way. I managed to make it through the flight. No panic-induced heart attack.

No matter how much I fly, I always, always locate the emergency exits when I get to my seat. I do this because I am an anxious flyer. I also do this because the research shows that when people locate the emergency exits during the plane safety briefing, they respond more effectively in actual emergency situations.[85] They have the information. Their brains remember—because our brains cling to survival information, like the rabbit with the snare.

So, consider this your birthing safety briefing. I am pointing out the illuminated floor path, the exit doors, and the life vests under your seat. In the, probably, hundreds of thousands of miles I've flown in my life, I have never needed to use the emergency exit door that I located. And I don't think that you will need to fight an evil, white-coated doctor who is trying to trick you into surgery. But if you aren't on the lookout, you might be less prepared to respond in an emergency situation.

I want to talk about consent outside of the medical world because even though this is a book on birth, you are a whole entire person whose life does not begin and end with pregnancy. Not all of us—in fact, most of us—were not raised with conversations about consent. Understanding consent is important for how we interact with the world. And it is important for anyone who interacts with or raises kids.

What children learn about consent will impact how they let others treat them when they get older. For example, if very young children are forced to hug family members when they do not want to, it teaches them that their bodily autonomy doesn't matter. Consent isn't always sexual. Consent has to do with having your picture posted on someone's social media. Or having your picture taken in the first place. Making consent a part of the conversation early on can help protect children as they age and increase their confidence.

Types of Consent

Consent
Everyday
Legal
All parties agree to an action before it occurs

Informed Consent
Healthcare and Research
Ethical
All the information is given, and you are told you have the right to change your mind

Complete Consent
Therapy
Compassion and Empathy
Ensures that not only is all the information given ahead of time, but there is complete understanding, including the possible outcomes.

In my work outside of birth, I teach kids about consent using ice cream sundaes. I have kids get in pairs and make sundaes for their partners. This gives them the opportunity to ask questions in a low-stakes, safe situation. What do you want? What don't you like? Is this ok? One of the things we talk about is consent versus enthusiastic consent. If you like strawberry ice cream but your partner likes vanilla and they say, "Just get vanilla. Do it. You'll be cooler if you get vanilla like me," and you agree to the vanilla; it may have been consent, but it wasn't enthusiastic consent.

You should be excited when you give consent. Of course, we are humans, and sometimes, adults in committed relationships consent without enthusiasm—like yes, of course, you can put on your Fantasy Football podcast during the entire road trip—because it makes life a little easier. But that shouldn't be the model. Saying yes to something you do not want to do to make a situation end or to avoid something that might be worse is not consent. Saying yes because someone is bullying or belittling you, is not consenting. Saying yes because you are scared or don't see any other option is never consent. All relationships require consent, all the time. Marriage, partnership, or raising a child together does not entitle someone to act without consent. If you are unsafe in your relationship, there is help. You can contact the National Domestic Violence Hotline at 1-800-799-7233, chat on their website, thehotline.org, or text "start" to 88788.

Saying NO

No is one of the first words toddlers really latch on to. It's short. Easy to pronounce. And it holds so much power. The word "no" is control. As young children learn that they can influence the world around them and that they have autonomy over themselves, "no" is the key that puts understanding into practice. Though sometimes it's the practice that leads to the understanding.

No. Glorious. Two little letters. One syllable. The power to change. That may be why it is so quickly phased out of the vocabulary of people raised female. When I was studying sex therapy and sexual health education at the University of Michigan, one of my lecturers said something from Carol Gilligan's *A Different Voice*, that hit me like a ton of bricks.[86] He said, "If you ask a little girl what she wants on her pizza, she'll tell you. If you ask a teenage girl, she'll say, 'I don't know.' If you ask an adult woman, she'll say, 'I don't know, what do you want?'" I felt both fully seen and completely attacked. It was a change I had experienced in myself and witnessed in others around me.

If you were raised female, it is likely not shocking to you when I say that females are taught to be small. Not to take up space. Be amenable and kind. Smile more. Smile when people tell you to smile. Smile when people tell you to smile, even when you don't feel like smiling. Accept the hug you don't want. Accept the touch you don't want. Accept the emotional labor you aren't compensated for. Accept less money for the work you are compensated for. Let the guy at the gym tell you that you really should shave your legs before working out because, of course, the only reason you are at the gym is for him to look at you.

Being raised female is great in many ways. And it's awful in many ways. Reclaiming your "no" can be one of the ways to make it less awful. Melissa Spamer taught me the tomato trick, and I would like to share it with you. Before you ask, yes, I did actually do this in public over the course of years until it stopped feeling awkward.

Go to the grocery store—you can go when it isn't very busy. Pick up a tomato, look at it, and say "no." Then, put it down and pick up another one. When you practice saying no, you will find that not all "no's" are created equally. Some "no's" are frantic or argumentative. Some are too quiet. Some sound unconvincing—because we are taught that our "no's" are negotiable. They aren't. No is a complete sentence. No. No justification, explanation, or apology needed.

I encourage you to **PRACTICE SAYING NO**. If going to a grocery store seems too intense or too public, start at home. Painting your nails? Pick up a color you aren't going to use and tell it, "No." Different mugs for your morning coffee. Different forks in the drawer. Different television shows you don't feel like watching. There are so many opportunities to practice saying no. But how often do we really do it? It can be so much easier for "I don't know," to slip out of our mouths. Or a simple shrug. Hell, it's sometimes easier to just do the thing you wanted to say no to, rather than saying no. And that is the problem.

Well, it's all the problem. But going along because it's easier than saying no doesn't just strip people of their autonomy. It's dangerous. It's dangerous in social situations, in sexual situations, and in medical situations. I want you to have a good, strong, complete, comfortable "no" for every aspect of your life. But I *need* you to have a good, strong, complete, and comfortable "no" for your birth. Consent doesn't really matter if your "no" has been chained up inside you over a lifetime of being taught to be agreeable. Someone can ask for your complete consent a thousand times, but if your "no" is stuck it won't do much good.

You 100% do not need my permission for anything. But sometimes it helps to have a scapegoat—someone that you can point at and say, "I would never normally do this. This isn't me at all. I'm really a very agreeable person. But…Dr. V said…" If using me will help you, do it. Practice. It helps. If someone asks you to wash the dishes while you're pregnant say, no. And if you need to, say, "Dr. V said it's really important that I practice saying no and stick to it." Get to a place where it is easy. So, when someone comes into your birthing space and tells you to do something that you don't want to do, that "no" glides from your lips more easily than all those smiles you were forced to fake.

If all of this felt like a lot—and it really can—there are two other ways to practice before enlisting produce in your No journey. You can practice with a friend or a support person. Role-play different situations. They don't have to be serious situations. "Do you want fries with that?" They don't even have to be realistic, "Would you like to ride this unicorn to the land of Zorzaplop?" Okay, that one might be hard to say no to. Get weird. Have fun.

If even forming the word in a playful situation feels like too much, and for some of us, it is. Practice writing the word. Write it 100 times every day until it starts to feel easy. Saying no can be extremely difficult. If you have a history of your "no" being ignored, especially in sexual situations, it can be even more challenging. Go slow. Be patient with yourself and kind to yourself. If this practice feels deeply or viscerally upsetting and those feelings linger, I recommend seeking out professional help.

And while we are talking about professional help remember that therapists are not above your "No." I cannot say this enough, so I am going to put it in bold. **If you do not like your therapist, stop seeing them.** I know this is easier said than done in the age of predatory insurance, but a bad therapist is damaging and possibly dangerous. There are a lot of bad therapists out there. I know some of them. I went to school with some of them. And there are incredible therapists who are not the right therapist *for you*.

Here's the trick to knowing if someone is a good therapist. They will understand when you tell them it isn't a good fit. A therapist who gets upset or tries to argue with you not to stop seeing them—is not a good therapist, and you should find a new one. A therapist who says, "Ok, I wish you the best"—is a good therapist who also totally understands. You have not hurt their feelings. Basically, you do not need to worry about changing therapists because only the bad ones will take it personally. I hope that helps alleviate the guilt a lot of people feel when they want to switch therapists.

How do you know if the therapist is right for you? That can be a difficult question to answer because therapy is hard. It is work. Therapy doesn't always make you feel good. Sometimes you leave feeling like shit. But there is a difference between the work bringing up discomfort and the therapist making you uncomfortable. Your therapist should never make you feel bad about yourself. Your therapist should never make the session about them. It can be helpful for you to explain some things to your therapist if they come from a different background, but it is never your job to educate them. They should maintain good boundaries both for you and for themselves.

I've left therapists before because we simply became too close, and they started giving opinions like friends instead of therapeutic guidance. If your therapist is ever inappropriate or takes advantage of the inherent power dynamic, don't just leave—if you feel able to do so—report them to their licensing board.*

Remember, a therapist is someone you hire to provide a service to you. You are paying them. Sometimes a lot of money! There are no gold stars in therapy. You can't be the best at it, but you also can't be bad at it as long as you are trying. And if you have no desire to go to therapy, you can say, "No."

What is important when it comes to medical interventions—including going to therapy—is not what you choose; it is that you *are* choosing. As always, you do you! You are the only person with all the information about where you are and what you need right now. Therefore, you are the only person whose opinion matters when it comes to making decisions about how you want to give birth.

RED LIGHT/GREEN LIGHT

This is an activity to help you keep track of everything you learn about in this book. You'll take a sheet of paper and label it "Red Light/Green Light." Then, draw three columns. Label the columns green, yellow, and red. Things you are

---

*Licensing boards are different for different types of therapists. You'll be able to use the letters after their name MSW, LMFT, AASECT etc. to do an internet search and find their specific licensing board for your state.

excited about and want to try, whether that's medical interventions or CAM—which we will get to in the next section—write them under the green section. Things you absolutely are not interested in go under the red section. Things you aren't sure about or would like to learn more about, go under the yellow section. Use the intervention cheat sheet to get quick information about medical interventions. Revise this as often as you need to. Remember, you are always allowed to change your mind and make new decisions.

Let's take a moment to talk about prenatal vitamins and MTHFR. MTHFR is a gene mutation that an estimated 150 million people in the United States live with. Most people don't know they have it. I personally didn't know I had it until I was doing infertility workups. To understand what it is, let's talk about what happens when people don't have this gene mutation.

When a person eats food that contains folate or folic acid their bodies start a process where they methylate the folate or folic acid into methylated folate. Methylated folate is then used for many vital processes in the body. It is now even becoming widely accepted that high folate levels protect against HPV.[*] If you have MTHFR, your body cannot methylate, so folate and folic acid just kind of gunk up your system, and you develop a vitamin deficiency.

When you became pregnant you probably started taking a prenatal vitamin. You probably heard the term folic acid more than you'd ever heard it before. Folic acid is the synthetic form of folate. It's cheaper to manufacture, so it's more common.

You may have noticed that a lot of foods, including bread, cereal, and most things covered by WIC, have added folic acid. That's because babies who do not get enough methylated folate develop Spina Bifida and other neural tube defects.

In the 90s, The March of Dimes advocated for the addition of folic acid into foods, making them "fortified." The intention was to reduce the rates of Spina Bifida and neural tube defects, and it worked. If you have MTHFR, though, that folic acid isn't helping whether it is in your cereal or your prenatal vitamin.

If you want to be sure the baby is getting the correct nutrients, you have two options. You can get bloodwork to determine if you have MTHFR, or you can switch to a prenatal vitamin with methylated folate. There are a lot of them out there. I recommend switching because it's easy and it doesn't involve needles. If you are getting prescription prenatal vitamins, talk to your provider. One last thing about MTHFR. It is linked to tongue tie. So, if you know you have it, and you end up having a baby with latching difficulties, it is a good idea to get them checked for tongue tie.

*[Piyathilake, C. J., Macaluso, M., Chambers, M. M., Badiga, S., Siddiqui, N. R., Bell, W. C., Edberg, J. C., Partridge, E. E., Alvarez, R. D., & Johanning, G. L. (2014). Folate and vitamin B12 may play a critical role in lowering the HPV 16 methylation-associated risk of developing higher grades of CIN. *Cancer prevention research (Philadelphia, Pa.), 7*(11), 1128–1137.]

Support Report

- Birth is often categorized as "natural" vs. everything else, but defining "natural" is unclear. Binary categories are unhelpful and can lead to judgment, exclusion, and unnecessary tribalism among birthing people. People should support each other regardless of their birth choices, as many factors influence these decisions.

- There are two types of essential people during birth: a support person and an advocate. Support people should focus solely on you and handle their own needs. Advocates ensure your wishes are respected and challenge medical professionals when needed. Doulas are highly recommended as advocates due to better birth outcomes.

- C-sections save lives but can be medically unnecessary and sometimes pushed for convenience or lawsuit protection. Having an advocate is critical for asking the right questions and making informed decisions.

- Pain medications can be given orally, intravenously, or through inhalation. They prevent feeling pain, which is good. They can also have side effects.

- Epidurals block pain signals from the spine, which is good. They can slow birth and lead to higher cortisol levels, which impact bonding and lactation.

- Nitrous oxide (laughing gas) is commonly used in other countries that have excellent maternal and infant mortality rates.

- Internal and external monitors are used to track contractions and fetal heart rates.

134 Sam Vaive, Ph.D.

- Internal monitors provide more accurate data but can limit mobility and feel invasive.

- Synthetic oxytocin is not the same as naturally occurring oxytocin. Synthetic oxytocin (Pitocin) can induce or speed up birth but may lead to fetal distress, increasing the likelihood of emergency c-sections due to the Cascade of Interventions.

- Forceps and vacuum extraction are used to assist difficult births but carry risks like tearing or injury to both the birthing person and baby.

- Membrane sweeping is a procedure used to induce birth. It can be uncomfortable and is often performed without consent, which is another reason it is important to have an advocate.

- There are three types of consent. Consent, informed consent and complete consent.

- Power dynamics in a medical setting can complicate consent. Advocates can help prevent you feeling pressured into choices you don't want to make.

- The power of "no" is vital in birth and life. Practice saying no in your daily life.

Journaling Prompts

- What qualities make a good advocate? What qualities make a good support person? What will you need from your advocate and your support team before, during, and after birth?

- Who's on your support team? Why did you pick them? Look to your eco-map for inspiration.

- Does "no" come easily to you or do you have a hard time saying no? What situations make no easier? Harder? How does it feel to say no? What can help you be confident in your no?

Complementary Alternative Medicine

I have always been an exceedingly anxious person. After Lockdown, I felt my anxiety rise to a new level. The first time I went to meet a friend and was out long enough that I had to drive home after dark, I panicked. I had to call my spouse before I even made it out of the parking lot. I was so afraid, that I thought I wouldn't be able to safely drive home. Then, the thought that I wouldn't be able to get back home—home, the only place that had been safe for so long—made me more panicked, which made me feel less safe to drive. On and on. The mind does love a good fear spiral.

I did make it safely home and was met with an overwhelming sense of relief. It was a brief glimpse of what would become my mantra in life. Four words that would get me through the hardest moments. Can we get tacos? No wait. Not that. Though tacos can be great when life gets hard, or when life gets awesome, or because it's Tuesday or Friday, or a day that ends in y.

This is not forever. This is not forever. It seems simple. And probably pretty obvious. I think the most effective ways to cope usually are. Complex coping skills are hard to implement when you need them most. When a plane hits turbulence, I would start to remind myself that this is not forever. When a phlebotomist jabbed my arm over and over because my veins do not like to give away blood. This? It's not forever.

I am grateful to the practice of Yoga for instilling this lesson in me. That chair pose that has you dripping in sweat, the pigeon pose that has you soaking in tears. They end. They end, and you will be okay, and life will go on. This is not forever.

It is theorized that this is one of the reasons Yoga is so effective at improving the childbirth experience. The temporary nature of discomfort gets engrained in you. This is not forever. So, when a contraction comes rolling through your body, you know deep in your mind's experience of your body, that the pain will end. This is not forever.

In the United States, our conventional medical practice is called Western Medicine. This is distinguished from Eastern Medicine. Western Medicine is focused on diagnosing and treating *illnesses*, whereas Eastern Medicine is more focused on the *person*. If you've made it this far in the book, you know I am going to say that there are pros and cons to both. Fortunately, Western Medicine has started to recognize the benefits of non-conventional medicine. While there is not a universally accepted definition, generally, we call these practices Complementary Alternative Medicine or CAM.

We are going to talk about some of these methods that have been shown through research studies to be beneficial for childbirth. CAM is diverse. It's a big umbrella term that lumps together things we normally wouldn't think of as being related, like massage and counting. There are so many different options that they might not all appeal to you. That's okay. Focus on the ones that do. Also, because there are so many practices, we won't get to talk about all of them. We will touch on all the ones that I consider to be major players in improving the childbirth experience based on the research. There are others. So, if you like the idea of CAM but these particular types of CAM aren't doing it for you, go explore. There's more out there to discover.

Distraction Technique

I volunteer at a wildlife rescue. It seems that no matter what I am doing with my life, I always find myself doing something to work with animals. After Lockdown, I found myself at a particular wildlife rescue that works with fawns. Working with animals is wonderful. It is also not without its shortcomings. One of those is *zoonotic diseases* or illnesses that effect both animals and humans. After getting a particularly nasty intestinal parasite from one of the cute baby deer, I found myself in urgent care.

I was extremely dehydrated. So much so that over the course of two hours, they tried to get blood from me and were never able to. I don't have great veins for blood draws to begin with. As I took a deep breath to brace myself for the first poke, I began to sing *Semi-Charmed Life* by Third Eye Blind, in my head. Why that song? I don't have a good answer other than that I've always found it pretty distracting.

After we left urgent care, my spouse was very concerned about my arms. He explained to me that the guy had been digging and digging around, trying—and failing—to get a vein. He almost had to leave because he couldn't watch it. I was completely oblivious to any of it until I noticed all the marks and bruises on my arms. This is an example of a Distraction Technique.

I love this technique because not only is it effective, but it can also be anything. Doing a puzzle, telling jokes, shredding paper, dancing, watching a movie, singing an early 2000s pop song. It encompasses whatever works for you. One study found that, in general, Distraction Techniques are very effective at reducing how painful people rate an experience.[87]

Another study looked at two groups of women giving birth. One group was taught to use Distraction Techniques including movies, music, books, and puzzles. The other group was the control group, and they were not taught about Distraction Techniques. At the end of the study, there was no statistically significant difference in length of delivery, use of synthetic oxytocin, or fear of childbirth scores, yet the Distraction Techniques group experienced significantly less pain during birth. The groups had very similar experiences of birth, yet those using Distraction Techniques rated it less painful.

I highly recommend adding Distraction Techniques to your birth toolkit. Hazel Gale is an ADHD researcher who developed a game to help people manage their ADHD. They also developed a method for helping people with ADHD sleep. I find it to be a very effective distraction technique as well. You pick a category: animals, produce, movie titles, etc. Then, you go through the alphabet. A is for apple. B-broccoli. C-clementine. D-dragon fruit. E-eggplant and so on. Of course, there will be some letters you can't always get like X. Don't worry about those. Just skip them. Gale says this game is effective because it focuses the mind enough to keep it from wandering onto other more active topics, but there aren't high stakes in the game—like thinking about a work presentation—so your mind doesn't become too active. Give it a try if it sounds interesting to you, especially if general pregnancy discomfort is making it difficult to sleep. If you find it useful, add it to the Green Light section of your Red Light/Green Light list.

Another technique I like is called "Counting Colors." There are two ways to do this. One way is to pick a color and then count the number of things you can see that are that color. In this version, you are just counting: one, two, three, etc. The other way is to name the items that are that color: water bottle, sweatshirt, car out the window, etc.

Distraction Techniques don't need to be complicated. They can be very simple. They can also be more passive than the examples I just gave. If you've ever been sick and zoned out watching *The Price is Right* or a random movie, that is using a Distraction Technique. In some ways, they are so integrated into our lives that we can forget how powerful they are at reducing pain.

One thing to make sure of is that you will be able to access your chosen Distraction Techniques where you are giving birth. If you want to watch a movie, you need the movie and a device to watch it on. You will probably also need a charging cord and access to an outlet. If you want to do a puzzle, you'll need a puzzle. Another technique that I really like can be done without needing anything but your body.[*] It focuses on the senses of the body to reground yourself in the here and now. It is especially helpful if you have had a traumatic birth in the past and feel yourself being pulled back into that space.

NOTICING

Close your eyes—if that feels good, otherwise keep them open.

Take a slow, deep breath.

Notice what you can hear. Say it out loud or in your head.

Notice what you can smell. Say it out loud or in your head.

Notice what you can taste. Say it out loud or in your head.

---

[*]This is technically an embodiment technique and not a distraction technique, though I believe they work the same.

Notice what you can feel. Say it out loud or in your head.

Now, open your eyes.

Notice what you can see. Say it out loud or in your head.

When you notice these things, try to just notice them without judging them as good or bad. Maybe the thing you feel is a contraction. That is not a bad thing. It is a temporary thing. It will pass. It will bring you closer to being done with birth. It means your body is functioning. It is just a thing.

Music and Sound

Music is often used as a distraction technique, but it is powerful in its own right. Listening to music has been shown to be effective at reducing pain and anxiety during childbirth.[88] One study found that it is most effective when the music is personal to the person listening to it.[89] It makes sense. If I played you random elevator music or call-holding music, it probably wouldn't be as enjoyable for you as music you actually like. If I played you a recording of my niece playing the piano, it might not be as appealing to you as it is to me. But if you listened to a recording of your own child playing the piano, it might be very effective.

Another study found that music is more effective when you can move your body.[90] This article has since been retracted, meaning we can't use it to inform us as published research. Still, I think there is something to be said for the value of moving your body. Spontaneous movement is so good for birth. Music inspires the body to move. So, if your music makes you want to move, I say do it, even if I can't say that the research says you should.

If you plan to use music during childbirth, always have multiple playlists with different kinds of music. Preferences change during birth, and something that you thought would be soothing or inspiring may feel very grating. You may also find that, in the moment, you want the opposite of music. You may want complete silence.

My friend had a whole musical plan for her birth, only to ask her midwife to turn the music off the second it started. She couldn't stand it. She wanted complete silence. If you are giving birth in a hospital or somewhere where you will not be able to control the ambient noise, I recommend packing some earplugs or noise-canceling headphones, just in case.

In addition to music, you may also want to think about sound therapy. As a sound therapist I am a big supporter of sound therapy. Sound therapy uses specific instruments that alter your mind and body. To understand how sound therapy works, you need to understand that—on a cellular level—everything vibrates. Everything is always vibrating. Vibrations have frequencies, which can impact and change the frequencies they come into contact with.

I was trained to break sound therapy into two categories: tuning forks and Himalayan Bowls/Gongs. First, let's look at tuning forks. If you play an instrument, you may be familiar with these metal "forks" that vibrate with a specific frequency when struck. Medical-grade tuning forks also exist. They are used in medical testing both for hearing and to identify bone fractures. Medical-grade tuning forks are used in sound therapy, and they come in two varieties. Non-weighted tuning forks are used off the body and can be quite loud. Weighted-tuning forks have round discs on the top of their tines, and they are very quiet. You can't really hear them when they are struck, but you can feel them. They are designed to be used directly on the body.

Both types of tuning forks encourage the body to "puff" nitric oxide. Nitric oxide—not to be confused with nitrous oxide, which we talked about in the medical interventions section—is naturally created by the cells in your body. Many cells of the body, including immune cells, produce nitric oxide. We call this puffing. It is incredibly important for the health and functioning of the body, which is why cells do it all the time, unless you're tired, or stressed, or sick... As you can imagine, they might need some extra help. Thankfully, we have tuning forks to stimulate the production of nitric oxide!

We also have bowls and gongs. The frequencies from bowls and gongs do not cause puffing, but they do some other very cool things. They stimulate the production of anandamide, which is also called the bliss chemical. Anandamide binds to the endocannabinoid receptors in the brain. This is the same part of the brain that cannabis—or marijuana—binds to. The production of anandamide makes people feel blissful—hence the name bliss chemical. People often feel a sense of being high, floating, joyous, and deeply relaxed.

Bowls and gongs also facilitate deep relaxation by moving the brain waves from beta waves—the active state or "monkey mind," as my teacher Julie calls it—to theta and delta waves.[91] Theta and delta waves are associated with deep relaxation and sleep. Sound therapy creates binaural beats. This occurs when the brain hears two slightly different frequencies in each ear, which the brain perceives as a third frequency, changing the brain waves and shifting the body into a state of sleep, relaxation or focus.

Sound therapy is awesome. If you get a chance to experience it in person, I highly recommend that you do. If you can't experience it in person, the recorded versions also work very well. I use recordings of my instruments to make custom sound baths for people, and I can tell you that listening to the recordings over and over while I'm mixing the tracks definitely has an effect. Also, this isn't just me saying that sound therapy is relaxing. It's in the research.[92]

If you decide to seek out a sound therapist, look for one who has been through training and is certified. Anyone can buy these instruments online. People may watch a few YouTube videos and decide to call themselves sound therapists. I recommend those who have been trained by Wind Willow Sound Health, Sage Academy of Sound, Diane Mandle, Richard Rudis, or Dr. John Beaulieu. It is super important that **if you are pregnant, no one touches your body with tuning forks**. They can use them off the body, but they should never put them directly on your body. They can stimulate contractions in pregnant people.

Massage

The next CAM we are going to talk about is massage. Multiple studies have shown that massage is effective at reducing the experience of pain during childbirth.[93] The main theory—and it is just a theory—behind why massage works is called Gate Control Theory. It isn't universally accepted yet. It is also very complicated. The easiest way to think about it is like this. Your body is full of nerves. But not all nerves are able to transmit pain signals. If you stimulate the nerves that don't transmit pain signals, then they override the nerves that can transmit pain signals.

I believe there are two other reasons why massage is effective. It's relaxing. When you are relaxed, cortisol levels stay low. Low cortisol levels mean pain doesn't feel as painful as it does with high cortisol levels. Massage is also a Distraction Technique, and we know that those are effective. Here is where it gets really interesting, though.

One study found that massage not only decreased pain levels: it shortened birth duration, decreased rates of cesarean sections, and increased satisfaction with childbirth. But when the massage used chamomile oil all those effects were even stronger.[94] Another study found that massage with ginger oil was more effective than massage alone.[95] These researchers believed the reason is because ginger strengthens the central nervous system.

For our purposes, it doesn't really matter why massage works, only if it works for you. Test it out before birth to see if massage is helpful for reducing your pain—like back pain or sore feet. Try ginger and chamomile essential oils and see if they make it more effective. Try back massage, shoulder, foot, and hand, and notice if any location is more helpful. The more you practice, the better your support person will be at giving massages.

Aromatherapy

Ginger and chamomile aren't the only oils that can have a positive impact on the birth experience. Aromatherapy is another complementary alternative medicine that uses smell to illicit health benefits. Multiple studies have found aromatherapy with essential oils to be effective at reducing childbirth pain and anxiety.[96] There are mixed results as to what is most effective, but here is a list of scents that have been included in the research that had a positive effect:

- Ginger

- Lavender

- Chamomile

- Peppermint

- Bitter Orange

- Sweet Orange

- Frankincense

- Clove Oil[*]

- Rosa Damascene

- Jasmine

- Geranium

- Clary Sage, when combined with Mandarin Orange

----

*Clove oil is great for numbing localized pain. It is commonly used for toothaches by applying a small amount to a cotton swab and touching it to the affected area. It can also be mixed with a carrier oil and used on the body. Though I recommend using it as a spot treatment in specific areas rather than as a full body oil as it can be quite intense.

There are several ways to do aromatherapy with essential oils. You can use a diffuser. These can be electric or a stick-style diffuser. The electric ones need to be plugged in, and they create a more intense scent. Stick-style diffusers use a bottle of oil with reeds in it, and the scent is far less intense. If you are giving birth in a hospital, they might have rules about diffusers, so make sure to check ahead of time. You can use aromatherapy jewelry. These are typically bracelets or necklaces that have special beads that hold the oil to make sure the scent lasts a long time. Essential oils can also be used with carrier oils and rubbed onto the body like we saw with massage. You can also just inhale the oil straight from the bottle if you want to keep things simple.

Use a high-quality essential oil, not a fragrance. Fragrances are usually synthetic and not effective. When using essential oils topically, you need a carrier oil. This is an oil that the essential oil is mixed with, diluting it. It helps with absorption and decreases the chance of irritation. Carrier oils include coconut oil, jojoba oil, almond oil, olive oil, and even aloe vera. They all have their own smell and feel, so try them out before giving birth.

Most importantly, smell whatever essential oils you might be using during birth BEFORE putting them on your body. It can be difficult to remove the scent once it is on your skin. Preferences change during childbirth. You may have loved a particular scent every day for your whole life and then realize that you hate it during birth. You want to know that before you use the oil. Take a small whiff of the oil from the bottle to determine if it still smells good to you. Also, check for allergies, not just yours, but anyone else in the room—especially if you are using a diffuser.

Acupuncture

If you've never had acupuncture before, it might seem pretty freaky. I was so nervous the first time I went in for an acupuncture treatment. I had read so many studies on the benefits of acupuncture that I gathered all my courage and went in for an appointment. Now, I am in love with acupuncture. After my magic wand gets paid leave for everyone giving birth for at least a year, my next move is to make all insurance cover acupuncture. Then make insurance free...I digress. Point being, acupuncture is amazing if you can get through the door.

Acupuncture is part of Traditional Chinese Medicine and has been practiced for over 2,500 years. The practice involves inserting very thin needles into specific points on the body. Traditional Chinese Medicine believes that illness and pain occur because qi—a vital life force—is blocked or disrupted. There are certain points along the body that can access or manipulate qi, and in acupuncture, that is done with needles. Acupressure works in the same fashion, but pressure is applied instead of needles.

According to the research, acupuncture prior to birth significantly reduces childbirth pain and makes the whole experience more satisfying.[97] Acupuncture also shortened the length of birth and reduced the need for synthetic oxytocin.[98,99] Acupuncture is generally seen as good for mood and anxiety. Pregnant women who received acupuncture were less stressed which can lead to a more positive birth experience.[100] If acupuncture seems like too much, know that one study found that ear acupressure during childbirth reduced pain and shortened the length of birth.[101]

Yoga

I could write a whole book on the benefits of Yoga for childbirth. The relationship between Yoga and childbirth was a significant part of my doctoral research. I will keep it brief here, but please don't mistake brevity for lack of importance. Yoga might be one of the best possible things you can do for your pregnancy. It is up there with prenatal vitamins. So, to keep my excitable nature on topic, we are going to focus on four things in this section: the benefits of Yoga during pregnancy, the theories as to why, safety, and what it looks like.

Multiple studies have shown that a Yoga practice during pregnancy reduces fear, depression, and anxiety.[102] Fear and anxiety are related to cortisol levels, which a Yoga practice during pregnancy has also been shown to reduce.[103] Since cortisol levels were reduced you won't be surprised when I tell you that pain levels were also reduced.[104] You may also remember the relationship between cortisol and birth length, so it makes sense that women who participated in Yoga during pregnancy had shorter birth lengths.[105]

Participants in Yoga during pregnancy had fewer preterm deliveries, lower rates of cesarean sections and inductions.[106] They even had fewer ruptured episiotomies— this is when the incision tears, causing it to become larger than intended.[107] If all of that wasn't enough, Yoga was also shown to increase self-efficacy.[108] Women believed in themselves more and their ability to birth confidently. Just to recap, there is less fear, anxiety, depression, and pain. Shorter birth length with fewer interventions and complications, plus more confidence. I'm sold.

That is a lot to promise, how is it that Yoga can do all of that? There are four main theories from the research as to why Yoga is so beneficial. It increases strength and flexibility in the waist, perineum, vaginal muscles, pelvic muscles, and sphincter, likely making contractions more effective, leading to shorter birth length.[109] Yoga moves the body in a way that causes cerebrospinal fluid circulation. The circulation stimulates the release of endorphins and serotonin, easing fear, anxiety, and depression while naturally relieving pain.[110]

A big part of Yoga is breath work—called Pranayama. Regulated breathing increases oxygen and decreases carbon dioxide.[111] This activates the parasympathetic nervous system. When the parasympathetic nervous system is activated, the brain goes, "The bear is gone! Now it's time to rest and repair." That chronic sympathetic nervous system activation goes away, and with it comes a reduced perception of pain. The breath is the only part of the autonomic nervous system that we can consciously control. When we control our breath, it unlocks an ability to alter our experiences.

Finally, Yoga teaches you to sit with discomfort. Yoga is uncomfortable. Sometimes it feels amazing. It should never feel painful. But often, it is not very pleasant. It can be downright awful. You're gritting your teeth while a serene Yoga teacher calmly tells you to breathe into the discomfort. You might look at that teacher and have a lot of very not serene thoughts. You might constrict your breath, making the pain worse. Or squeeze your fists super tight. But eventually, you get guided out of the pose. Sometimes, to do the other side...still the situation that was causing you to feel that way, it ends.

Yoga teaches that everything is temporary. Yoga Asana—the poses—teaches that discomfort is temporary and

that you are strong enough to face it. No wonder it increases
self-efficacy. This? This experience that I do not like that I
want to end, it will end. This is not forever. When you know
that the discomfort will end, that the contraction will end,
that birth will end, and that you have the ability to sit through
physically and emotionally difficult times, it turns the
mountain of birth into a hill.

    I would never recommend something that wasn't
safe. In my experience as a Yoga teacher there are many
postures, I would never suggest a person do while pregnant.
These poses are contraindicated for pregnancy. Yet, some
researchers were like, "Let's have pregnant women do these
poses so we can see what happens in their bodies!" There are
two studies that looked at what happened when pregnant
women participated in a rigorous Yoga practice. One study
found that blood pressure, heart rate, pulse oximetry, and
uterine tocometry all remained safe during an advanced
practice, even among women with no previous Yoga
experience. The study also showed that the practice did not
have any negative impacts on fetal heart rates.[112] A second
study also showed no negative impacts on fetal and maternal
heart rates, and uterine activity remained safe.[113] The first
study used a ridged pose to neutral pose style called a 26-
Poses practice. The second study used a moderate-intensity
Vinyasa—or flow—style practice. These two styles are
extremely different, which begs the question, what does
"Yoga" look like?

    It's an excellent question because the answer is not
clear. In every study I analyzed during my research, the
practice of Yoga looked different. Who taught it? How long
each session was? How many sessions over what length of

time? Even the poses and the styles were all different. And yet, they all found a benefit for birth.

So, what kind of Yoga should you do? Well, whatever kind you like. Despite the research on safety, I still recommend staying away from contraindicated poses, working with someone trained to work with pregnant individuals, and taking time for spontaneous practice. Spontaneous practice is when you just move with your breath. Think of a really good stretch that just overtakes you.

Spontaneous Yoga is not trying to get anywhere. There is no peak pose. No shape you have to twist your body into. There is only going where your body leads. It's like dancing. Sure, we can learn the tango or ballet, and we can do choreographed dances. A routine that has a beginning, middle, and end always in that order. Or you can put on some music and just dance. Both are beneficial in different ways. If taking a Yoga class doesn't feel like something you want to do or have time for, try spontaneous Yoga. Start with three minutes. Put on a song you like, and let your body move with your breath. Slow and stretchy. Undulating. Strong and steady. Whatever movements and shapes feel right.

Whatever type of Yoga you are practicing always, always, listen to your body. Let your body decide what poses are okay for you at that moment and which ones aren't. It doesn't have to be the same on both sides of the body. Remember, what poses are accessible to you changes every day whether you are pregnant or not. That may be another reason Yoga practice helps prepare people for birth. It teaches you that you can't control or rush your body. You have to accept where your body is in the moment and let the frustration go. Yoga in the west often is very focused on the Asanas, the poses. But fundamentally, Yoga is breathwork. It is movement combined with breath. As long as you are moving with your breath, you are doing Yoga.

Pranayama

Breathwork in Yoga is called Pranayama. Various types of Pranayama have been shown to have a positive impact on birth. Before you engage in any Pranayama, it is important to first practice belly breathing. You want to make sure your shoulders don't rise and fall with your breath, as this can create extra stress on the body. It goes back to that old part of the brain. Our necks are very vulnerable, so when we feel threatened, our shoulders rise to protect our necks. We can't be fully relaxed with our shoulders up by our ears.

To practice belly breathing find a comfortable seat—you can also stand or lay down—and see if you can straighten your spine. If you are sitting, having your back against a wall can provide extra support. Place a hand on your belly. Alternatively, you may want to place your hands on your shoulders to see if they move. Or have a support person place gentle pressure on your shoulders. As you inhale, attempt to expand the belly out as much as is comfortable. On the exhale, imagine touching your spine with your belly button. In my Yoga classes, I describe the spine and the belly button as star-crossed lovers forever drifting together but never quite meeting before parting ways. When you feel like you have a comfortable expansive belly breath, you can move on to practicing the other Pranayama.

NADI SHODHANA

Also called Alternate Nostril Breathing, is one of my most favorite Pranayama. It involves breathing through one nostril at a time. I find it very soothing—especially on a turbulent airplane. Although, I will say when I first started practicing it, I would get a little panicked. If this happens to

you, stop. Try again later, maybe keeping your eyes open.
This technique is known for its calming and balancing effects
on the mind and body. It reduces stress and anxiety by
calming the nervous system.[114] It enhances respiratory
function and improves lung capacity.[115] It also balances the
two hemispheres of the brain, promoting mental clarity and
focus.[116]

Your "dominant nostril"—the one that air flows
more strongly through—changes. This is called the nasal
cycle, and it is part of the autonomic nervous system. You
know when you have a cold, and you can only breath through
one nostril? This is like a very mild version of that. This
optimizes nasal functioning. I was taught that when you
practice Nadi Shodhana it confuses your brain since your
brain no longer knows where it is in the nasal cycle. This
leads to a reset, like restarting a computer.

To Practice Nadi Shodhana:
Find your comfortable seat with a long spine
Close your eyes if it feels good
Take a few deep belly breaths
Bring one finger by your left nostril, and another by your
right. I make the "Shaka" sign with my hand. I put my pinkie
by the left side and my thumb by the right. This is not the
traditional way to do it, but it is the only way that doesn't
make my hand cramp. You can do it however works for you.
Exhale
Plug the right nostril by softly pressing it closed
Inhale through the left nostril
Hold at the top of the inhale
Plug the left nostril by softly pressing it closed
Release the right nostril

Exhale through the right nostril
Hold at the bottom of the exhale
Inhale through the right nostril
Hold at the top of the inhale
Plug the right nostril by softly pressing it closed
Release the left nostril
Exhale through the left nostril
Hold at the bottom of the exhale

That is one cycle. I aim for at least eight cycles when I practice. See if you can make the inhales, and the exhales the same length. Then, try making the exhale just a little bit longer. Notice how that feels. Play around with the length of the inhales and exhales maybe starting with a count of 5. You can also play around with the lengths of the hold. Maybe it's 1 second. Maybe it's 4. **When you have finished your cycles, exhale through both nostrils and take several deep belly breaths**. Feel the changes in your mind and body. Sit with them for a bit before moving on with your day.

UJJAYI

Also called Victorious Breath, is common in most active Yoga classes. This breath creates a noise like a soft hissing sound. It requires a slight lift of the soft palate. Imagine you are trying to fog up a mirror. You can practice in front of an actual mirror, use your hand as a "mirror," or just use your imagination.

When you do the fogging-up action, your soft palate naturally lifts, and you make a "hah" sound. Once this feels comfortable, do the exact same thing but with your mouth closed. That's Ujjayi breath. Ujjayi breath is great because it increases oxygen intake—which we saw in the Yoga section activates the parasympathetic nervous system.[117] Ujjayi breath, in particular, is associated with increased parasympathetic nervous system activity, reducing the experience of pain.[118,119]

Again, make sure your breath is moving through the belly and not through the shoulders. Ujjayi breath can be practiced while you are doing anything once you have the belly breathing down. It is great for practicing Yoga, but you can also do it while you are washing the dishes or taking a shower. There is something to be said for focused practice where you sit comfortably and close your eyes, all your attention on your breathwork. There is also something to be said for practicing while doing other things because, likely, during childbirth, there may be some stuff going on.

If the practice is only effective in a perfectly controlled environment that is silent, then it won't be much help.* The more you practice while other things are going on, the easier it will be to access the skill during birth. It also feels really good. So, if Ujjayi breathing makes you feel better while washing the dishes, then do it while washing the dishes.

The last Pranayama we are going to talk about is the easiest and the most important.

BHRAMARI

Also called Bee Breath gets its name from the buzzing sound that it creates. Bhramari reduces anxiety and feelings of agitation, creating a sense of calm.[120] The practice releases

---

* Melissa Spamer talks about being in India with a group practicing Yoga. Many people complained. It's too hot. It's too loud. There are too many smells. "How am I supposed to meditate with all of this distraction?!" Ah, but isn't that the point? Anyone can do anything when everything is perfect. It is the overcoming when things are not perfect that creates growth and expands your capacity.

endorphins, reducing pain.[121] The practice of Bhramari lowers
blood pressure.[122] Specifically, when pregnant women
practiced twice a day for 10 minutes at a time for 8 weeks,
they were protected against developing preeclampsia.
Furthermore, practicing just 5 minutes daily and then for 10
minutes at regular intervals throughout birth improved
postpartum hemorrhage, hypertension, eclampsia—a severe
complication of preeclampsia—pre-term delivery, anxiety,
and insomnia.[123] That is some serious benefit for something
that is so simple.

To Practice Bhramari:
Start in your comfortable seat, and begin your deep belly
breathing
Close your eyes if you like
You may also choose to gently plug your ears with your
fingers, though it isn't necessary
Take an inhale
On the exhale, hum like a bee
     That's it. That's all you have to do. Repeat it for
however long you want to practice. I personally—to help
keep me focused—practice moving the location of the
vibration. I imagine it coming from my forehead, throat,
chest, diaphragm, low belly, and pelvic floor. Sometimes, one
at a time. Sometimes like a wave rolling through each
location. Sometimes bouncing around. You get to make it
work for you.
     Remember that Pranayama is a branch of Yoga just
like Asana. And just like Asana—Yoga poses—Pranayama
takes practice. You wouldn't walk into your first Yoga class
expecting to go from a down dog to a handstand to a plank,
would you? If these Pranayama seem confusing or hard,

spend some time with them. Practice. The benefits of doing so are very real. And if it's just not for you, then don't sweat it. There are many other types of CAM out there.

I encourage you to look around and do some research. Find out what is available in your area and what might work for you. Ear acupressure, saffron, and hypnosis are all other methods of CAM that have been found effective for childbirth.[124] I find it really interesting, though, that one study found that education was more effective than hypnosis.[125] While education is not technically CAM, it does improve the childbirth experience. You are already improving your experience just by reading this book! Everyone is going to be different, so get out your Red Light/Green Light list and organize what CAM you are interested in and definitely not interested in.

Support Report

- When things are difficult, I find it helpful to remember "this is not forever."

- Western Medicine focuses on diagnosing/treating illness; Eastern Medicine focuses on the person. CAM (Complementary Alternative Medicine) includes diverse methods that have been shown to benefit childbirth.

- Distraction techniques have been shown to reduce the experience of pain.

- Music has been shown to reduce anxiety and childbirth pain.

- Sound therapy promotes relaxation, reduces pain, and causes the body to produce bliss chemicals.

- Massage during birth has been shown to reduce pain, shorten the length of birth, and reduce the rate of c-sections. Adding ginger or chamomile essential oil has been shown to increase the benefits of massage.

- Aromatherapy has been shown to reduce pain and anxiety during childbirth. Aromatherapy can be administered through diffusers, special jewelry, or topically with a carrier oil like coconut or olive oil.

- Acupuncture prior to birth has been shown to reduce pain, shorten the length of birth, and reduce the need for medical interventions. Ear acupressure (done without needles) performed during birth provides similar benefits.

- Yoga has been shown over and over to reduce childbirth fear and anxiety, depression during pregnancy, shorten the length of birth, and improve outcomes. It is believed that Yoga is beneficial because it increases oxygen and decreases carbon dioxide triggering the parasympathetic nervous system, increases cerebrospinal fluid circulation, increases strength and flexibility, and teaches you to sit with discomfort. Despite all of the benefits, some Yoga classes or teachers might not be good for you. Only take classes that make you feel better. Or opt for spontaneous Yoga practice done on your own.

- Pranayama, including Nadi Shodhana (alternate nostril breathing), Ujjayi (victorious breath), and Bhramari (bee breath), reduce anxiety and pain, and improve birth outcomes. Practicing ahead of time is vital.

- Do what works for you and leave the rest. You get to decide.

Journaling Prompts

- A coping skill is anything you do to help yourself feel better during stress or difficulty. It can be anything! Deep breathing, listening to music, eating ice cream, masturbating, jumping rope, doing a puzzle. Not all coping skills are healthy, and any coping skill can become unhealthy if you do it too much—even exercising. Some people like to add numbers together. Some people like to name all the colors they can see. Some go through the senses, naming something that can see, hear, smell, touch, and maybe taste. What are some coping skills you have or would like to try? Are they positive or negative? Can do it while pregnant/giving birth? What might you need for the coping skill?

- Think about ways you can use your senses during birth to help you. What might you want to look at? Listen to? Are there things you'd like to touch or hold? What about smell or taste?

- What do you think about CAM? What did you like? What didn't you like? What are some other ideas you'd like to look into?

Birth Positions

In that image of the woman screaming during birth that you've seen in movies and on television, is she lying on her back? The answer is, most likely yes, as this has become the most common way people give birth in the United States. This is called the supine position. The shift to lying on the back during birth is relatively recent. Historians say the change started in the 17th century and became more common in the 19th and 20th centuries. Why did this shift happen, and how were people giving birth before? Let's find out.

Everyone's body is different. We say this all the time, but we don't always grasp how different. During one of my Yoga teacher trainings, we were discussing how Yoga poses can't work the same for everyone because everyone's body is different. The guest lecturer for the module explained how someone close to her has an extra half vertebra. Vertebrae are the bones that make up the column of the spine. When someone slips a disc, they are referring to the cartilage pads between the vertebrae. The vertebrae and discs are integral to how we move our bodies.

This person didn't just have an extra vertebra, but half of one. It only developed on one side. It's called a hemivertebra, and while rare, it occurs in approximately 0.3% to 1% of the population.[126] It does happen. A whole extra vertebra is called a supernumerary vertebra. People with an extra vertebra may never even know that they have one because it can be asymptomatic. Yet people walk into Yoga classes or throughout life thinking all our bodies—at the very least, our bone structures—are the same. They aren't, so why would we expect our bodies to behave the same? Or be capable of doing the same things in the same way? Or comfortable doing them in the same way?

You can imagine that if every body is different, then there must be a lot of different ways to give birth. So why is everyone lying on their back? Historically, that wasn't the case. Birthing positions varied, with people doing whatever felt most natural and most effective for their bodies. People can successfully give birth by sitting, squatting, standing, or on their hands and knees.

Some of these positions may be helped by having certain tools. Sitting birth can be facilitated by a birth chair. These look like chairs with a U-shaped seat. They kind of look like if you put a toilet seat on a stool. Birth stool use has been documented as early as ancient Egypt, indicating that they have been used for thousands of years.[127]

Squatting and standing births can be aided by an anchor. An anchor is something you hold onto for support. This can be your support person if you loop your arms around their neck or waist. It can be a sturdy bed frame or table. It can be a tree if you are birthing outside. It is what makes you feel steady and supported, that won't slip. Some hospital beds now have bars that pop up when someone wants to give birth in a position that requires an anchor. If you plan to give birth in a hospital, ask them if their beds have birthing bars.

Birthing in these more upright positions means the birth is aided by gravity. As you push the gravitational pull of the Earth is helping to draw the baby out. It can be hard to imagine that that makes much of a difference, but just for fun, imagine with me that you could hold a handstand for hours with ease. Imagine being in a handstand was as easy for you as lying down. Now imagine trying to give birth in a handstand with gravity pulling the baby up and in. It would create a lot of unnecessary work, right? Now, flip the body in the other direction. That same work that was created by gravity, is replaced by the aid of gravity. Some hospitals now even offer birth stools. So, if this is something that interests you, make sure to contact your birth location—or your midwife if you are doing a home birth—to see if they have birth stools.

You can also give birth on your hands and knees. This is how many animals give birth. Which may be why it fell out of popularity. I am musing here when I say that humans have done many things over the centuries to distinguish themselves from animals and to be more "civilized." I imagine the look of horror on Portia Featherington's face if Penelope wanted to give birth on her hands and knees—or some other representation of high society if *Bridgerton* isn't your thing. But hands and knees can be a more comfortable way to give birth. In fact, if giving birth upright puts too much pressure on the pelvis, switching to hands and knees can relieve the pressure. When giving birth on your hands and knees, you may need something soft to cushion the floor beneath the knees. You may want to put down a folded Yoga mat, some blankets or pillows, or even be up on a mattress.

Lying down to give birth doesn't always mean giving birth on your back. It can mean lying on your side. When people first moved to giving birth on beds, it was more common for them to do so on their sides. The supine position became more common with the switch from midwives to doctors. This position gives doctors more control and is best for interventions like instrument delivery and epidurals. Unfortunately, it also goes against the natural mechanics of birth. That's why it was historically uncommon and is not seen in other mammals.*

It is important to be aware that giving birth on your back actually narrows the birth canal. Not only does this make it harder to push the baby out, but it can also lead to longer birth and increased pain. It can put pressure on major blood vessels, leading to decreased blood flow and lower blood pressure. It can also reduce the oxygen supply to the baby. Now, if you are more comfortable on your back or you are having an intervention that requires you to be on your back, then go for it. Many, many, many people have given birth on their backs.

If you are open to other positions, I suggest you try them. Let your body be the guide. Use spontaneous movements, just like you practiced with spontaneous Yoga, and see where your body takes you. If you become tired and you need to lie down, try lying on your side instead of your back and see how that feels. If you need to get up and move, get up and move. If something starts out feeling good but stops feeling good, change it up. You get to decide. Like we say in Yoga classes, don't try to make your body do something that doesn't feel right just because someone else's body is doing it.

---

*My dog Rain loves to be on her back. She sleeps on her back, in the bed, head by the pillow like a human would sleep. It's adorable. It's her favorite way to sleep. But there is no way she could ever give birth like that. Cats and dogs typically squat or lie on their sides to give birth. Cows, horses, and sheep tend to stand or lie on their sides. Non-human primates usually give birth squatting or sitting.

Switching from upright to hands and knees is a good example of a pivot you can be prepared to do. Remember that as much as we are going to prepare, plan, and advocate for the birth you want, sometimes changes need to be made. Sometimes, there is too much pressure on the pelvis, and you won't know until you are actively giving birth. Being prepared with pivots ahead of time makes it easier to make changes in the moment because you don't have to think. You just have to look at your plans. In the moment, it can be hard to remember what your options are. Looking at the list makes it so you don't have to remember. When working on your birth toolkit, provide yourself with pivots whenever you can.

Going to the hospital

We started this journey together, talking about the way we've seen childbirth portrayed in the media. But what about going to the hospital? How many times have you seen a show or a movie where the woman's water breaks, and then she's rushing to the hospital, screaming, or giving birth in the back of a taxi? So let me ask you. When should you go to the hospital?

In the book *Girls & Sex* by Peggy Orenstein—which I highly recommend. I recommend all her books—she recalls sitting in the classroom with Dr. Paul Wright, professor of communications science at Indiana University.[*] He asks his classes about their experience the first time they attended a "kegger." His students reported similar experiences of standing around the keg in a specific way. Then he asked how they knew to do that. The answer? *American Pie.* If you have not seen this very cringy movie, it definitely lacks in consent and does not hold up. It was once extremely popular and is now regaining notoriety thanks to the song *So Highschool.* It was *the* quintessential teen movie in 1999.

This is Dr. Wright's way of getting students interested in script theory. For us, it is yet another reminder of how

---

[*]Peggy Orenstein's books lend great insight into the female existence and how sexuality impacts us. Orenstein is an investigative journalist using interviews and sometimes first-hand experience to shed light on the complex realities of being sexual and gendered beings. While I love all her books, I want to take a moment to mention *Cinderella Ate My Daughter.* This book was inspired by Peggy's personal struggles to not raise her daughter in princess culture, yet no matter her efforts, her daughter wanted nothing more. It is a fascinating look at princess culture, gender, and "little girlhood." If you are raising a child living in this society as a girl, it's definitely worth the read.

media influences our behavior. Going to the hospital is no different than screaming birth or keg parties. We are susceptible to altering our actions based on what we see others do, even if those others are fictional characters written and scripted for drama or comedy, not realism. Like screaming birth, the portrayal of when to go to the hospital—if you are giving birth in a hospital—is not only inaccurate, it can also be damaging.

You'll see in this section why timing matters. When you go to the hospital can impact your experience. But we can't talk about going to the hospital without talking about a major change that occurs, signaling you are closer to giving birth. That big change? Mucus. That's right, it's time to talk about mucus plugs!

This is a fascinating and essential part of pregnancy that often doesn't get much attention. The mucus plug is exactly what it sounds like—a thick plug of mucus that forms in the cervix during pregnancy. Its primary role is to protect the uterus and growing baby from bacteria and infections. The mucus plug forms early in pregnancy, soon after conception. It acts as a seal for the cervical canal, preventing any harmful pathogens from entering the uterus.

Changes to the cervix occur the closer a person gets to birth. The cervix begins to soften, shorten, and dilate, which eventually causes the mucus plug to pop out. Losing the mucus plug can happen all at once or gradually over several days. It might look like a thick, jelly-like discharge and can be clear, slightly pink, or blood-tinged. This is sometimes called a "bloody show." Losing your mucus plug is a sign that your body is getting ready for birth, but it doesn't necessarily mean that birth is imminent. It could still be days or even weeks before contractions start.

I spend a lot of time bemoaning the negative impact of media on birth, so I do want to take a moment to give credit to *Brooklyn 99*. This comedic television show—in its last season—was very upfront and honest about the childbirth experience, including speaking frankly about mucus plugs. It was done in a humorous context, but it mainstreamed the conversation and taught a lot of people something they knew nothing about. Media has the power to make pregnancy and birth better for people. If you work in Hollywood or make movies, remember the impact of the content you create.

So, your mucus plug is gone. Your water broke. Or maybe it didn't, but it's your due date. Your bag is packed. Now what? Speed to the hospital, driving recklessly, while everyone screams and panics? That's not necessary. Despite what we've seen in films and on television, after someone's water breaks, they may not need to go to the hospital for days. This can be especially true for first-time births as they can have a longer gestational period than later pregnancies. About 75% of first-time births occur between 37 and 42 weeks. One study of healthy individuals giving birth for the first time found that only 50% had given birth by 40 weeks and 5 days.[128]

Part of the problem with due dates—while we get some strong information from seeing development through ultrasounds—is that they are based on the last menstrual cycle. Basing pregnancy on menstrual cycles comes with a lot of assumptions. It assumes that everyone's cycle is approximately 28 days. This is not true for everyone, and even people who regularly have 28-day cycles don't always have 28-day cycles. As I'm sure you've experienced, cycle length can be influenced by travel and stress.

It also assumes that everyone ovulates at the same time in their cycle—day 14—which is also not true. Even when it typically is for someone, it can fluctuate. In the book *Taking Charge of Your Fertility,* Toni Weschler shares the story of a young couple who chose to wait for marriage to have sex for the first time. The sex that occurred the night of their wedding resulted in pregnancy. Now, weddings can be quite stressful and exciting and full of all kinds of emotions that can impact someone's cycle. The young woman in the book was not tracking her cervical mucus or basal body temperature.[129] She was unaware of when in her cycle she ovulated. When she gave birth, her husband's insurance claimed she had become pregnant before their marriage because of her gestational length. I can't imagine the confusion and frustration of an insurance company claiming you had sex before you did.

If you do not know when you ovulate. You don't have a great window on when fertilization happens. Without this information—but also with it, too—due dates are estimates, not facts. It is okay to accept the information given to you by an external source as long as you realize it could be wrong.

Back to breaking waters—which, by the way, has nothing to do with water. The fluid is neither water nor pee. It is a protective liquid contained in the amniotic sac to provide cushion and exchange nutrients. Sometimes, the amniotic sac ruptures before birth starts. This is called "premature rupture of the membranes" or PROM. Because the amniotic sac creates a protective seal around the baby, there is some concern for infection 24 hours after the water breaks if birth hasn't progressed. Antibiotics and expectant management—waiting to see if birth progress on it' own—

can be an option. If your water breaks and your contractions haven't started or increased in 18 hours, it is best to talk to your healthcare team. They know your specific situation and can give advice on how to proceed.

In the medical interventions section, we discussed that hospitals are businesses that have limited space and resources. So, what happens if you go to the hospital just because your water breaks? You can end up taking space and resources. Going to the hospital early, in the best case, can lead to them sending you home, which is annoying and possibly uncomfortable because you have to get in and out of the car and in and out of the car, and then back in to go back to the hospital again. But at its worst, it can lead to unnecessary interventions focused on speeding up birth.[130] If your water hasn't broken, and you go to the hospital simply because it is your due date, you are more likely to have your sac ruptured or your membranes stripped.[131] The good news is that this is an easy risk to avoid.

Don't go to the hospital early—this is even easier to avoid if you are having a home birth. Talk to your healthcare team early—especially your doula if you have one—about when to go to the hospital for your specific situation. Typically, it is suggested that first-time pregnancies go to the hospital when the contractions are roughly 5 minutes apart, lasting for 1 minute each, continually for at least an hour. In later pregnancies, it is typically suggested to wait until the contractions are 3-5 minutes apart. But again, this is general information; you might have specific circumstances that require something different.

You can also check to see how dilated your cervix is. If your arms are long enough, you can do it yourself. You can also have a support person check for you. It might be a little hard to wrap your mind around, especially if you don't already have a relationship with your cervix. But someone is going to check. Personally, I would prefer it be me or someone who loves me before I rush to have a stranger rooting around. The latent phase of birth is considered 0-6 cm. The active phase is from 6-10 cm. At 10 cm, pushing typically begins. Fingers can be used to measure the cervix, by lubricating and inserting them into the cervical opening. Remember, everyone's body is different. Fingers aren't always a specific size, and while 10 is the magic number, it's not 100% all the time always. Generally, two fingers are about 3 cm. If the two fingers can be—gently—pulled apart inside the cervical opening, there is approximately 4 cm of dilation. When the two fingers can be pulled apart as far as the finger webbing allows, it is a good indication of 7 to 8 cm of dilation. At 10 cm, the cervix should no longer be visual, and you will be able to see part of the baby—typically the head, unless the baby is breech.[132]

That was a lot of information to take in. Use your Red Light/Green Light sheet and your intervention's breakdown as guides to help you keep track. You don't need to make every—or any—decision right now. Revisit your guides in small bites. Reread about one intervention at a time, digest it, process it, before moving on.

Most importantly ask questions! Explore your options. Talk to your support team and your advocate, if you want someone else weighing in. If you don't, then don't. If you have concerns about interventions to speed up birth, discuss them with your healthcare team early and often. Remember that if your healthcare team isn't taking your questions seriously—or is doing anything else you do not like—it is okay to replace them. Demand full and complete consent every time you are touched. If you do not understand what they are doing or why, they need to explain it to you first. Finally, if something feels wrong whether or not your water broke or you've reached your due date, talk to your healthcare team. Never ignore what your body is trying to tell you. You are the expert when it comes to you and your body.

Support Report

- Lying on the back during birth (supine position) became common in the 17th century, more so in the 19th and 20th centuries. Historically, birthing positions varied, allowing people to give birth in ways most natural and effective for their bodies.

- Every body is different. The best way to give birth for your body will be unique to you.

- Other birthing positions include lying on the side, sitting, squatting, and on hands and knees. Birthstools or anchors can be used. The supine position works against gravity and narrows the birth canal, leading to longer birth, increased pain, and reduced oxygen supply to the baby. It is the best position for medical interventions.

- When possible spontaneous movement should be encouraged.

- Be prepared to make adjustments.

- There is no immediate need to rush to the hospital just because your water breaks. Arriving at the hospital too early can lead to unnecessary interventions. There can be concern for a risk of infection 18-24 hours after the water breaks if there is no progress in birth. Generally, first-time births should go to the hospital when contractions are 5 minutes apart and last for 1 minute each for at least 1 hour. Or 3-5 minutes apart for subsequent pregnancies. Talk to your medical care team to make a plan about when to go to the hospital.

• Replace healthcare providers you are not comfortable with, and demand full and complete consent for all procedures.

Journaling Prompts

• What are your thoughts on different birth positions? Is this new to you? Are you interested in exploring other birthing positions, or would you prefer to give birth on your back? What is your reason for your decision?

• How familiar are you with your cycle? Did you track your cycle before your pregnancy? Did you monitor your cervical mucus? Is this something you want to do in the future?

• How do you feel about waiting after your water breaks? Have you discussed when to go to the hospital, birth center or other location, if you are going? What will you do to pass the time after your water breaks if your contractions have not started?

After Birth

Placenta

You've just birthed a baby. Okay, not really, but let's pretend for a minute. You did it! The baby is out in the world! You made it through! You're done...sort of. Just in case no one told you—because they don't always—after the baby comes the placenta.

The placenta is amazing, and honestly, they are quite beautiful. I know a lot of midwives and doulas like to photograph them. If you can get past the, *it's a squishy thing that was inside my body and is now outside of my body* part of it, placentas really are incredible to look at. If you're curious, you can find lots of them on Instagram. Before anyone can photograph yours—or do any of the other things that can be done with a placenta, it has to come out of your body. This means more pushing.

I know, not cool. You already did the important part. You got the baby out. But think about all the critical work the placenta did for the baby. The placenta provides nourishment and stores nutrients to be used when needed. The placenta gives oxygen to the baby, who would not be able to breathe without it. The placenta takes what the baby no longer needs and removes it away from the baby back into the pregnant person's body to be removed. Carbon dioxide goes to the lungs. Urea, creatinine, and bilirubin go to the kidneys. The placenta produces progesterone, estrogen, and other hormones. The placenta acts as a protective barrier against changes in the pregnant person's blood pressure, ensuring the baby's environment stays safe. The placenta protects from viruses and bacteria and transfers antibodies from the pregnant person to the baby, providing passive immunity to protect the baby from infections after birth. That is a lot of very important work. So, when you birth the baby and realize there is more work to come, just remember everything the placenta did for the baby. When you approach birthing the placenta with gratitude rather than frustration or annoyance—can you guess what happens? Your cortisol levels will stay lower!

Once you deliver the placenta, you have a couple of options. You can do nothing. The placenta will be examined for abnormalities and to ensure all of it has been delivered. Then, typically, the placenta will be disposed of as medical waste. But, you can also keep the placenta! Why? Great question. You can have it dried and kept as a keepsake. The placenta can be used as a stamp to make cool art. You can also find pictures of this on social media. You can have a ceremonial burial. This is common in some cultures. The Balinese have a very significant ceremony involving the burial of the placenta. You can eat it. Don't pull back. You do not *have* to eat it. But you can.

It is called placentophagy. There isn't good modern research on how effective the body is at using the nutrients from the placenta. In Traditional Chinese Medicine, this practice is called ziheche. In this context, people have been consuming placenta for centuries. In Traditional Chinese Medicine, the placenta is steamed, dehydrated, and ground up. Now, you can also have your placenta freeze-dried and put into capsules for easy consumption, should you so choose. It's all anecdotal, but I know people who swear by it.

Okay, we can be done talking about eating placenta now. But here's another important thing to know about the placenta. Once the placenta is out, the uterus is left with a wound where the placenta had been attached. This area—known as the placental site—needs to heal to prevent infection and excessive bleeding. So, what happens next?

After the placenta is delivered, the uterus continues to contract. These contractions help compress the blood vessels at the placental site, reducing blood loss and aiding in the healing process. These contractions can feel like afterpains. They may be more noticeable during BBC feeding due to the release of oxytocin. It's also normal to experience vaginal bleeding, called lochia, as the uterus sheds the remaining tissue and blood from the placental site. Lochia progresses from a heavy, bright red flow to a lighter, pinkish discharge and eventually to a whitish or yellowish color over the next few weeks. The placental site gradually heals over **6 to 8 weeks**. During this time, it's important to monitor for signs of infection, such as foul-smelling discharge, fever, or increased pain. If you notice any of these symptoms, contact your healthcare team.

During this time, it is also important to rest. You are healing. Even if you have the most perfect, easy, intervention-free, tear-free birth, you are still healing. That is the nature of birth and the nature of the placental site. Embrace the rest. I know it is not possible for everyone—seriously, someone get me that wand—to stay home and do very little for 8 weeks. If you have other kids to care for or are returning to work or both, or anything else, rest when you can. Be patient with yourself. It's easy to think, "The baby is out. I'm back to pre-pregnancy state." You're not. Sorry. If you can't rest, find other ways to nourish your body. Good food. A foot soak. Soothing essential oils. This is not forever.

Postpartum

Rest is crucial during the postpartum period. The body needs time to heal from childbirth and the delivery of the placenta. Avoid heavy lifting and strenuous activities to support the healing process. Proper nutrition and hydration are essential for recovery. Eating a balanced diet rich in iron, protein, and vitamins can help replenish the nutrients lost during childbirth and support overall health. Remember, too, that if you are BBC feeding, producing milk requires a lot of calories.

Postpartum is NOT the time to worry about getting your "pre-baby body back." Honestly, *never* is the time to worry about that. Bodies change. Constantly. Whether you give birth or not. They are supposed to change over time. But if you are concerned about weight loss, try to keep those concerns at bay until your body is done healing. Healing can take a full eight weeks after birth, if not more depending on who you are and your body. When the body is healing—from anything—it needs care and attention, not discipline. The body can be like a distraught child, requiring compassion not punishment.

Emotional support is also exceedingly important postpartum. Your support person(s) doesn't lose that role once the birth is over. Even the smoothest, easiest, most joyful birth is still a major bodily event. The body needs to recover. Just like someone can take first place in a marathon. They did the thing! Not only did they do it, but they did also it the best of everybody! Wooh! Now, are they just going to go back to training the next day? No, of course not. They are going to give their body some time to recover. Ice bath. Massage. Eat all the delicious stuff. Sleep. So much sleep.

Zone out watching a *Schitt's Creek* marathon. The same is true for the post-birth body. Well, maybe not the ice bath. That's up to you.

It can be easy to be swept up into "parent mode" if you are parenting or "get back to normal mode" if you are not. That makes perfect sense, except…You are a whole entire person. Birth happened in your body. *Your* body. Pregnancy can feel like being a beautifully wrapped candy. Everyone looks at you with anticipation. But once birth happens…? Well, the baby is the candy, and what happens to the beautiful wrapper? It gets tossed. At least, that's the way it can feel.

I know a doula who worked with a very young mother who kept getting pregnant over and over. As soon as she gave birth, she would get pregnant again. She wasn't in a financially or socially stable situation. Social services had come in with birth control education and access to resources. Still, she kept getting pregnant. So, this doula thought to ask her, "Why do you think you keep getting pregnant?" She said, "When I'm pregnant, I'm special. Everyone wants to take care of me. The second I give birth, people only care about the baby." Heartbreaking. And it can be so true.

You are not a wrapper. You are not just a vessel for birth. You are a whole entire person with hopes and dreams, favorite foods and favorite movies, and needs. Your needs matter. You are valuable beyond birth. You require recovery support even when there is a baby to take care of. Before you give birth, we are going to make a plan so that you get what you need, too.

Help

Help can look a lot of ways and not all of them are helpful. Postpartum help needs to be clearly defined. If not, people will make assumptions or just ignore the difficult tasks. In this section you will find a sample **POSTPARTUM HELP CALENDAR**. I suggest you bring one to your shower or diaper party or whatever event you are having.* Leave it somewhere central and make an announcement (you don't have to be the one to make the announcement) for everyone who can and wants to sign up for a shift or shifts. That way, when you are home and resting, you will know who is doing what, when, and what you may need to reach out to family and friends for.

Having this specific list is important. It lets you know what to expect—you do not need people coming into your home at random times. It also sets clear expectations for what help looks like. We can say things like, "I think I'm going to need help with laundry," and people say, "I'd love to help!" But when they show up, they don't ask for your laundry basket. They ask for the baby.

It is great to have someone else hold the baby if you are experiencing touch fatigue, which is when you've been touched too much, and you don't want to be touched

---

*If you are not parenting after birth, you still deserve a party. Birth and postpartum are a lot of work, no matter what. Register for comfy pajamas and cozy socks. Herbal tea and lavender hot packs. If you are parenting, you can register for those things too; it doesn't have to all be about gifts for the baby. I have also seen a new trend in postpartum prep parties where a group gets together to make padsicles (menstrual pads with witch hazel, aloe vera gel, and essential oils that are frozen. They are soothing to wear after vaginal births), mix up herbal teas, make freezer meals, etc.

anymore, or you want to take a shower or enjoy some food. However, holding the baby is not inherently "help." Especially, if you are doing chores. I listened to a doula recount her horror at showing up for a three-day postpartum check. She entered the house, and a family member was holding the baby. She asked where the new mother was. The person with the baby pointed to the bathroom so she assumed the mother was taking a shower. Turns out she was on her hands and knees scrubbing the bathroom.

UNACCEPTABLE!

I don't care if you love cleaning the bathroom. If it is the single greatest joy in your life. You will have plenty of time to clean bathrooms after your body has recovered from birth. This is what can happen though, if you don't make a plan. People want to "help," but their help isn't always helpful. Thus, the postpartum help calendar. You get to decide what you will need. You set clear expectations, and it is up to your support circle to help you.

Honestly, people aren't guaranteed time with your baby. People need to earn those chubby cheeks and wiggly toes. You can also set clear boundaries that work for you. For example, if someone is bringing food, you can ask them to leave it on the porch and send you a text message. If someone offers to do laundry, ask if they can pick it up from your garage and bring it back or come in a back way so they don't disturb you. Just because someone is helping does not mean they are entitled to come in and hold the baby. They are helping because they care about YOU. The whole person,

who existed before they birthed this squishy new person.[*]
Also, remember that emotional labor is work. So, if a friend
comes over and wants to talk to you about the annoying thing
their boss did, that is placing a burden on you. One you are
more than welcome to accept, *if* you want to. Be aware,
though, that it will impact you because emotional work is
work.

When possible, I recommend staying in a dimly lit
room that is quiet/soothing while holding your baby skin-to-
skin. This will allow your baby to attune to you as a person
existing outside of a sac filled with amniotic fluid. Even if you
had months and months for your baby to bond with you
from the inside, they need time to bond from the outside.
Now let's talk about what I mean when I say skin-to-skin and
why it is so extremely, incredibly, superbly important.

---

[*] If you are a non-birthing parent reading this book, postpartum
help applies to you, too. Adjusting to bring a new person into your
home is a lot. Babies are a lot. You are allowed to ask for help even
if you aren't recovering from birth.

Postpartum Help

	)	)	◗	●	◖	(	(
MON							
TUES							
WED							
THURS							
FRI							
SAT							
SUN							

) BRING FOOD   (

) LAUNDRY/DISHES   (

◗   ◖

●

Birther: Complete the list of tasks you want help with and a time window that works best for you.

Helper: Select a task. Write your name under the task column with the time you plan to complete it.

You can print out this version at
mindbodybirthbook.com or you can make your own.

Skin-to-Skin

Skin-to-skin contact is the act of holding a baby with no barrier between their skin and the skin of the person holding them. It is literally skin touching skin. It's typically done by placing the baby—naked or in a diaper—on the exposed chest of a caretaker. Anyone can do skin-to-skin, not just the person who gave birth. However, if you are direct-feeding—meaning the baby latches to a person's nipple—that person should be the first and most frequent person providing skin-to-skin contact. If this is of interest to you, I go into greater depth about this in the BBC feeding section.

When I say anyone can do it, I mean that. Skin-to-skin is so beneficial for babies. Touch, in general, and being held lets babies know that they are safe. It helps them to attach more securely. There is this outdated idea that you can spoil your baby with too much contact, and they won't be able to self-soothe. Or that they will be clingy or overly attached. In reality, securely attached children feel safe and confident, so they go out and boldly explore the world. They know that their caretakers will be there, so they feel empowered to step away from them. Denying touch is harmful to babies. It triggers the part of the brain that responds to all stress like it is a bear. This part of the brain remembers a time when being left alone to cry meant something very bad happened. We cry—and not just as children—when we feel abandoned. And when we feel abandoned, being further ignored is not the solution. Hold the baby.

Now, if you are in the middle of a shower. Or you just took the first bite of food that was actually hot. Or your special someone just kissed your neck, and for the first time since birth, it filled you with excitement instead of dread, then it is okay for the baby to cry. Babies cry. It's how they communicate. It's not like they are skilled in the art of spoken word poetry. They have different cries and different volumes, but crying is the extent of their abilities.

No one's existence is perfect. No one's needs get met exactly when they need them met 100% of the time. That's not realistic. It is okay for babies to spend a little bit of time waiting to have their needs met if it means you are having *your* needs met. As long as overall, in general, the baby's cries are responded to, and the baby is being touched and held, it is okay not to jump into action with Wonder Woman-like reflexes at every squeal of discomfort. Now, if holding them is good, what makes skin-to-skin better? Oh, so many, many things!

Microbiome

The microbiome is a collection of bacteria, fungi, and viruses that live in and on the body. Sounds gross? It's not! It's super cool. These microorganisms do a lot to keep people healthy. They break down certain nutrients that the human body is not capable of digesting on its own. They train the immune system to determine what is healthy and what is harmful. They help heal wounds on the skin. They can also influence the metabolism. And because there is limited space in and on the body—and the microbiome takes up a lot of it—there isn't space for harmful pathogens to flourish.

You may have experienced the loss of your microbiome if you've ever taken antibiotics and ended up with a yeast infection. In addition to the skin and gut, many other parts of the body have a microbiome, including the vaginal canal. Antibiotics kill off the microbiome throughout the body. Sometimes when people take antibiotics, it kills off enough of the microbiome in the vaginal canal that space is created for yeast to grow, resulting in a yeast infection. If you've ever had that experience, you know how awful life is without the microbiome. Even more fascinating, we now know about the gut-brain axis, which allows the microbiome to communicate directly with the brain! That's right, microorganisms, including fungus living inside your gut, talk to your brain. Being a human is super weird, and awesome.

Okay, but how does all this stuff get on your skin in the first place? Excellent question. We talked about how the vaginal canal has a microbiome, and the skin has one too. When babies pass through the vaginal canal, some of the microbiome from the vaginal canal and from the rectum transfers onto their skin.[133] Thus, we are born in possession of a microbiome. Unless we aren't born vaginally. Cesarean section babies do not receive the initial microbiome transfer, which can impact the strength of their immune system. They need other ways to get a microbiome. Luckily, human milk, saliva, and skin can all provide microbiome transfers. Which brings us back to skin-to-skin contact.

In addition to transferring the microbiome, skin-to-skin provides other amazing benefits. It increases oxytocin levels, helping to create a sense of connection and bonding for both the baby and the person providing the contact. It also decreases cortisol levels for both.[134] Remember, both sexual and non-sexual touch lowers cortisol levels. If skin-to-skin contact with a support person during childbirth sounds appealing, it can be a great way to reduce cortisol.

Skin-to-skin helps babies regulate their body temperatures, heart rates, and breathing.[135] This is particularly important for low birth weight and premature infants. Skin-to-skin contact can raise the body temperature of a premature infant up to two degrees while regulating their breathing. This is warmer than if they were put in a baby warmer.[136]

The World Health Organization's official stance is that skin-to-skin contact should be the primary intervention for premature and low birth weight infants.[137] This is the primary intervention in other countries. However, it is not— at the time of this writing—in the United States. This method of using skin-to-skin to care for premature and low birth weight infants is called Kangaroo Parenting or Kangaroo Mother Care, in reference to kangaroos who intentionally give birth to underdeveloped, embryo-like, babies and then care for them in their pouch until they are fully developed. Why do they do this? Because their babies are the size of jellybeans. For all my talk of the wonderful experience that birth can be, I'm sure if humans had the ability to safely give birth to jellybean-sized babies that would be the preference.

Skin-to-skin contact has lasting impacts. Not only are babies physically healthier thanks to the microbiome, but they are emotionally healthier. One study found that children who had 6 hours of skin-to-skin during the first week of life and 2 hours a day for the first month of life, had better relationships with their mothers when they were 9 years old.[138] Another study found that one hour of daily skin-to-skin contact from birth until 5 weeks old led to fewer behavioral problems at 3 years old, and greater empathy as teenagers.[139] Skin-to-skin can also impact maternal well-being. So, let's talk about PMADs, what to be on the lookout for, and how skin-to-skin and other tactics can help.

PMADs

You may have—I truly hope—heard of postpartum depression. It is gaining in awareness, though in the past, many people were left confused and alone. I remember my first postpartum project. I was interning at Bright Beginnings in Denver, Colorado, during my Master of Social Work program. We were working on getting fathers more involved, so I created a little manual for dads, a big part of which was on postpartum depression. At the time, most people didn't know what I was talking about. Thankfully, it has gotten better. In the beginning of this book, I said I have seen a profound sense of loneliness in pregnancy and birth. That experience is rivaled by postpartum.

Postpartum depression is depression that occurs after giving birth. According to the Centers for Disease Control and Prevention, the rates of postpartum depression can be as high as 20%.[140] If you know five people who have given birth, it is very likely you know at least one person who experienced—or is experiencing—postpartum depression. We now acknowledge that the mental health impacts of giving birth can expand beyond depression and have begun to use the term Perinatal Mood and Anxiety Disorders or PMAD.

There are several different types of perinatal mood and anxiety disorders, including depression, panic, obsessive-compulsive, post-traumatic stress, bipolar, and psychosis. All these PMADs are real and serious. They can—though not always—lead to harming oneself or the baby.[141] I am reluctant to say that. Sometimes people do not want to seek help because they are afraid others will assume they have tried to hurt their baby. I do say it because it is important to understand how serious this can be. Even if it is "just" loss of pleasure and impaired mental functioning, it is still serious. We, as humans in this society, can be slow to seek help when we think only our joy is at risk. So, I am telling you how bad it could be because I want you to be aware that it is always serious, and it is also potentially dangerous.

Whether or not it becomes dangerous, there is never any shame in experiencing PMAD symptoms. They are medical conditions like preeclampsia or cancer. Just like cancer, there are things that can help prevent PMADs and factors that can contribute to them. Also, like cancer, sometimes for seemingly no reason, it just happens to some people, and there was nothing anyone could have done. PMADs are never your fault. Postpartum depression has been the focus of most studies, so we will focus on that. However, there is a lot of similarity across PMADs.

Some symptoms are normal after birth. For example, being tired is both normal and a symptom of postpartum depression. Some sadness is also normal due to hormonal changes. Sadness can also be caused by the focus shifting from you and onto the baby. There can be very real sleep deprivation. However, if symptoms do not go away, increase, or impact your functioning, it may be PMAD. Here is a list of other symptoms to be aware of:

- Feeling depressed/anxious or being observed as depressed/anxious most of the day
- Loss of interest or pleasure most of the day
- Difficulty sleeping or sleeping too much
- Difficulty thinking or making decisions
- Changes in weight or appetite

- Impaired mental functioning or physical functioning
- Feelings of guilt or of being worthless
- Being tired or having no energy
- Thinking about death or wanting to die

This is another time that your support team becomes super important. They should be taking notice of changes in your mood and behavior. It is not their job to accuse you of anything, but it is their job to pay attention. They can use the **POSTPARTUM TRACKER** at the end of this section to keep track of changes. Keeping a record can help you determine if it is time to seek out professional help. The tracker can also be of help to your healthcare team if you do seek help.

There are medical treatments available. Those treatments are beyond the scope of this book. Instead, we will talk about contributing factors to be aware of. If you experience a contributing factor, that does not automatically mean you will experience postpartum depression or PMAD. It does mean that you—and by you, I mean your support team—should be extra vigilant in watching for signs of PMAD.

PMAD is not your fault. It doesn't mean you did anything wrong or that you are a bad person or a bad parent. It is nothing to be embarrassed or ashamed of. Mental health conditions never are.

The research highlights several factors that are linked with higher rates of postpartum depression. A history of depression—or other mental health conditions—indicates that you have a greater risk of developing postpartum depression.[142] Even if your depression has been under control, be aware that birth might trigger it. Gestational diabetes—which can be impacted by sleep deprivation—is linked with higher rates of postpartum depression.[143]

Cesarean sections are a "complex factor." Some research shows those who have cesarean sections are more likely to experience postpartum depression.[144] However, it is possible that it isn't all cesarean sections, just emergency ones.[145] If that is the case, then we do not know if it is the cesarean section that causes postpartum depression or if it is some other factor that occurs, such as feeling scared or out of control. People also may feel judged and ostracized for not having a "natural" birth, leading to feelings of depression. It may also be that cesarean sections delay—and sometimes decrease the amount of—skin-to-skin contact, resulting in lower levels of oxytocin and higher levels of cortisol. The lack of bonding hormones and the increase in stress hormones may make people feel more anxious.

Pain is also an important factor when it comes to postpartum depression. Several studies have noted that the higher women rated their pain during birth, the more likely they were to experience postpartum depression.[146] This was still true three days and six weeks after birth.[147] We also know from a meta-analysis done in 2020, looking at 85,928 patients, that epidurals did not protect against postpartum depression.[148] That means even if we numb away the pain, it does not appear to reduce the impact that pain has on postpartum depression. The truck is still on the road, even if the road is blocked. This is another reason why reducing pain through an understanding of the fear-pain cycle—rather than through medication—is so important.

There are also ways to protect against postpartum depression. Having a strong support system can help. This is true for a variety of reasons, including getting more sleep, more emotional support, and eating better when people bring you food. Of course, not smoking and eating well are good ways to lower your risk of postpartum depression and to keep you healthy in general.

Again, getting enough sleep is a protective factor. Sleep is important. Always. It can be so hard to rest in our society because it is seen as not being productive. But sleep is productive. It heals you and keeps you healthy. You can't contribute if you aren't healthy. You can't contribute well when you are sleep deprived. Prioritize sleep. Always. It is good for you. It is good for your relationships. It is good for your impact on the world.

With that in mind let's take a quick moment to talk about sleep deprivation. Sleep deprivation doesn't just occur after birth. Discomfort, pressure on the bladder, and stress are among the reasons that sleep can be elusive during pregnancy. Fear of childbirth is also linked to less sleep during pregnancy.[149] Sleep is important. Always. But especially, when creating a person out of your blood and thin air. Lack of sleep during pregnancy can affect the metabolism increasing the risk of gestational diabetes.[150] It is also linked to higher blood pressure, which can contribute to preeclampsia.[151] Sleep is needed to keep the immune system strong, meaning lack of sleep increases the risk of infections.[152] Chronic sleep deprivation can affect fetal growth, lead to preterm birth, a longer time in birth, and a higher likelihood of delivery by cesarean section.[153]

How can you make sleep more accessible? Prioritize it. That's not a guaranteed fix, but not prioritizing sleep will definitely not help. I get it. It can be hard to prioritize sleep because there is so much to do. And if you're like me, you really value the time you get to spend with your partner at night watching *Taskmaster* or whatever else is currently top of the list. I've lost track of the number of nights I've sacrificed sleep for the soothing comfort of shared time. It sucks. But like rollercoasters and spontaneously taking up horseback riding, there are things that have to be held off for your safety and the baby's safety. Other ways to improve sleep are:

1. Using pillows/pregnancy pillows to increase your comfort.

2. Hydrating earlier in the day and limiting liquids closer to bedtime.

3. Relaxation techniques include breathing, meditation, sound therapy, and Gale's alphabet game from the CAM section.

4. Limiting caffeine, especially later in the day.

5. Limiting screen time and/or using blue light blocking glasses. It may help to keep your phone out of the bedroom if your lifestyle allows that.

6. If safe for you, walking during the day or other tolerated gentle exercise.

7. Lavender and chamomile tea. I like to add some mint as well when I make it.

8. Aromatherapy.

9. Sweet pea flower essence (I like the one from Green Hope Farm) can help with sleep. Always talk to your medical team before taking anything new during pregnancy.

10. Soaking your feet in warm water.

Finally, Yoga. Yoga has been shown to reduce rates of postpartum depression and depression during pregnancy.[154,155] As depression during pregnancy is a risk factor for postpartum depression, it makes sense that something that lowers the risk of depression during pregnancy would also impact postpartum depression. We already talked about the wonderful ways Yoga can improve the birth experience, but this is another one. I highly, highly, recommend a Yoga practice during pregnancy. This doesn't have to mean going to a formal class or working through Asana. It can be spontaneous. Moving with your breath and letting your body tell you what feels good. No matter what you do, make choices to prioritize your wellbeing during pregnancy and after.

Postpartum Watchlist

Monitor your birthing person after birth for symptoms of postpartum depression. Put a check under the day you notice a symptom. Add a + if the symptom is getting worse and a - if it is getting better but still there. Talk to your healthcare team about what you notice. Continue to watch for signs up to a year after birth.

Symptom Day	1	3	5	7	9	11	13	15
1. Crying								
2. Self-Blaming								
3. Unable to find enjoyment								
4. Not laughing or finding things funny								
5. Anxious for no good reason								
6. Feeling scared for no good reason								
7. Difficulty sleeping								
8. Withdrawing from friends and family								
9. Hopelessness								
10. Difficulty concentrating or making decisions								
11. Intense irritability								
12. No interest in enjoyable things								
13. Changes in appetite								
14. Mood Swings								
15. Difficulty bonding with the baby								
16. Feelings of worthlessness, shame, or guilt.								
17. Restlessness								
18. Thoughts of self-harm or harming the baby								

Adapted from Mayo Clinic Postpartum Depression and the Edinburgh Postnatal Depression Scale

Support Report

- The placenta does several vital jobs, including nourishing the baby, supplying oxygen, removing waste, producing hormones, and providing protection. After the baby is born the placenta still has to be delivered. The placenta can be kept for keepsake art, ceremonial purposes or consumed. The placental site in the uterus must heal which can take weeks. Bleeding and pain may occur as it is healing.

- You will be healing postpartum for several weeks. Give your body time.

- Emotional support from your support team is critical after birth. Rest and self-care are as important as baby care. Don't rush into "parent mode" or normal life activities without considering your own recovery.

- It's great when people want to help, so long as their help is actually helpful. Have helpers drop off meals, do laundry, and clean.

- Skin-to-skin contact is vital for newborns, promoting bonding, regulating temperature, and improving health outcomes, especially for low birth weight or premature babies. It can help reduce cortisol and increase oxytocin levels. Babies who have skin-to-skin contact are emotionally healthier and show better long-term development.

- The microbiome is a collection of viruses, bacteria, and fungi that are vital for human health. Babies born vaginally receive their initial microbiome from the birthing person's vaginal canal, which supports immune system development.

Babies born via C-section can receive microbiome transfers through skin-to-skin contact, human milk, and saliva.

- Perinatal Mood and Anxiety Disorders, or PMADs, cover a variety of mental health conditions that occur postpartum. Symptoms include depression, anxiety, loss of interest or pleasure, sleep issues, appetite changes, impaired functioning, feelings of guilt, and thoughts of death or suicide. PMADs are never your fault. They are a medical condition like cancer that requires professional help. There is no shame in seeking help for PMADs.

- Pain during birth increases the risk of postpartum depression.

- Prioritize sleep and eating well to reduce the risk of PMADs. Lean on your support team for help. Yoga during pregnancy can help prevent postpartum depression.

Journaling Prompts

- What kind of help will actually help you after birth? Who can you depend on? How will you handle people who only want to hold the baby but don't actually want to help?

- What does it look like when you're sad? Are there certain things you do or don't do? How might someone else know you are sad? What should your support team look for after you give birth to make sure you are doing ok?

- What makes you feel better when you're sad? What do you wish someone knew to do to cheer you up? What might your support team try to help you, if you are feeling a little sad after giving birth?

BBC Feeding

When it comes to feeding, there is one thing I want to establish right away, which is the pro side of formula. It can give you freedom and flexibility. Ultimately, the most important thing to know about feeding is that you get to make the decisions that are right for you and your family. No one else is in your circumstances, so their opinions do not get to count—unless you want them to. Never forget that you are a whole person. You existed long before becoming pregnant, and you will live a whole life long after your children are done feeding and even living in your home. You get to make decisions for you. You do not have to justify them to anyone.

Some people reading this may want to BBC feed but cannot due to physical, medical, social, or economic complications. For that, I am deeply sorry. We will talk about donor milk in this chapter, which you might find to be a compelling alternative. If you have a medical or physical complication, I encourage you to talk to a lactation specialist—one that makes you feel good about yourself—to see if you have options, if BBC feeding is important to you. For example, many people with inverted nipples may believe they cannot BBC feed, but that is not true. There are techniques and devices, like nipple shields, that can make BBC feeding possible.

If you have a social complication, such as discomfort around body feeding—which we will discuss more in this chapter—reach out to your local La Leche League or other breastfeeding support groups, or to a qualified therapist. If you have an economic complication, including needing to go back to work right away, not really being offered time or space to pump, or storage for expressed milk, contact your mayor, governor, representatives, union leaders, and state attorney general. There is a form letter in the back of this book you can use as a script to contact them. No matter your situation or what your feeding desires are, remember to vote. Informed voting is the best way to make progress in women's issues and issues for people with pregnant bodies.

If you know you are going to be using solely formula, then there is no need to read this section. Skip ahead and get started on your birth toolkit!

***

If you are BBC feeding and you find yourself increasingly stressed out by it, I want you to give yourself permission to stop. Remember when we discussed cortisol—the stress hormone? Being stressed out is not good for you, and it's not great for the baby. BBC feeding—when it stresses you out—causes you to stay in the active sympathetic nervous system state. Staying in that state is not good for your health. We all struggle with being chronically stressed out—I recommend the book *Burnout* by Amelia Nagoski and Emily Nagoski to learn more about this. This is a big problem in our society, so if BBC feeding is keeping you in that state of chronic stress and you want to stop, I am telling you that do not have to BBC feeding.

If that is not enough to help you make that decision, know that research shows when women are very stressed out, their human milk has high cortisol levels. There is reason to believe that high cortisol levels in human milk can impact how infants behave.[156] Cortisol levels in human milk have also been shown to impact the body composition—the ratios of fat, bone, muscle, and water—of infants.[157]

Stress changes human milk. Human milk includes long-chain unsaturated fatty acids and medium-chain fatty acids. In general, long-chain unsaturated fatty acids are released by the body in times of stress. This goes back to our bear analogy. If a person is running for their life or hiding from a bear, they cannot stop to think about eating. So, the body uses up the stores of this type of fat.

In human milk, long-chain unsaturated fatty acids are essential for the growth and development of the baby. When there are high levels of cortisol in human milk, there are also high levels of long-chain unsaturated fatty acids. This is perfectly fine—and a healthy response—in the short term. The problem is when this becomes chronic. Over time, the body of the person feeding—and their milk—will become depleted of long-chain unsaturated fatty acids. It can take time to refill those stores, meaning the milk will be missing a vital component.

Medium-chain fatty acids are also an important part of human milk. Research shows women who had high stress levels had fewer medium-chain fatty acids in their milk.[158] Medium-chain fatty acids in human milk do not come from the mother's diet or fat storage in the body. They are made in the mammary gland, so changing your diet will not change the amount of medium-chain fatty acids in your milk. Only reducing your cortisol levels will. In short, high levels of stress make human milk less nutritious. If you are stressed out and want to stop BBC feeding, STOP. And throw those facts about fatty acids at anyone who gives you flack about it. If you think this describes you, skip to the section on donor milk or go straight to building your birth toolkit.

If you plan on BBC feeding, but you read the last few paragraphs, and now you're panicking because what if you get stressed out and it changes your milk...Breathe. Seriously, put the book down. Take a deep breath.

Did you do it? Now, do it three more times.

This is all just information. And information is power. When I tell you that high maternal cortisol levels are linked to low LATCH scores and suckling behaviors, I am not telling you that to freak you out.[159] I am telling you so that if there is an issue with latching or suckling, you now know to think, "Okay, am I very stressed out right now? Might my cortisol levels be high? What can I do to bring them down?"

Knowing what the problem might be will help you find the solution. If you want to continue BBC feeding and you find yourself chronically stressed, then you might want to think about ways to reduce your stress level, especially around feeding times. Take deep breaths. Listen to soothing music. Create a peaceful environment to feed—when that's possible. And keep BBC feeding because exclusive breastfeeding decreases cortisol levels.[160] The long-chain fatty acid increase is perfectly fine in the short term. Stick with it. Let the act of BBC feeding reduce your cortisol, and the long-chain fatty acid issue will correct itself.

The body is amazing—especially when left to its own devices. There is an ebb and flow. Some cortisol is needed to start lactogenesis (milk letting down). Your body needs some cortisol for birth. Good thing it is part of the childbirth process. Then you BBC feed your baby, and the cortisol goes away. It's all quite beautiful when you think about it. So do not panic. You are in good hands. Your own.

Next, we are going to go over the upside of human
milk, the downside of formula, how bottle-feeding human
milk is different than direct feeding human milk, and donor
milk.

The Pros of Human Milk

Breastmilk is considered the gold standard of infant nutrition by the World Health Organization.[161] Human milk is perfectly formulated to exactly meet the nutritional needs of the infant. Saliva from the infant goes into the skin of the nipple, triggering the body to change the makeup of the milk to what the infant needs (remember, this can be impacted by stress!). There are numerous benefits for the baby and for the person producing the milk.

First let's look at the benefits for the baby. Human milk improves their immune system. If the infant is exposed to a disease, the milk will change to contain antibodies to fight that disease. Human milk passes on immune cells.[162] It colonizes the microbiome—this is especially vital if the baby was not birthed vaginally and did not receive any microbiome organisms through the birth canal.[163] Not only does the infant's saliva let the body know what antibodies the baby needs, but it also mixes with human milk, releasing antibacterial compounds, including hydrogen peroxide.[164] It is not safe for babies to straight up drink hydrogen peroxide, yet, when it is created by human milk it is perfectly formulated for the health of the baby. Human milk produced in the evenings even contains melatonin to help babies regulate their sleep cycles because young babies do not have a circadian rhythm. Utterly incredible, right?

Research shows that children who were human milk fed have better motor skills, language abilities, and cognition when compared to kids who were formula-fed.[165] Being fed human milk decreases rates of asthma, obesity, type 1 diabetes, poor mental health, severe lower respiratory disease, ear infections, Sudden Infant Death Syndrome, gastrointestinal infections, necrotizing enterocolitis, and childhood leukemia.[166] That is a lot of benefits.

It makes sense. Over the course of human existence, humans have evolved to produce a food that would increase their offspring's chances of survival. Human milk does just that. It makes babies healthier and improves the skills necessary to keep them safe. One study found that longer BBC feeding is associated with lower cortisol levels in children at 8 years old.[167] Exclusive BBC feeding also appears to decrease cortisol levels in both the baby and the person feeding.[168] But the benefits for people feeding don't stop at cortisol levels.

The benefits for the person producing the milk are quite astounding. They will have lower rates of high blood pressure.[169] Likely, due to oxytocin, which is produced during feeding. Oxytocin is a vasodilator, which helps to widen the blood vessels, reducing blood pressure. Oxytocin also produces a sense of calm and relaxation. There are also lower rates of type 2 diabetes, ovarian and breast cancer among people who BBC feed.

Employers that provide lactation support have lower healthcare costs, absenteeism, and turnover. They also experience higher morale, job satisfaction, and productivity, with a return on investment of nearly three to one. [U.S. Breastfeeding Committee. (2019). *Breastfeeding saves dollars and makes sense.*]

BBC feeding also decreases the likelihood of developing postpartum depression. Postpartum depression is real and serious. There is more information in the PMADs section of this book. BBC feeding and postpartum depression have what's called a bidirectional relationship.[170] So, the more you BBC feed, the less likely postpartum depression is to occur, and the less you BBC feed, the more likely postpartum depression is to occur.[171] The oxytocin that is produced during BBC feeding can impact postpartum depression symptoms.[172] It is likely that the oxytocin is again doing the heavy lifting here.

Remember, research also indicates that stress and cortisol levels can actually trigger the release of oxytocin.[173] It is the body's way of combating pain, stress, and even loneliness.[174] I want to remind you again—until you are sick of hearing it—that if BBC feeding is overwhelming and stressful and you don't want to do it: Don't do it. Because even with that fancy research noted, lactation is not guaranteed to prevent postpartum depression. And stress is not good for preventing it either. So, no matter what the research says, always make sure you are making the best choices for you. Plus, skin-to-skin contact also releases oxytocin, so if you aren't BBC feeding, just cuddle your baby instead.

Human milk is packed with immunities. People use their milk to treat diaper rash, sunburns, rashes in general, and burns in general.

The Cons of Formula

Human milk is honestly a scientific marvel that we don't even fully understand yet. In fact, according to Dr. Hinde, there is more research on "coffee, wine, and tomatoes. We know over twice as much about erectile dysfunction" than we do about lactation and breastmilk.[175] We do know that formula lacks the health and developmental benefits of human milk. It is straightforward, so I would like to focus on a different negative of formula that is not always part of the conversation.

Formula has an extremely negative impact on the environment. There are three parts to this: the ingredients that make up the formula, the supply chain, and the packaging. Infant formulas are commonly made of cow's milk, vegetable oils, and supplements, resulting in an ultra-processed food with a complex supply chain.[176] This complex supply chain contributed to the United States formula shortage in 2022.[177] Infant formula production requires land clearing, water, and energy use. The results are pollution, methane gas, packaging, and food waste.[178] Infant formula should be of global concern as "a 2009 study showed that 550 million infant formula cans, comprising 86,000 tons of metal and 364,000 tons of paper are added to landfills every year [and] the formula industry has more than doubled since then."[179]

The garbage alone from infant formula is enough to make me stop in my tracks. Sure, one could argue that if you are a person who is BBC feeding their child, you might also be drinking milk, eating hamburgers, and producing a lot of trash. If you made that argument, you would be right.

However, with BBC feeding only one person is generating trash.

Formula feeding has as much as a 72% higher environmental impact than feeding human milk.[180] Research shows that if the United Kingdom started supporting mothers in feeding human milk, it would have the same environmental impact as taking between 50,000 and 77,500 cars off the road every year.[181] Infant formula in just Australia, South Korea, China, Malaysia, India, and the Philippines was responsible for 771,978 tons of CO_2 in 2012.[182] Bear in mind that the industry has doubled since that research was conducted. If toddler formulas are included—which research shows are unnecessary with the potential to be harmful—these six countries generated a total of 2,893,030 tons of CO_2 in 2012 from formula.[183]

According to NASA, global warming caused by human-made greenhouse gases is worsening and will result in sea levels rising, stronger hurricanes, increasing droughts, heat waves, more wildfires, and changes to growing seasons.[184] If the goal is to give our children the best future possible, then it is not enough just to look at the impact BBC feeding has on their bodies and minds. We must also think about the world they will be living in.

There are risks associated with feeding babies formula that are just not risks for feeding them human milk. Formula is subject to both supply chain issues and recalls, like the one in 2024. It requires access to clean water. Human milk cannot spoil. It cannot make your baby sick. Human milk is made from the blood. This is important to be aware of because we often think in terms of "you eat something, that becomes human milk." While diet can impact human milk, it happens through changes in the blood. Large and rapid consumption of alcohol can affect human milk, but this happens because alcohol alters your blood alcohol level. Not because it goes directly from your digestive system into the milk.

There are certain medications that can go into human milk, so, if you are on medications, you always want to tell whoever is prescribing those medications that you are feeding a baby. Even better, check with a lactation consultant or a doctor who specializes in feeding human milk as not all people who prescribe medication are versed in what is safe for human milk. Doctors tend towards being overly cautious, which can be good. But if people are stopping BBC feeding because they have been falsely informed that their medication is going into their milk then overly cautious is not helpful. This happens all the time so if you take medications make sure the information you are getting is correct.

While medications can sometime transfer, antiretroviral therapy does not. It is now generally accepted that individuals with HIV who have undetectable viral loads and are on antiretroviral therapy can BBC feed. In fact, it is the recommendation of the World Health Organization that people with HIV do BBC feed their babies for the first six months of life.[185]

Supplementation

Supplementation is when formula is fed in addition to human milk. This often happens when there is concern about supply or when lactogenesis—the letdown of milk— is delayed. It is common and is completely okay to do. Especially if a lactation specialist—one you like and feel comfortable with—recommends it. However, supplementation should not be the default. There are several reasons why feeding both isn't the ideal choice. Formula can impact overall BBC feeding success. Using formula decreases milk supply because there is less demand put on the body. The body rises to meet the demands of the baby. If the baby is eating less, the body makes less. In addition to impacting the body of the person feeding, doing both impacts the baby. Introducing formula can delay the onset of lactation and increase the likelihood of discontinuing human milk feeding.[186]

BBC feeding and bottle feeding use different muscles in the baby's mouth and throat. Introducing a bottle before a baby has a solid latch can prevent successful latching. Formula is digested differently than human milk. When both enter the infant's digestive system even spaced hours apart, it can negatively impact digestion overall. It is far better to pick one route and stick with it.

Sometimes, formula is introduced directly after birth. If that happens and you still want to BBC feed, it's okay. Just try your best to make sure all formula feeding is stopped before the infant is one week old. If you stop by one week, research shows you can avoid the long-term effects that formula feeding has on human milk feeding success.[187]

At one time, it was standard for infants to immediately be given a bottle of formula upon birth. This was less a best practice for infant health and more a product of companies like Nestlé working to get formula introduced in the hospital. We saw a lot of reasons cortisol levels can be high. Cortisol can lead to delayed lactation.[188] Now, imagine your cortisol is high, so your milk isn't letting down. Then, someone tells you that your baby is going to starve. What is that going to do to your cortisol levels? Probably increase them, which will only delay lactation more.

Take a deep breath. Babies are born with a lot of fluids and "brown fat"—or brown adipose tissue. This reserve fat helps keep the baby warm. It also keeps babies nourished in the event lactation is delayed. Childbirth and BBC feeding is about as evolutionarily old as it gets for humans. Our bodies are designed with safeguards. Lactation specialists are taught that ideally babies will start gaining weight at three days old, but they have enough fat reserve for seven to ten days without consuming anything.[189] So, there is no need to immediately offer formula.

In fact, blood sugar changes typically don't happen until day two, so your baby won't really experience hunger before that. I know it seems really scary, especially if your baby is crying, but if you plan to BBC feed, hold off on formula and follow the advice of a lactation specialist. If latching is the problem—not lactation—milk can be hand-expressed onto a spoon and then fed to the baby. In short, stay calm and feed on.

Premature and Low Birth Weight babies do NOT have brown fat. They cannot wait as long as other babies to feed and may need formula.

Bottle Feeding versus Direct Feeding

Regardless of what is inside the bottle, there are some things to know about bottles. Suckling on a rubber nipple is not the same as suckling on a human nipple. It requires the use of different muscles in the mouth and throat. The muscles needed to feed need to be developed, just like the muscles to sit up or rollover. While babies may have some muscular development of the mouth from sucking their thumbs in utero, they still need to learn to use and develop the muscles to latch.

When using a rubber nipple, babies are strengthening different muscles. It isn't bad. It's just more work. It's like riding a bike to get better at swimming. This means using both human nipples and rubber nipples can lead to some difficulty with latching. This is sometimes called "nipple confusion." It can lead to infinite frustration for all parties involved, including a lot of "Why won't you just eat!" being shouted into the ether. The baby isn't being difficult or bad at eating. There is just a lot being asked of someone so new to eating. Be patient. When it's possible, direct feed early and often to build strength. Then, transition to bottles, especially if they will be a necessary part of life.

There are two other things to be aware of with bottles. When bottle feeding, the baby's saliva isn't going into the skin to change the makeup of the milk. If the baby is sick, I recommend direct feeding as much as possible to ensure they are getting the most effective milk makeup. Also, babies don't just nurse for food. They do it for comfort. This isn't bad, or lazy, or weird, or wrong. They are getting oxytocin. They feel protected and cared for. It might not always feel great to be someone's self-soothing device, but it can also be really great. Embrace it when you can. Your child won't always want you to comfort them. You may miss it someday. This is not forever.

Widström's Nine Stages

We've already talked about how important Skin-to-Skin contact is. If you are BBC feeding, the person(s) who is doing the feeding should be the person(s) holding the baby first, and most often. Skin-to-skin will release oxytocin, which is necessary for lactation. It will also help that person, and the baby feel bonded. Skin-to-skin contact also allows the baby to move through Widström's Nine Stages.[190] We often think of babies as being born helpless. They are capable of doing some amazing things right away. Did you know babies can crawl within two hours of being born? Not in the traditional sense, because humans are born with heavy heads, but when placed on the body, they will crawl to the nipple. Incredible.

Widström's Nine Stages outline the sequence of behaviors that babies exhibit right after birth when given undisturbed skin-to-skin contact, resulting in latching and feeding. This process can take up to two hours. The first stage is the birth cry. This happens quickly after birth and helps clear their airway. It is an intense cry that transitions the baby into breathing air.

The next stage is the relaxation stage. The baby rests. You won't see any activity in the mouth, head, arms, legs, or body. We often think about the impact on the birthing person of having a large thing move through a tight space. We don't really think about the impact on the baby of being a large thing moving through a tight space. Babies produce pain-relieving chemicals during birth because there is a lot of pressure on their skulls. This chemical is called catecholamine, and during the relaxation stage, the baby is processing and reabsorbing it. During this time, the baby is listening intently to the heartbeat of the person providing the skin-to-skin contact. If the baby is disturbed during the second stage, they will cry.

In stage three, the awakening stage, the baby begins to show signs of activity. There will be small movements of the limbs and shoulders. They will move their heads around, going up and down and side to side. These movements are exploratory. The baby is getting ready for the active stage.

In stage four, the baby is making determined movements. They will push with their limbs, though they won't shift their bodies. They begin the instinctive behavior of rooting. If the corner of the baby's mouth is touched, they will turn their head in that direction and may make sucking motions. Do not move the baby to the nipple. The baby is good. Great really. Just let them do their thing undisturbed.

You may have noticed that nipples change during pregnancy. The darkening of the skin color makes them more visible to babies. The change in position makes latching easier. Babies can also recognize the smell of the nipple because of the way scent is transmitted through the amniotic fluid. The nipple will also smell like amniotic fluid. It is okay if the person doing the feeding is not the person who birthed the baby—we will talk more about this in Induced Lactation—the baby will still be able to find the nipple. They just may need a little more time. This brand-new baby has just done a lot of work. Rooting and shifting. Smelling. When they hit stage five, it is time for a little rest. There may be some activity, like sucking on the hands, but there is significantly less movement than in stage four. Resting will start to occur throughout the following stages whenever the baby needs to rest. Let them take their time. They need to conserve their energy.

Crawling! I told you it was going to happen. In stage six, the baby crawls. The baby's legs will push against the abdomen or wherever they are placed on the feeding person. They will use an instinctive movement—called the stepping reflex—to move themselves closer to the nipple. This action is reflexive. There is no conscious awareness that it is happening. The stepping reflex fades around two months as voluntary movements develop.

In stage seven, the baby has reached the nipple, and their mouth is in a good position. They will now begin familiarization. The baby will brush, lick, or massage the nipple, becoming familiar with it. This stage can take 20 minutes or longer. It can feel nerve-wracking because the baby is right there but not latching. Don't be concerned. They need time to learn. When they are ready, they will start stage eight.

Stage eight is the suckling stage. The infant latches and officially begins their first feeding session. They may stop and start. They may even completely disengage from the nipple. They aren't finished, however, until they reach stage nine—the sleeping stage. Let them keep feeding in their start-stop pattern until their eyes close, and they fall into a deep sleep.

Congratulations! Your baby has now had a successful first direct feeding! You can see how important uninterrupted skin-to-skin contact is. If at any point the baby is taken away, they won't complete the transition through the stages. I know you might be very tired, and a nurse saying, "Let me take that baby and lay it down," might sound so appealing. But, giving your baby time to move through the stages at their own pace is not only important for successful BBC feeding, it is so fucking cool. It will blow your mind. Plus, it will fill you with all the oxytocin warm and gooeies.

Barriers to BBC Feeding

Unfortunately, despite how primed babies are to BBC feed, there are a lot of barriers to BBC feeding. We just saw how interrupted or delayed skin-to-skin can impact movement through Widström's Nine Stages. Let's look at some other barriers, starting with birth experience.

Birth Experience

Birth experience can impact BBC feeding which is why we are talking about BBC feeding long before you give birth. Having this knowledge can help you make decisions about the kind of birth you want to have. It can also help you understand why you might be experiencing some difficulties, so you are prepared to get what you need. What you need may be as simple as time.

Among the many other issues associated with long birth duration, it delays the onset of lactation.[191] There is an increase in cortisol levels, which impacts oxytocin production.[192] Cortisol is also associated with low LATCH scores and weak suckling behavior. We also know that fasting increases cortisol, which means longer birth in a hospital setting is a longer time without eating.[193] BBC feeding takes a lot of calories. Producing milk is hard. I wouldn't want to run a marathon on an empty stomach. I could with sympathetic nervous system activation, but it isn't ideal. Be prepared to be hungry. Also, be prepared for it to take a while for your appetite to come back. Both are normal.

Medical interventions can be a huge barrier to BBC feeding. Pain medications can increase birth duration—which delays the onset of lactation.[194] They can decrease the baby's ability to suckle and latch.[195] They can also impact the baby's heart rate, making it more difficult for them to move through the nine stages.[196] Pain medication can decrease oxytocin and prolactin production, both of which are vital for lactation, leading to a delay in lactation.[197] The decrease in oxytocin is not something that can be fixed with synthetic oxytocin. Synthetic oxytocin appears to cause more problems for BBC feeding.[198] Cesarean sections can delay skin-to-skin contact, which can impact the nine stages. Cesarean sections are also associated with reduced suckling behavior and lower milk supply.[199]

None of this is to say that if you have a cesarean section or use pain medication you can't BBC feed. You absolutely still can. You just need to be prepared that it might not go the smoothest or quickest in the beginning. That's okay. That's what lactation specialists are for. That's what staying calm and taking your time is for. If your oxytocin levels are low, just hold the baby more. Although, sometimes, just holding the baby is easier said than done.

Birth can be painful. Even if you do not have a cesarean section, it can be physically difficult to hold your baby. One study found that 89% of women who did not have a cesarean section still had too much pain to easily breastfeed.[200] Cesarean sections, of course, can cause a lot of pain and come with pain medications. Pain during active birth is negatively correlated with LATCH scores.[201] This means the higher women rated their pain, the lower the LATCH scores of their babies were. Yet another reason why it is so important to stop the fear-pain cycle.

Pregnancy

Another barrier can be pregnancy. You may be aware that pregnancy can cause sore nipples. If your thought is, "Yeah, but so does BBC feeding," pitch that idea from your mind right now and see the box to the side. Hormones in pregnancy can cause your milk supply to drop.[202] Eventually, milk will change into colostrum—the milk that babies need immediately after birth. It won't hurt an older child, but it will taste different. They may choose to wean because of the change in taste. If you have a high-risk pregnancy or you're having twins, you may be advised not to BBC feed during pregnancy, as BBC feeding causes mild uterine contractions.[203] If you have a lengthy BBC feeding goal—and there really isn't such a thing as feeding for too long—you may want to delay future pregnancies. You may have a "number of children" goal, too, and delaying isn't something you are excited about. Just know one may impact the other. If you are not planning to have another child right away, make sure you have a birth control plan. BBC feeding is not birth control.

> BBC feeding should not be painful. There can be some initial discomfort, and of course, babies can bite. But this whole idea that you need to "toughen up your nipples," is not correct. If BBC feeding is painful, there is something else going on—likely issues with the latch. Seek out a lactation consultant right away. In the meantime, know that the baby's mouth should be all the way around the entire areola—the outer part of the nipple. Their lips should be flared out, kind of like a fish or Instagram duck-lips. The nipple should be hitting way back in the throat. If you have pain, do not suffer. That is not good for anyone. Check your latch and get some support.

Systemic Barriers

Systemic barriers also impact people's ability to BBC Feed. Systemic barriers look like no paid parental leave and lack of access to locations for pumping and storing milk. Not to mention, not being given practical time to pump. It is one thing to say you are allowed to pump, but if you aren't given the time because your work is so busy—or they schedule meetings when you need to be pumping—you aren't really being given time to pump. Even when systemic barriers don't cause a direct problem, they can lead to stress, which leads to cortisol, which impacts milk and lactation. Remember, there is a form letter in the back of this book that you can use to contact your elected officials to let them know that systemic barriers to BBC feeding are a problem.

Body Image

How people see their bodies can impact their feeding decisions. According to the research, mothers with body image concerns are less likely to start BBC feeding. When they do start, they are less likely to reach six months than mothers without body image concerns.[204] The research also shows that those with more positive body image had lower levels of psychological distress and higher rates of initiating BBC feeding.[205] As someone who has lived pretty much their whole life with body image issues and body dysmorphia, I think this sucks. Body image should not be the reason people make decisions about how to feed their babies. Although, a lack of government oversight shouldn't be either…

Concern about weight is not always grounded in health. There is so much focus in Western society on what our bodies look like, especially the bodies of women and AFAB people. It shouldn't be surprising that the research shows that self-objectification and body image concerns were associated with anxiety and depression, as well as lower self-efficacy of BBC feeding.[206] How we feel about our bodies shouldn't determine how good we think we will be at BBC feeding or how confident we feel. Yet people are so objectified in our society that the way they feel about their bodies—which has been projected onto them—impacts the choices they make about how they care for their children. With that in mind, let's get into sexualization and objectification as barriers to BBC feeding.

> What the research says isn't always helpful. Remember, research typically looks at populations of people and then notes trends and patterns. Not every person falls into those patterns. However, if you do live with body image concerns, then you may want to prepare yourself with some extra support if you plan to BBC feed. This can look like working with a lactation specialist, seeing a therapist, or seeking out a support group.

Sexualization

We saw how sexualization can impact the experience of childbirth. You likely won't be shocked when I tell you that sexualization can impact the experience of BBC feeding as well. Before we look deeper at sexualization, let's strip all the sexualization away. Some human bodies come equipped with mammary glands. They serve a primary purpose: to feed offspring. Humans are the only primates—or mammals of any kind—where this chest area tissue occurs from puberty on. In science, this tissue is called permanent adipose breasts.

When two mountain lions decide to mate, one isn't looking at the other and thinking, "Yeah, look at those breasts. Nice teats. That's who I'm mating with." The breasts of other mammals aren't visible until pregnancy occurs. Even in other apes, the breast tissue only becomes visible during pregnancy and through the feeding period. This is not the case with humans. Mammary glands get bigger during pregnancy, but to varying degrees, they are always visible. However, they still serve the same primary purpose as the mammary glands of all other mammals, which is, just to remind you, feeding babies.

I am not here to yuck anybody's yum. If you or your partner(s) think boobs are a super fun, sexy turn-on, or that lactation is a super fun, sexy turn-on, great! You deserve a happy, fun, fulfilling sex life. If boobs add to that, more power to you. The problem is that the sexuality of breasts has come to precede the function of them. We have started to think of breasts as sexy first and a system for feeding our offspring second. This wouldn't be a problem, except it is also paired with a society that has a lot of opinions on sexuality and female-presenting bodies. I have heard women say, "I can't breastfeed. My breasts are for my husband." If we had no concerns about sexuality, then this sexual first, feeding second mentality wouldn't really matter because there wouldn't be any stigma. As it stands, sexualization highly impacts decisions around BBC feeding, so there is a problem.

I want to be able to say that everyone can disconnect BBC feeding body parts as sexual from BBC feeding body parts as nurturing. I want so badly for that to be the world we live in. But it isn't. We live in a hyper-sexualized society where BBC feeding body parts are primarily seen as sexual body parts. When you think about it, this is quite ridiculous, since they have nothing practical to do with reproduction and everything to do with feeding babies.

I know what you are thinking, "But Sam! They respond to sexual stimulation." Well, guess what? The back of the knees is also considered a major erogenous zone, and the world doesn't fall to pieces when people go out in shorts. Yet a person BBC feeding in public can lead to all kinds of drama. I mentioned previously that we are able to separate sexual kissing from loving kissing. This same liberty is not extended to BBC feeding body parts. It is almost as if society feels some sort of ownership over the body parts of women and AFAB people. Imagine that...

In her TedTalk, Sophia Jawed-Wessel explains that objectification is

> the foundation of sexism, and we see it reinforced through all facets of our lives. We see it in advertisements. How many of you have seen an advertisement that uses a woman's breasts to sell an entirely unrelated product? Or movie after movie after movie that portrays women as only love interests?

> These examples might seem inconsequential and harmless, but they're insidious, slowly building into a culture that refuses to see women as people. We see this in the school that sends home a ten-year-old girl because her clothes were a distraction to boys trying to learn. Or the government that refuses to adequately punish men for r*ping women, over and over and over (0:51).[207]

Objectification is also the foundation of sexualization. The American Psychology Association classifies sexualization as occurring when a person is treated as a sexual object.[208] You are not an object. No one has any right to make you into one—unless it is part of consensual sexual play.

Sadly, as Jawed-Wessel noted—and you've likely experienced—objectification is everywhere. It is also a big reason people decide to stop BBC feeding. The research shows that mothers feel ashamed to BBC feed in public.[209] When public feeding is disapproved of, it can become difficult to separate the caretaking and sexual roles of the body.[210] Objectification and sexualization are so bad one study even found that mothers were embarrassed to show their BBC feeding body parts to healthcare professionals.[211] I haven't seen any research, but I would have to imagine that objectification and general "gawking," also contribute to the decision of non-binary people, AFAB people, and trans men to not BBC feed as well.

Objectification and sexualizing people is treated as a different issue than body image in the research, but I see them as connected. Without objectification, people would not have body image issues in the same way. We exist for ourselves. We are not things for other people. We need to stop seeing ourselves as existing to be viewed by others. Instead, we need to learn that we exist to enjoy life. That is your purpose in being here. To get to experience the weird, wonderful, ugly, beautiful, sticky, sweetness of existing in a human body.

My old housemate came home one day from the gym. A guy had approached her while she was lifting weights— probably more weight than the guy could lift. He stopped her in the middle of her workout to tell her she should really shave her legs before coming to the gym. What? Who was that guy? And how did he feel so entitled to not only her body but her time? He interrupted her. He invaded her space to pass judgment on her existence. There was no world in which this guy would ever have been granted an opportunity to touch her legs, yet he still felt her body hair was his business. She left the gym without finishing her workout. I don't blame her. Who would want to hang around with that? In the end, though, it wasn't his workout that was disrupted. He didn't leave feeling icky. If anything, he got to finish his workout without having to look at her apparently offensive body hair. This makes me angry.

Female presenting bodies aren't treated like they are allowed to just exist. But here's the thing, you don't owe anyone anything. You don't owe anyone hairless legs. Or pants with no pantie lines. Or a dress size below a certain number. You do not have to earn the space you take up by fitting into some standard defined by someone else without your input. You get to exist. You get to take up space. You get to feel beautiful. You get to feel sexy. You get to feel not beautiful and not sexy and still go out and take up space. And you sure as shit get to feed your baby with your exposed body parts in public, and everyone else can fuck the right off. I mean it.

You have legal protections. All 50 states plus the District of Columbia, Puerto Rico, and the Virgin Islands all have laws that specifically allow people to BBC feed in any public or private location. Concerts, restaurants, park benches, your father-in-law's living room. That doesn't mean people won't be shitty. It doesn't mean it won't be hard or uncomfortable. It takes all of us, working together to improve

the experience. We can stop *The Big Lie* and change our
assumptions of the childbirth experience. And we can stop
"the stare" by BBC feeding in public so often that it becomes
part of everyday life for everyone. Thus, improving the
experience for future generations. When young people
experience BBC feeding in their lives, rather than people
hiding away in another room, it creates a learning opportunity
helping them to be better prepared when their time comes.
Finally, if this section didn't make me angry enough, let's get
into another infuriating barrier to BBC feeding.

Greed and Money

The last barrier to BBC feeding we will be talking
about is corporate greed. Formula is a multibillion-dollar
industry. Companies stand to gain a lot when people choose
formula, and they stand to lose a lot if they don't.

In other developed countries, health organizations
encourage BBC feeding. They also go out of their way to
protect people from corporate interference. Formula samples
are not given out at the hospital. There are far fewer types of
formula available in the stores. How and where formula is
displayed in the store is also taken into consideration. The
displays are far less prominent, so formula doesn't act as an
advertisement for itself. It is something you have to
intentionally seek out because you have a need for it.

Compare this to America, where people, regardless of
their intention to BBC feed, can be given formula samples in
the hospital. State regulations and hospital policies are
regulating the unsolicited handing out of formula to new
parents, but it still happens. Formula companies will also
provide supplies and other incentives to hospitals, including
supplies that would be difficult for the hospital to provide for

the new parents without the "donations" from corporations. The catch? These products are often covered in advertisements. New parents will even receive formula samples in the mail that they did not request. Formula is widely advertised across all advertising platforms and is prominently displayed in the store.[212] Plainly put, formula and predatory advertising are everywhere.

Let's go back to one of the first things we talked about in this book. People are suggestible. Historically, we've had to depend on the stories we are told for our own survival. Our brains are not designed for a society where we are being manipulated for profit. As cynical as we may think we are, our brain processes are built to trust. It doesn't make us bad or stupid or even naive, but it does make us easy to influence.

Corporations spend billions of dollars every year finding ways to convince us to keep buying their products. In a better world, that manipulation might be reserved for luxury items, like fancy cars or overpriced bottled water. It should not be the case that how you care for your infant—and food is healthcare—is seen for its marketability. It would be great if only people with very specific needs used formula. Then we wouldn't need to talk about it at all. But, unfortunately, people with babies are not being given all the information, and people with shareholders to appease are working very hard to keep formula sales up.

According to the American Psychological Association, advertisements impact the diets of children.[213] It makes sense, right? Kids see commercials for things, and they tend to want them. This is a problem for produce companies, as they simply do not have the advertising budgets required to keep up with the processed food companies. The result is that children end up eating more sugary, high-calorie, highly processed foods. It can be a marvel to watch a child who has never had a certain food begging, demanding, and tantruming over access to it. How do you know you want Cheetos or Skittles? Well, aside from the colorful packaging and the cartoon characters—which are also forms of advertising that a lot of money is spent to develop—it's commercials. But it isn't just children who are susceptible to advertising. It's all of us. That's why it is such a high-powered industry.

When you see ads for formula and are handed formula without asking for it, you are being directly targeted as a consumer. Not a parent caring for their new child, but a means to make money. You might say, "Hey, that's capitalism," and shrug it off. And if it was sports cars, I'd be inclined to let it go. But it isn't. When you are making choices for your child, no one should be manipulating you so that they can make a profit. Feeding is a personal decision, and it should be made that way.

It's also important to talk about the financial impact of feeding, or rather not feeding, human milk. More than 17 billion dollars are spent annually on healthcare and premature death costs that could be avoided if 90% of infants were fed human milk exclusively for the first six months of life.[214] Exclusive BBC feeding for six months would likely save more than 3,000 lives annually by disrupting a cycle of preventable death.

Currently, 41.7% of Americans are not receiving any human milk at six months.[215] As BBC feeding exclusively for six months decreases rates of obesity, it is likely not a coincidence that 42.4% of Americans are obese.[216] In 2016, the aggregate medical expenses due to obesity cost the United States of America $260.6 billion.[217]

Additionally, female breast cancer accounted for $29.8 billion of national expenditures, a condition that can be reduced by BBC feeding.[218] By increasing BBC feeding rates, the United States has the potential to save hundreds of billions of dollars.

On top of all of that, we have PMADs. Not only can the symptoms of PMADs be devastating, but a cost-of-illness mathematical model also found that perinatal mood and anxiety disorders cost fourteen billion dollars over the first five years after birth.[219] That is a lot of money—and lives— that can be saved.

It would be nice to think that everyone had your and the child's best interest at heart, but sadly, that is not true. The formula industry makes a lot of money. The global infant formula market in 2019 was estimated to have made 57.12 billion dollars. The companies that make formula are interested in making money. Nestlé is in the top three largest formula manufacturers in the world. In 1974, Nestlé was labeled "baby killers." They advertised that formula made babies healthier while fully knowing that human milk is almost always better for infants. They would have sales representatives dress up as nurses and hand out free samples. Nestlé knowingly gave impoverished women in Africa only enough free formula to stop them from producing milk to force them to buy more formula. The problem with their plan was that the women could not afford formula, and their babies died of starvation.[220]

Today, when women in impoverished areas are unable to afford formula, they switch to "bear milk," a Nestlé creamer that is not suitable for infant nutrition but is cheaper to obtain. These mothers unknowingly jeopardize their children's health because they are taught that formula is better than breastmilk.[221] Nestlé also promoted formula in areas where there is no access to clean water, leading to infants dying from disease due to drinking contaminated water.

Women, particularly women of color and those with a lower socioeconomic status, are simply used as a means to profit. Now there are many larger issues here about global poverty, clean water access, and lack of literacy education for women in poor countries. But these children would have had a better chance at life if their parents were never introduced to formula.

Just like we talked about the experience of seeing childbirth in television and film impacting your perception, there are other ways in which feeding behavior is subtly manipulated. This includes:

- Companies sending formula samples or bottles directly to your home.

- The hospital forcefully offering formula or attempting to scare you into making sure your infant eats immediately.

- The hospital not providing you with access to lactation specialists.

- The hospital sending you home with formula.

I will say that in 2022, Nestlé stopped advertising formula globally for babies under 6 months of age, and they have stopped offering free samples. Although this is a choice made by the company not a regulation. They continue to advertise formula for babies over 6 months, which can still impact people's perceptions of formula as important for babies. While there is a place for formula, and people have a right to access it should they desire to—advertising and forced free samples can manipulate people into choices that are not right for them or their families.

Access

We discussed a lot of barriers to BBC feeding, but there are also ways to increase the accessibility of BBC feeding. Having a support system and working with a lactation specialist—one you like—are great ways to increase BBC feeding success. Holding your baby to increase oxytocin is another. You can also increase oxytocin in other ways, like petting a dog, listening to music, or hugging someone you love. There is one thing that the research shows combats several of the barriers to BBC feeding. Can you guess what I am going to say?

Yoga! We saw how depression can impact BBC feeding. Well, Yoga decreases rates of depression in pregnant people.[222] We know that BBC feeding decreases postpartum depression. Yoga can act as a bridge to decrease depression until BBC feeding decreases it. If you are experiencing depression during pregnancy or are at risk for postpartum depression, starting Yoga now can help to prevent gaps in BBC feeding and reduce depression symptoms sooner.

We also saw how body image impacts BBC feeding. Yoga has been shown to increase body image satisfaction in women.[223] One study found that after only 3 weeks, women saw results. They had higher body appreciation, body connectedness, body satisfaction, and a more positive mood.[224]

There is some belief that Yoga stimulates milk production though there is not good research on this. The idea is that Yoga kneads the tissue, stimulating milk production. If it works for you, it works for you. So, if you want to increase production and you like Yoga, give it a try.

I do need to make one caveat about Yoga, especially when it comes to body image. Not all Yoga is beneficial. Some instructors or studios are toxic. I know. I've worked for them. You can leave feeling worse about your body than when you got there. Sometimes, this judgment is internal and has nothing to do with the instructor. We can easily get caught up in comparing ourselves to other people in the room. This is a real issue in the Western fitness-focused Yoga that is so common.

Yoga fundamentally teaches about turning inward, feeling your body and your breath. It is very hard to do that when our attention is focused on others. If the Yoga studio, class, or instructor is not making you feel better, try a different one. If none of them are working for you, go back to spontaneous Yoga. Let your body and breath guide your movements. When the focus is *feel,* there are no correct poses or places to get to. It simply is right if it feels right.

Induced lactation

Did you know you do not have to give birth to
lactate? You don't even need to have a uterus or ovaries.[225]
How cool is that?! If you are a non-birthing person who
wishes to lactate, it is possible. It is not always the easiest, but
it can be done. Hormones similar to those found in birth
control can be prescribed, though they can be hard to get in
the United States.

I attended a lecture once from a person who induces
lactation for sexual purposes. She travels to Canada to see her
doctor. I find this to be such a badass example of taking
control of your life, body, and sexuality. She and her
partner(s) find lactation a turn-on, so she made a conscious
choice to prioritize her sex life. She made a conscious choice
to alter her physiology. She travels to another country to do
so safely. She is living her best life. I think that is very cool. It
is important to note that—like with all medications—there
can be risks and side effects, so they are not recommended
for everyone, and usage should be monitored.

Medications are not always required to induce
lactation. Supplemental Nursing Systems can be used. They
work by placing supplemental/donor milk in a container that
is hung around the feeding person's neck, attached to their
clothes, or hung from an IV pole. Thin tubing goes from the
container and is taped near the nipple. The baby then suckles,
drawing the supplemental/donor milk through the tube. The
baby is nourished, and the suckling stimulates milk
production. Supplemental Nursing Systems can induce
lactation without medication, though it can take longer.

There are other ways to induce lactation that can be
done on their own or in conjunction with Supplemental

Nursing Systems. Consistent nipple stimulation several times a day is always important, no matter the method of induction. Pumping using an electric pump every 2-3 hours, including once at night, can be an effective way to induce lactation without medications or a baby present. Herbal supplements called galactagogues such as fenugreek, blessed thistle, and fennel are also believed to promote milk production. Although, this is not universally accepted and taking them on their own will not spontaneously induce lactation.

It is recommended to work with a lactation specialist. When seeking out a doctor to prescribe medications or a lactation specialist to induce lactation, do some research before scheduling. You don't necessarily want to take the first appointment that you can find. Depending on the circumstances that are leading you to induce, you may find that people can be judgmental, mean, or sadly, even dangerous. It can be best to look for a progressive, LGTBQ+ friendly, doctor or lactation specialist. If you can, find one who is familiar with your specific circumstances as a non-birthing person.

Cons of Human Milk

There are downsides to human milk. The downsides have more to do with the person doing the feeding than the infant. But the person doing the feeding is just that, a person. Any downside to them is important.

Time is the first major impact of BBC feeding. Not only does it take a lot of time, but it demands specific time. You can't BBC feed for twelve straight hours on Monday and then not do any on Tuesday or Wednesday. It just doesn't work like that. You need to have time every single day, multiple times a day, to feed or pump. You might experience pain or leaking if you are unable to express milk when your body wants you to. I want to be clear that leaked milk is totally normal and not at all gross. That doesn't mean it won't make you feel embarrassed. I wish I could take that away, but I can't. We, as a society, seem to have issues with anything that naturally comes out of estrogen-based bodies. But blood, milk, and poop are all things that come out of bodies. You do not need to be embarrassed.

We discussed objectification and sexualization. Those are major downsides. I can say let's rally, and fight, and stand up. That doesn't mean it isn't exhausting. BBC feeding is exhausting in general. Just calorically, it is demanding on the body. It can also take an emotional toll. An emotional toll that is increased when you have to worry about people's judgments and stares.

You can also experience touch fatigue, which is when you've been touched too much, and you don't want to be touched anymore. Touch fatigue can happen whether or not you are BBC feeding. If you are BBC feeding, it can be even harder to get space away from touch because you are both a food source and a source of comfort.

BBC feeding is hard. Even in a perfect world with paid leave, lots of support, and no one having opinions about what you do with your body. If all of that were true BBC feeding is still demanding on the body. There will be less sleep as baby's brains are not designed to safely sleep through the night. Co-sleeping can reduce some of that sleep disruption. Safe co-sleeping is beyond the scope of this book, but if it interests you, I encourage you to do more research on the topic.

Even though there are downsides, there are so, so many upsides. But it would be unrealistic and unfair of me to disregard the actual toll it can take. Remember, you do not have to BBC feed if it is detrimental to your health and well-being. You do not need to minimize your own needs. If you want to strike a balance between the health benefits of human milk and the impact of BBC feeding on your life, then donor milk might be your answer.

Donor Milk

Donor milk is human milk that is donated to people who need access to human milk to feed babies. Human milk is so beneficial that in the event that traditional BBC feeding is not possible—for whatever reason—The World Health Organization recommends the use of donor milk over formula. The CDC recommends that human donor milk is sourced through the Human Milk Banking Association of North America.[226] Unfortunately, there are not very many locations. Only 25 states have a member bank. So, the CDC can recommend it, but it isn't always practical.

Prior to the HIV epidemic, donor milk banks were extremely common. Today, they are still common in other countries. The fear of HIV did a lot to damage the public's opinion of milk banks. People were terrified that their baby could drink HIV-positive milk and become HIV-positive. While this was possible back then, we can now test milk to make sure it is safe. The argument can be made that if milk banks had the social acceptability they had prior to HIV, there really would not be a considerable need for formula.

When the formula shortage happened in 2022, there was an explosion of milk-sharing groups on Facebook. There are some legalities around this. Human milk is a biological waste product, like blood, which means there are regulations for it. Fear of HIV-positive or drugged-filled milk is likely one of the reasons it is not typically encouraged for people to get milk off of the internet. However, I do not believe there are people out there living with HIV intentionally giving out HIV-positive milk to harm babies. That sounds an awful lot like "there are razor blades in Halloween candy" or "people are giving free weed gummies to children." As the meme goes, "Drugs are expensive. No one is giving them away for free to children." Pumping milk is hard. I don't believe anyone is out there doing it for malicious reasons.

So, I personally do not believe there is a huge HIV risk when exchanging milk with people you know. But I am not a doctor—well, not that kind of doctor—and I am not the government, and this whole book is about encouraging you to make your own decisions. I am definitely not telling you to take or not take donor milk from a non-regulated milk bank. I *am* telling you that donor milk is an option. Even if you do not live near a Human Milk Banking Association of North America member bank. There are other ways to get donor milk, especially now that we can freeze dry human milk to make it shelf stable. Some Human Milk Banking Association of North America member banks even ship milk. Donor milk can be a great option if you have low supply or if BBC feeding isn't right for your life, but you still want your baby to have the benefits of human milk.

Support Report

- Using formula provides freedom and flexibility. You have the right to choose what's best for you and your family. You do not need to justify your decision to anyone. You are always allowed to change your mind.

- High cortisol levels can change the composition of human milk. Try to keep your stress levels low when BBC feeding. If BBC feeding causes you significant stress it is okay to stop.

- There are several barriers to BBC feeding. They can be physical/medical, stem from body image and/or sexualization, or be systemic. Lack of paid paternal leave, places to pump, and places to store milk, as well as needing to work multiple jobs, can all make BBC feeding more complicated.

- Human milk is incredible. It provides the best nutrients tailored to the baby's needs and has been shown to improve motor skills, cognitive abilities, and the immune system. Feeding human milk reduces the risk of postpartum depression, as well as the risk of certain cancers, and it lowers blood pressure.

- Widström's Nine Stages are the steps babies will go through to latch and feed if given uninterrupted skin-to-skin contact after birth. It is amazing. It is also very important that babies are given the time they need to work through the stages.

- BBC feeding is hard. It takes a lot of work, emotionally and physically. Be patient with yourself. Seek help when you need to and lean on your support team.

- Lactation can be induced. You do not need to have given birth or even have ovaries to lactate. There are hormonal and non-hormonal methods to stimulate milk production.

- Donor milk is recommended when BBC feeding isn't possible. The Human Milk Banking Association of North America can help you find donor milk. Donor milk can now be freeze-dried to increase the shelf life and ease of shipping.

Journaling Prompts

- What have you learned about breasts? Do you see breasts as sexual? If they are sexual, what does that mean to you?

- What were you taught explicitly about breasts, and what did you learn from just living? What did the media teach you? What did your experiences teach you? Were your feelings different when you were younger, or are they the same now?

- What did you learn about "breastfeeding?" Do you have experiences with others BBC feeding? How were they treated?

- How do you balance the sexual aspect of breasts with the nourishing aspect? How does your relationship with your own body influence your opinions?

- What are your feeding plans? Will you be working? Do you plan to pump? Where will you pump? Where will you direct feed? Where will you store milk? Who will support you, and what will you need?

Creating and Using Your Birth Toolkit

I love to hike. I feel most at peace when I am hiking. It is also physically demanding. There are days—due to EDS—that I can't walk around the block. Yet, whenever I'm in the woods, I find the ability to not only walk but climb mountains. It's primal. My body knows. My body craves it. I hike for hours on these uphill journeys. Sometimes scrambling. Sometimes, stopping and needing to rally myself. When I get to the top, to the goal, the breathtaking view. Whatever it is. I breathe a deep sigh. I take it all in. All the joy of what has been accomplished. And then...I keep going. Once you reach the top, you don't just sit down and live there forever. There is still more to come. The "hard part" may be over, but the hard part isn't over. You go back down, which also takes work.

This is how I like to think about birth. The primal experience of climbing a mountain. Working, straining, stretching. Finding strength you don't possess at other times. Birth calls to the body just like the desire to return to nature. Once you reach the peak, you breathe that deep sigh. You gaze upon the breathtaking view that is a tiny new human. Then, you start the journey back down. You birth the placenta—or have your cesarean incision stitched up. You experience your body chemistry change, your hormones shift, your brain rewires. It's hard. And wonderful. And brutal. And amazing. It's all the things. Sometimes you think, "Why did I do this?" And sometimes you think, "I can't wait to do it again."

Our bodies are capable of so much. Our minds are too. You now know the inexplicable power that exists within you. Use it. Use it to have your best birth. Use it to get through a bad day or a stressful time. Use it to change your outlook. You *can* have a joyful, amazing, wonderful birth.

You are incredible. You can change your mind, "change the story, [and] change the world."[227]

You Did It!

You did it! You made it to the end. You have learned so much. I hope you are proud of yourself. I am proud of you. It wasn't easy to get here. You have a life. You're probably tired. You're maybe, just maybe, trying to avoid thinking about birth for as long as possible. You still did it. Now, it is time to put together everything you've learned to build your birth toolkit. If you've been doing the activities along the way, you're already well on your way to completing your birth toolkit. If you haven't started yet, don't worry. The activities are still there for you. In this section we are going to go over the parts that make up the birth toolkit and how to use it.

How is a birth toolkit different than a birth plan? Imagine you're planning a hiking trip through that mountain. A birth plan is like a map; very important for how to get from point A to point B. But a map is just a map. The birth toolkit is more like a guidebook. It includes the map but also information about how the weather impacts the trails and what edible—or poisonous—berries you might pass along the way. Sources of water. How to read animal tracks. Stopping points with beautiful outlooks. Maybe a recommendation for great pancakes right off the trail.* We need the map.

---

*I went to college in Great Barrington, MA. The Appalachian Trail went right through our very tiny downtown. One year, a magazine published that GB Eats, the very small diner right on Main Street, was a must-stop for pancakes when hiking the trail. That place got so packed. This has literally nothing to do with childbirth, but I often think about that. What it must be like to be hiking sometimes for months and then step off the trail, squeeze into a tiny booth, and inhale the scent of those pancakes. The overwhelming joy it

We also really benefit from all the other stuff that is not on the map. Especially because sometimes, even when you bring the map, you don't end up on the path you planned. The birth toolkit brings all the other stuff that you don't technically need to get from point A to point B, but that will impact the kind of experience you have as you go on your adventure. And it's really useful if you look around and realize you're not on the map anymore.

A birth plan is a written summary—sometimes a very in-depth one—of what you want your birth to look like. A birth toolkit includes a version of a birth plan that is created from all the information you gained from this book and all the knowledge learned from your personal exploration through the accompanying activities. A birth toolkit also includes what you will need before, during, and after birth to keep your cortisol levels low. As well as strategies for if things do not go according to plan. A birth toolkit is very personalized, so they do take a little bit of work to put together. I wish I could just give you a completed one, but that would look like what works for me. And what works for me might not work for you. So, let's get started!

---

must bring. Okay…maybe this doesn't have literally nothing to do with childbirth.

In the table of contents there is a list of the activities and journaling prompts that were given throughout the book. If you haven't done them yet, do them now. Not all at once. That might be quite overwhelming. Make your way through them. Skip any that you truly do not want to do. When you are done, come back and then we will start the birth toolkit.

Changing the Story

Way back at the beginning of this journey together we talked about how you've been lied to. You've been told that childbirth is painful and maybe even awful. We discussed the self-fulfilling prophecy and the science behind it. We learned about the fear-pain cycle. Fear produces cortisol, and cortisol makes you feel pain more strongly, which causes more fear, which causes more cortisol, and so it goes. But you now know it doesn't have to be that way. I can't tell you what kind of childbirth you will have. I can only show you the science that says these negative narratives do not have to control you. Which means you can write your own narrative.

So let's change the story. Get a sheet of paper, a journal, a laptop, some magazines, or a dream board—whatever media works for you—and write your birth story. The birth story you want. Get as detailed as you can. When you're finished, read it. Read it over and over. Write it again. Write it as many times as you're moved to. Ingrain it in your brain. Share it with your birth team if you feel comfortable doing so. If you don't want to, don't. Use it as an opportunity to practice your boundaries.

Focus your mind on this best birth. Write down the emotions you feel when thinking about this best birth. Rewrite screaming birth into ecstatic joy birth. Will you get this birth exactly? Maybe, maybe not. It's not about manifesting a particular birth story. It's about changing the story you've been told—the story we've all come to believe—so that when your childbirth begins, you can go into it from a place of happiness and excitement instead of fear. Thus, preventing the cortisol spike and the endless fear-pain cycle.

Let your experience be controlled by your story and not someone else's.

Mapping Your Team

You worked on an eco-map to help you visualize the social aspects of biopsychosocial. We are going to use that map to map your team. Take a sheet of paper and draw a small circle in the center. That center is you. You can identify it with your name, the word "you," a picture, or whatever you would like. Then, draw 6 concentric circles around you, like the rings of a tree. Moving from the inside to the outside, label the rings: Birth Team, Helpers, Visitors, Check-Ins, and No Thank Yous. Of course, you can always use different labels if you prefer.

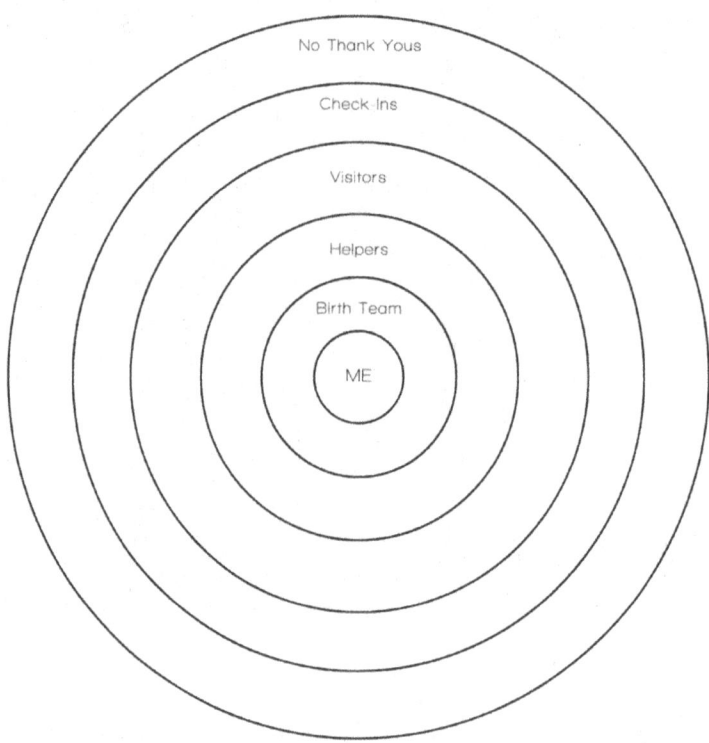

Birth Team includes anyone who will be in the room with you when you give birth. Your support person(s), doctor or midwife, and your advocate or doula.

Helpers is for all of the people who will be helping you. These are people who signed up on the Postpartum Help schedule. It might also include a family member or friend who is staying with you. Or the person you are going to call to vent to when you are tired, and life feels hard. Anyone you can depend on to truly help you goes here.

Visitors are people who will be visiting either you or the baby. They are people who you expect to come by either directly after birth or in the coming days to weeks. You aren't planning on them being helpful, but you are going to allow them to show up anyway.

Check-ins are people who likely won't come by but who you will check in with. Either because they check in on you or because you reach out to them. This can look like the people who respond to your birth announcement on social media or the people who receive a mass text. They aren't helping per se, but sometimes it's nice to share your news with others.

No Thank Yous are the people you don't want to deal with during postpartum. You get to decide who is on this list. Maybe it's an overly personal boss who isn't good with boundaries. Maybe it's a family member. Or a neighbor who goes through your trashcans. Whoever will prevent you from your goals—staying calm, bonding, healing—goes on this list and they do not get your energy. If they are someone you can ignore, ignore them. If you really can't ignore them, assign one of your helpers to be the point person. They can send messages on your behalf. Support People also make good No Thank Yous buffers.

Once your map is complete, take some time to reflect. Was it easy to make? Are you surprised by what you see? What tasks are priorities to you? Do you have enough helpers? If you do not have enough helpers, are there other people you can reach out to, or would they only create more stress? Reach out to new parent/postpartum groups in your area and see what support resources may be available to you.

Birth Details

On a new sheet of paper start your Birth Details. Put your due date near the top and the location where you plan to give birth. List your birth team, including their contact information and their role at your birth. Be as clear as possible. Imagine a scenario in which a random person had to organize your birth. This person needs to get everyone on your birth team to your birth location, prepared and ready to fill their roles. The Birth Details list is a quick reference so that all planning questions can be easily answered.

Birth Coping Skills

If you have not already completed your coping skills journaling page, do so now. When it is complete, take a look at what your coping skills are. If you haven't had a chance to practice them, try them out. When you have a good grasp on what coping skills you might want to use during birth, it's time to make another list. Label the top "Coping Skills." Then, make two columns. On the left side write "My Birth Coping Skills." Label the right side "What I Need for It." As you list your coping skills in the left-hand column, include what you need to accomplish that skill in the right-hand column. For example, if listening to music is one of your coping skills, you will need something that plays music, something to listen to the music—like headphones, and a charger(s). This is a quick reference sheet. If you were to say, "quick! I need a coping skill." Someone else should be able to look at this list and get you everything you need to complete that coping skill.

What Will I Need?

Your "What Will I Need" list includes everything from your coping skills list, your Red Light/Green Light list, plus anything else you will need. This may include knee pads or a Yoga mat if you plan to give birth on hands and knees. It can be fuzzy socks. Think of all the things you will need—especially if you are giving birth outside of your home. Your face wash or face wash wipes. Toothbrush and a flavor of toothpaste you like. Hair ties. This list is not specific to things for giving birth, though, it will include what you need for giving birth. Think of it more like a packing list.

Look at your Red Light/Green Light list. What have you decided you want for your birth? What will you need to accomplish what you decided? Do you need essential oils? A carrier oil? A book of puzzles or a weighted blanket? Whatever you need, include it on this list and include who is bringing it. Are you bringing it with you? Is a midwife bringing it to you? Does the hospital already have it?

Sometimes, this may seem self-explanatory. But it can be helpful to keep you organized. It also acts as a reminder to check. Will the hospital have nitrous oxide? A birth ball? A squat bar? Did you already download that playlist, or do you still need to? When everything is packed and ready to go—or you've ensured the hospital/midwife/doula is on top of it—put a check next to the item on your list.

What Are My Back Ups?

Now that you have your list, let's make another list! Things don't always go according to plan. If that happens, the best thing to do is stay calm. A backup list is everything from a different playlist to what questions you want your support person to ask—if you have a doula, they will already know this, but it is a good conversation to have with them ahead of time. This is where plans B, C, D, and E come in.

List your backups in order of preference. Refer to your coping skills. If plan C is an epidural, but you really, really do not want to have an epidural, what will you do to stay calm if you end up having one? This might be the hardest part of the whole birth toolkit. Take your time. Take breaks. Be patient. Planning for what you do not want is a lot less fun than planning for what you do want.

Get out your "What Will I Need" list and a blank sheet of paper. In the first column write, "What I Want." This can be a specific thing like a synthetic oxytocin-free birth. Or something less concrete that helps you feel in control. In the next column, write what you will need for it. This is where your list from before comes in. After that, write a column that has backup plans or pivots. If there isn't one, write what you will do to remain calm in that situation. If there is one, write the pivot—or multiple pivots if you have them, and then what you will do to remain calm if you need to use them.

Postpartum Help

If you used the postpartum help schedule you may already have a good grasp on postpartum help. If the schedule works for you and is easy to read, you can stick with that. Sometimes, it can be helpful to have the information presented in another way. This can be useful to generate what you want to put on the schedule and for a quick reference.

Take a sheet of paper and write Postpartum Help at the top. Make two columns. Label the left column "What I Need." Label the right column "Who Will Do It." Then, fill it out. This can be everything from making meals, to picking up groceries, to foot rubs, to supportive texts, and taking out the trash. Your support person can do some of these, but they should not be responsible for everything as they are also going to be exhausted and adjusting to a new person in the home.

What Will I Need for Feeding?

This is very similar to your "What Will I Need" list for birth, except now we are preparing for what comes after. No matter how you plan to feed, you will need certain things to feed successfully. This may include a pump, both electric and manual. Nursing bras if you so choose. Sports bras with holes cut in them if that is more your thing. Bottles. Or nipples that fit on mason jars. Formula if you are using it. A drying rack if you don't have one. It can be a little overwhelming to think of everything you'll need, but it is better to make the list now than once the baby is here. Talk to friends, local support groups, or lactation specialists to help make sure you have everything you need.

Feeding Coping Skills

Regardless of how you feed, feeding is labor intensive and can be frustrating. Having coping skills at the ready can help keep you calm. This is just like your birth coping skills, although you may find you have different coping skills when it comes to feeding. If you are giving birth in a hospital, you probably will have limitations for your birth coping skills that you won't have while feeding at home.

These can be skills you implement while you are doing the feeding, like watching a movie or soaking your feet. Or these can be skills you use at other times to help you feel ready to do the feeding. Going for a walk by yourself. Playing games on your phone in the bathroom. Eating candy in your car. Holding hands with someone you love. Just like before, take a blank sheet of paper and label the top with" Feeding Coping Skills." Then, make two columns. On the left side write," My Feeding Coping Skills." Label the right side "What I Need for It." List your coping skills in the left-hand column. Include what you need to accomplish that skill in the right-hand column. Be honest with what you need. There is no judgement. You don't have to show it to anyone. It's just for you.

Assembling Your Birth Toolkit

On to the fun part! Take all the parts of your birth toolkit and combine them. Maybe in a binder or a folder. Maybe you had them in a notebook or a journal. Now you get to decorate it. This is always one of my most favorite parts of my group workshops. Everyone with stickers and markers personalizing their birth toolkit. Make it special. Make it fun. Set aside some time where you will not be interrupted—if possible. Maybe put on some music or your favorite binge show. Preparing for birth can be enjoyable! I suggest gathering:

• Colored pencils or markers

• A variety of stickers

• Quotes

• Pictures

• Glue, glue dots, or tape

• Google eyes

• Stamps

• Washi tape

It doesn't have to look like anything in particular. It should bring you joy to create it and to look at it. Your birth toolkit is a coping skill in and of itself. Both because it contains what you need to stay calm and in control, and because looking at it should illicit a sense of joy. Go have fun! Make art!

Support Report

- A birth plan is like a map getting you from point A to point B. A birth toolkit is like a guidebook containing personalized strategies and quick references for what you will need before, during, and after birth.

- A birth toolkit is important for keeping cortisol levels low, so take your time with the activities. Have fun. Make it your own.

Journaling Prompts

- What do you want your life to look like after birth? What do you think your life will look like after birth? How do you feel about it?

- You've just taken in a lot of information. You've created a birth toolkit, and you are preparing for a fearless birth. How do you feel? How does it compare to when you started this book? What do you need? How can you get it?

Coming to a Close

I know I said it before, but you really, *really* did it. We are at the end of our time together. I hope you had as much fun reading this book as I did writing it. Actually... I hope you had more. I hope you feel better than you did at the start. I wish I could wave that magic wand and ensure that you feel awesome and that your whole entire life is perfect. But then, it wouldn't really be life, would it? How can we appreciate the highs without the lows? How can we grow if we are never challenged? How can we be brave if we are never afraid? Life is bitter and sweet. And you are about to bring a new one into the world! How incredible is that?

There is only one thing in this life that I know with absolute certainty. It is that every single person's experience is unique, and no one can ever truly fully understand what it is to live another person's life. Of course, we should try to approach each other with empathy. We should try to understand each other to the best of our abilities. But this will always be limited in some ways. If no one else can know your experience completely, then no one else can know what will be best for you.

You are the only person that really knows what you need. It can be hard to tap into that. Especially, when women and AFAB people are often taught to defer to the authority of others. In this process of childbirth and everything that comes after, you will be—if you haven't been already— surrounded by people telling you what you should do. They are not you. You do not need my permission, but if it feels like you want it, let this be me giving you permission to tell those people to kindly fuck off.

Life is hard. You are doing your best. We all are. Everyone's situation is infinitely more complicated than what goes into a course or a standard operating procedures manual. It is even hard for the people who write and enforce those rules.

I went to a Maternal Infant Health and Equity "town hall" put on by the Department of Health and Human Services in Michigan. One of the women running the event had adopted a child from Korea when he was five months old. Since the child was born, he had slept with a person on a mattress on the floor. That's the way it was done in his culture.

The baby arrived in another country on the other side of the world, in a completely different time zone, and he did not sleep. For days and nights. He. Did. Not. Sleep. In—what I am going to call—an impressive display of bravery and compassion, this woman from the Department of Health and Human Services made the bold decision to pull the mattress down on the floor and bed-share with her new baby.

As she told this story, she said, "I knew better." She was a nurse—I believe she had a background in social work as well. She knew it was against the "rules." She had been taught—she had taught others—that bed-sharing is bad. But now, she was more than a nurse. She was also a mother. A mother that knew what her child needed.

She and her husband lied at doctor's appointments and at home visits through the adoption agency. They could not let anyone know about the bed-sharing. There were too many risks. When you lie about one thing, the trust is already broken. The relationship weakens. This was the message she was sharing when she told the room full of healthcare workers, parents, and advocates the importance of approaching people holistically and with cultural sensitivity. She made a hard choice to do what was right for her family. She lived daily with all the complications of making that choice because other people had assumptions about how she was supposed to parent. She didn't let other people decide for her. She did the research. She made a choice.

Please know, when it comes to bed-sharing there are ways to make it safer and ways to make it very, very dangerous. If you intend to bed-share do your research. Just like with everything else in this book. Knowledge truly is power. When you have knowledge, you have the power to make the decisions that are best for your family, and to confidently let others know that you are doing what is best for your unique personal situation.

With that in mind, know that this book is not exhaustive. There is no way that it could be. Science and the medical industry are changing constantly. Aside from that every body is different. Everyone will have their own experience. I can say without a doubt this book does not have all the answers.

My hope is that you've learned enough to know what you want to know more about. You now have a starting place to go explore what is interesting to you, that you are confident in your right to ask questions and advocate for what you want, that you feel grounded in your power. That you not only know but believe that you do not have to be afraid. Because you are strong, and capable, and you deserve whatever kind of birth you want. You are strong and capable, and you deserve whatever kind of birth you want.

You are strong and capable, and you deserve whatever kind of birth you want.
You got this!

Now go climb your mountain.

Form Letter to Advocate for BBC Feeding Support

Your Name
Your Address
City, State, ZIP Code
Email Address
Date

Recipient's Name
Recipient's Title
Organization or Office Name
Address/Email Address
City, State, ZIP Code

Dear *Recipient's Name,*

I am writing to bring to your attention the critical need for increased support and resources for breastfeeding and human milk feeding individuals in our community. I believe that we must prioritize the health and well-being of both parents and infants by ensuring that everyone has access to the necessary resources to successfully provide children with the gold standard of nutrition.

The benefits of human milk are well-documented and include improved immune system function, better motor skills, enhanced cognitive development, and a lower risk of various health conditions such as asthma, obesity, type 1 diabetes, and childhood leukemia for the infant. As well as significant health benefits for the person doing the feeding including lower rates of high blood pressure, type 2 diabetes, ovarian cancer, and breast cancer, as well as a reduced risk of postpartum depression.

Despite these well-known benefits, many individuals face significant barriers, including a lack of workplace accommodations, insufficient parental leave, inadequate access to lactation support services, and social stigma. To address these issues, I urge you to consider the following actions:

1. **Support Legislation for Parental Leave**: Advocate for policies that provide adequate paid parental leave to allow parents the time they need to establish and maintain feeding routines. A minimum of six month after birth.

2. **Workplace Accommodations**: Ensure that workplaces are required to provide private, comfortable spaces for pumping, as well as sufficient break times for lactating individuals and shortage for milk.

3. **Access to Lactation Support**: Increase funding and resources for lactation consultants, postpartum doulas, and support groups, such as La Leche League, to provide essential guidance and assistance to new parents.

4. **Public Education Campaigns**: Promote public awareness campaigns that normalize feeding human milk and educate the community on its benefits, helping to reduce stigma and support feeding parents.

5. **Regulation of Formula Marketing**: Implement stricter regulations on the marketing of formula to

ensure that parents receive unbiased information and can make informed choices without undue corporate influence.

By taking these steps, we can create a supportive environment that allows parents to make the best decisions for their families and promotes the health and well-being of our community.

Thank you for your attention to this important matter. I look forward to your response and hope to see meaningful progress soon.

Sincerely your constituent,
Your Name

A bonus book for bodies with vaginas or vulvas.

I don't want to make any assumptions about who is reading this book or what kind of upbringing they have had. So, we are going to level the playing field here with a dive into some anatomy and other things that can be helpful.

Genitals

We often get told as kids or teenagers that boys have a penis, and girls have a vagina. This is, at best, not a whole truth. External genitalia refer to the part of the genitals that can be seen from the outside of the body. Some people are born with external genitalia, commonly referred to as a penis. They may or may not also have testicles that descend from the body protected in a sac called a scrotum.

Penises have a protective hood called a foreskin. This is the part of the body removed during a circumcision. Circumcisions are optional. They are not medically necessary, and they are medical procedure where part of the body is permanently removed. Like all medical procedures they can have complications. Circumcision was originally a religious/cultural practice founded by the Jewish community. While popular in the United States, non-religious circumcision is uncommon in most other countries. As with everything in this book I encourage you to make conscious choices when it comes to the genitalia of your children.

Some people are born with external genitalia, commonly referred to as a vulva. The vulva is what can be seen on the outside of the body of these individuals. This includes the labia both majora and minora[*]—or the folds of

---

[*] Outer and inner labia are now the preferred term. Major and minor imply size or shape. There is no consistent way labia or

skin that line the vulva. The outer folds—the labia majora—
may be covered in pubic hair to protect the vulva from
bacteria. The vulva is home to the urethra. This is the tube
that connects to the bladder so that urine can be removed
from the body.

The vulva includes the introitus, also referred to as
"the entrance." This is where penetration—or if we are using
Amanda Montell's anti-patriarchy language, which I prefer,
where envelopment—occurs.[228] It leads to the vaginal canal.
This is where the baby exits the body during a vaginal
delivery. Some people are born with MRKH syndrome, a rare
congenital disorder that can cause the vaginal canal to not
develop. Some individual may choose surgery or the use of
dilators to create a vaginal canal. Some individuals choose not
to and live happy fulfilling lives.

The vagina is only this internal canal. Vagina also
comes from the Latin word for sheath because that is where
the penis is *sheathed*. Annoying and offensive as that idea is, it
can help to understand which part is the vagina. At the top—
internally speaking—of the vaginal canal is the cervix. This is
the spongy tissue that separates the canal from the uterus.
The uterus is where babies grow.

The vulva also includes the clitoris—sometimes called
the clit for short—and the clitoral hood. The clitoral hood
protects the clitoris. The clitoris is the densest bundle of
nerves found across any type of body. As it is so sensitive, the
hood decreases direct contact. Without the clitoral hood, it
might be difficult to go about your day wearing pants. In

---

vulvas look. Major and minor can make someone people feel
uncomfortable if their inner labia are larger than their outer labia.
But all vulvas are unique and it is completely okay for inner labia to
be larger.

arousing situations, blood rushes to the clitoris the same way that it rushes to a penis, enlarging it and causing it to peak out from the hood.

In some countries, female circumcision is practiced. The clitoral hood, clitoris and possibly the labia are removed. It is considered a human rights violation and is also referred to as female genital mutilation, though some individuals claim it as part of their culture and take pride in it.

One justification for male circumcision is smegma. This is a white substance that is produced in the foreskin. It is also produced by the clitoral hood. People think of it as being dirty or gross, but smegma is the bodies way of protecting itself by reducing friction, protecting against dryness and self-cleaning to remove dead skin cells and oils. Just like the vaginal canal, the foreskin is self-cleaning. However, for overall health and hygiene it is important to remove this buildup of self-cleaning by product. All areas where smegma (and smegma byproducts) can build up should be kept clean, including the labia, armpits, between the toes, under the breasts and in piercing holes. When you think about all the places the body produces this style of buildup, it doesn't make very much sense that it is a justification for circumcision.

Not everything is either penis or vulva. Intersex people are born with genitals that are not immediately put into the penis or vulva box. It is estimated there are as many intersex people in the United States as there are redheads. This does not mean every person born with red hair is also intersex. It's there as a helpful comparison. If you have ever met someone born with red hair, then statically speaking, you've met an intersex person.

Also, know that genitalia are as unique as the people it belongs to. Like snowflakes, no two are the same. Pornography is often cited for creating this idea that genitals are supposed to look a specific way. They aren't. If you have never seen your own genitals, I encourage you to take a peek. This can be done using a hand mirror or the camera feature on your phone (just make sure your phone doesn't automatically share all photos taken with anyone that you don't want to have a picture of your genitals).

I love the website—popularized by the Netflix show *Sex Education*—All Vulvas Are Beautiful. This website shows—in a non-sexualized way—thousands of vulvas. As does the Labia Library. The goal is to make sure people with vulvas know there is no right or wrong way for a vulva to look.

There was a big uptick in the 2000s in "vaginal" plastic surgery—also due to porn—because people thought their labia were too long or big or they didn't like the color of their vulva. I am deeply saddened that someone could be made to feel so ashamed of their genitals that they would surgically change them to look like someone else's. Your body is beautiful.

The same is true for penises. They come is all shapes and sizes. Despite what your romantasy book says bigger is not inherently better. The average vaginal canal is only 3 inches before it stretches. Yet penises can be subject to just as much scrutiny and body shaming vulvas. As are genitals that don't fit into a binary box. All genitals are beautiful. All genitals are kinda weird. We are all in this beautiful weirdness together. So, be kind to each other and be kind to yourself.

That being said, we've been talking about people born with bodies that are determined to be male or female. But being male or female includes way more factors than genitals. It also includes hormones and chromosomes and probably other things we haven't discovered yet. Sometimes, people are labeled one way when that is not who they are. People who fall into this group often use the label trans to describe themselves or AFAB/AMAB (assigned female/male at birth).

Trans people make wonderful loving parents, just like gay, straight, cis, non-binary, queer, and asexual people. If you are a person, especially a person who cares enough to read this book or any book, you will likely make a wonderful parent. If you are a person bringing a human into this world for another family, you are doing an amazing, invaluable thing.

People make good parents. Bears, not so much. Well, they make great parents to bears. But I have a pretty strong stance that I do not advise bears raising human children. Humans, though, regardless of genitals, gender, orientation, or identity, should birth and raise children if that's what they want to do. And we should all support their choices.

If you're reading this, I am going to talk to you as though you have a uterus and maybe—but not necessarily—a vaginal canal. Because a uterus—at this time—is still a necessary component of pregnancy. You might not have a uterus, and you're reading this book to support someone else or out of pure interest. If that's the case, bear with me while I talk to you like you do.

I am going to encourage you—to the best of your ability for where you are in your life right now—to get to know your genitals. Not only is this empowering for life overall, but it is also especially important for childbirth.

Whether or not you get to know these parts of your body, someone will. It has never sat right with me that another person could have intimate knowledge of my body when I don't. Maybe you are well versed in your body. If so, that's great. Maybe this is not a step that you want to take right now. Maybe taking a peek with a mirror is too much. That's okay, too.

If you aren't ready to start exploring physically, I suggest you start thinking about the idea. Or start to think about thinking about the idea. What is happening is happening in your body. Childbirth will happen in your body. This book is here to help you take ownership of the process. It is not impossible, but it is harder to do that without ownership of your body. Just something to think about. Remember, everything in this book is information and a suggestion. You get to make every decision.

The Menstrual Cycle and Cervical Mucus

It's slightly frustrating to me that we refer to the "menstrual" cycle when it is also the fertility cycle and the creativity cycle—people tend to experience different levels of creativity through their cycle. The menstrual cycle is a series of natural changes in hormone production and the structures of the uterus and ovaries. It typically lasts around 28 days, but the average range is from 21 to 35 days in adults. Or it can be a totally different range. People are unique.

The cycle begins with the menstrual phase, during which the uterine lining, known as the endometrium, sheds if there is no pregnancy. This shedding results in menstrual bleeding and lasts about 3 to 7 days, with levels of estrogen and progesterone being low. Again, the whole 3-7 thing is a

thing that "they" say. They may have never talked to you or
your body. If you have bleeding that lasts longer than 7
days—and it causes you discomfort—you can talk to a
gynecologist or a licensed acupuncturist for help.

The follicular phase overlaps with the menstrual
phase—because this needed to be more complicated. This
phase lasts until ovulation, which occurs on average at day 14
of the cycle. But it can occur before or after that 14-day mark.
One study found that of 221 women, only 10% ovulated on
the 14th day.[229] During the follicular phase, the pituitary gland
releases follicle-stimulating hormone (FSH), which stimulates
the growth of ovarian follicles. Each follicle contains an egg,
and as they mature, they produce estrogen, which helps
rebuild the uterine lining. Ovulation is triggered by a surge in
luteinizing hormone (LH) from the pituitary gland. During
ovulation, a mature egg is released from the dominant follicle
and travels down the fallopian tube, where it may encounter
sperm and become fertilized.

Following ovulation is the luteal phase, lasting from
maybe day 15 to day 28. It all depends on your body. After
releasing the egg, the empty follicle transforms into the
corpus luteum, which produces progesterone. Progesterone
maintains the uterine lining, preparing it for a potential
pregnancy. If fertilization does not occur, the corpus luteum
breaks down, causing a drop in progesterone and estrogen
levels, leading to the shedding of the uterine lining and the
start of a new menstrual cycle.

You may notice as you wipe throughout your cycle
that you have different types of discharge. Or you may have
noticed a white patch in your underwear. This is cervical
mucus, and it changes. The cervical mucus cycle is closely
linked to the menstrual cycle. It provides important signs of

fertility. Throughout the cycle, the consistency and amount of cervical mucus change due to hormonal fluctuations. After menstruation, there is usually little to no cervical mucus. As estrogen levels rise during the follicular phase, the mucus becomes creamy and sticky, indicating the beginning of the fertile window. Near ovulation, cervical mucus becomes clear, stretchy, and egg white-like, creating an optimal environment for sperm to swim through the cervix and fertilize an egg. This type of mucus indicates peak fertility. After ovulation, progesterone levels increase, causing the mucus to become thick and sticky again, preventing sperm from entering the cervix.

Cervical mucus—and the discharge of it—is normal. It is also pretty cool. It's not gross or bad. It is not a health concern unless there is an odd color to it, you are experiencing itching or pain, you feel sick, or there is a distinctly different smell than typically. If you have any of these symptoms, talk to your healthcare provider. If you don't have symptoms, marvel at how incredible the human body is.

Steps of Conception

The journey from ejaculation to conception is a fascinating process that involves multiple steps and precise timing. When ejaculation occurs during intercourse, millions of sperm are released into the vaginal canal. From there, the sperm begin their journey through the cervix and into the uterus. Sperm can live up to five days, depending on the environment and cervical mucus.

The sperm travel through the uterus and into the fallopian tubes, where they may encounter an egg.

Interestingly, some sperm can rest and be stored in the crypts of the cervix. These cervical crypts are small pockets in the cervical canal that can provide a protective environment for sperm, allowing them to survive longer and maintain their motility as they wait for ovulation.

Ovulation typically occurs around the middle of the menstrual cycle. During ovulation, an egg is released from one of the ovaries and enters the fallopian tube. The egg then begins its journey toward the uterus. Fertilization usually takes place in the fallopian tube. When sperm encounter the egg, they attempt to penetrate its outer layer. Only one sperm will successfully fertilize the egg, resulting in the formation of a zygote. This process can happen within hours to a day after ovulation if sperm are already present in the fallopian tubes.

After fertilization, the zygote begins to divide and form a blastocyst as it travels down the fallopian tube toward the uterus. This journey takes about 3-5 days. The blastocyst consists of an inner cell mass that will eventually develop into the embryo and an outer layer of cells that will form the placenta.

Upon reaching the uterus, the blastocyst must implant into the uterine lining for pregnancy to continue. This usually occurs about 6-10 days after ovulation. The outer cells of the blastocyst, known as trophoblasts, attach to the uterine lining to establish a connection with the person's blood supply, allowing the embryo to receive nutrients and oxygen.

After implantation, the body begins to produce human chorionic gonadotropin (hCG), the hormone detected by pregnancy tests. This hormone supports the corpus luteum, which in turn maintains the production of progesterone. Progesterone is crucial for sustaining the uterine lining and pregnancy.

When we understand the timeline of fertilization and implantation, we can see that life doesn't begin at ejaculation. One of the key steps of developing a fetus is implantation into the uterine lining. Sometimes implantation occurs, but very quickly, the body expels the blastocyst, which leads to a chemical miscarriage. A chemical miscarriage typically occurs within the first 5 weeks of pregnancy when the evidence of pregnancy is based on biochemical evidence (positive pregnancy test) rather than clinical evidence (ultrasound confirmation), thus the name chemical pregnancy.

Chemical miscarriages are quite common, and many people may not even realize they experienced one, mistaking it for a late menstrual period. However, people tracking hCG levels may be aware of the loss. Chemical miscarriages can be devasting to people who feel the loss. At the same time, their experience might be minimized by others since it occurred so early on. The loss of a desired pregnancy is horrible, no matter when it occurs.

Ectopic Pregnancy

An ectopic pregnancy occurs when a fertilized egg implants outside the uterus, most commonly in a fallopian tube. This condition is a medical emergency because the growing tissue can cause the tube to rupture, leading to severe bleeding. Symptoms of an ectopic pregnancy include sharp abdominal pain, shoulder pain, dizziness, and vaginal bleeding. Treatment options depend on the timing and severity but often involve medication (methotrexate) to stop cell growth, or surgical intervention to remove the ectopic tissue. **Ectopic pregnancies are never viable and always require medical attention.**

How Abortion Medication Works

Abortion medication, commonly referred to as the abortion pill or Plan B, typically involves two medications: mifepristone and misoprostol. Mifepristone is taken first to block the hormone progesterone, which is necessary for pregnancy to continue. Without progesterone, the lining of the uterus breaks down. Misoprostol is taken 24-48 hours later to induce contractions—like menstrual cramps—and expel the pregnancy tissue through the vaginal canal. This method is effective within the first 10 weeks of pregnancy.

After taking mifepristone, most people feel normal and can go about their day as usual. Some may experience mild side effects such as nausea, dizziness, or mild cramping. It is important to follow the healthcare provider's instructions and contact them if there are any concerns.

After taking misoprostol, cramping and bleeding usually start within a few hours. The intensity of the cramps can vary, but they are often stronger than menstrual cramps. Heavy bleeding, including passing blood clots, is a normal part of the process and indicates that the medication is working. The heaviest bleeding usually lasts for a few hours, and then it typically tapers off over the next few days.

How D&C Works

Dilation and curettage (D&C) is a surgical procedure often used for both diagnostic and therapeutic purposes, including miscarriage management and abortion. During a D&C, the cervix is dilated, and a surgical instrument called a curette—it honestly looks like one of those things you use to get blackheads off your nose—is used to remove tissue from the inside of the uterus. The procedure is typically performed under local or general anesthesia and takes about 10-20 minutes. Recovery time is usually brief, with most people resuming normal activities within a day or two.

How Late-Term Abortion Works
&
Why it Might be Necessary

Late-term abortion—usually defined as occurring after 20 weeks of gestation—can be necessary for several reasons, including severe fetal abnormalities, risk to the birthing person's life, or significant health problems. The procedure might involve induction abortion, where labor is induced using medications, or a D&E (dilation and evacuation), which combines dilation of the cervix with surgical removal of fetal tissue. These procedures are complex and performed only when necessary to protect the health or life of the pregnant individual. If someone finds themselves in this situation, it is because of circumstances beyond their control. There is a severe risk to life involved. **This is not a situation anyone would ever choose.**

***

In each of these situations, it is important that people are kind to themselves. Whatever the reason, these situations can be difficult. They also don't have to be. If someone does not want a baby and they take medication to ensure their bodily autonomy and they don't have any negative feelings, that's great. You shouldn't have to have negative feelings when taking control of your life. If someone does not want a baby and they take medication to ensure their bodily autonomy and they have lots of negative feelings, that's okay too. If someone wanted the baby but they feel relief because their life was saved, that's a lot of complicated feelings. Any and all other scenarios, whatever your beliefs and how ever you feel about your experience, you are right. It's your experience and you get to feel however you feel about it.

Lube

Lube, short for lubricant, is a special liquid that is used to reduce friction on the body. There are several kinds that have different feels, tastes, and purposes. Some lube cannot be used with silicone (like the kind found in some adult toys), or it will destroy it. Some lube is specifically designed for trying to conceive. This does not mean that other lubes can be used as a contraceptive, though they do make spermicidal lube that can be used WITH a condom to reduce the chance of pregnancy. Some lubes are designed to be edible. If you have an allergy, for example, strawberries, always check the lube for scents and flavors before using.

Why would you want to use lube? Well, we typically think of lube being used for two reasons. One is older estrogen-based bodies who are no longer "getting wet" on their own. Or for anal sex. I will never forget my very first human sexuality class. I was just barely 18. The class was taught by a woman whom I would describe as an "elder." She was teaching us about lube, and using her fingers to demonstrate widening an opening, she said, "Remember! Vaginal tissue stretches. Anal tissue tears!"

For many years, that was my education. Vaginal tissue is self-lubricating (except when it isn't), but anal tissue requires lube. In graduate school, I took another class that expanded the use to include people with medical conditions. But it was when I was getting my post-graduate certificate in sex therapy and sexual health education that I learned a very important lesson that I hope you take with you.

While vaginal tissue stretches it is still subject to micro-tears. These are teeny tiny tears that you may not even feel. They heal on their own, but they need time. They also create an opportunity for bacteria or viruses to enter the bloodstream. It is also a good reason to keep nails short if they will be penetrating vaginal canals, as long nails can cause micro-tears. What does all this mean? If you are inserting something into the vaginal canal it is best to use lube. Every time. Even if you are "wet."

I want to take a moment to talk about "wet." "Wet," is the slang term for a lubricated vaginal canal. If you've read a romance novel or seen a sexy movie, you've probably heard something like, "Oh my god, you're so wet," or "I love how wet and ready for me you are." Wetness is not an indication of desire. It is a biological response. There are times when the biological and the psychological do not work together. People can be not "wet" when they have very high desire. And people can be "wet" when they have no desire.

There are also people who believe that they could not have been assaulted because their bodies responded, and they lubricated. That is not true. Consent is mental and emotional, not a biological response. The body may be protecting itself from further physical damage by lubricating. Lubricating is not consent. It is not inherently a sign of desire.

People can also not lubricate when they are very aroused and super excited for a sexual encounter. Desire is mental. Bodies do all kinds of crazy things that don't mean anything. There is nothing wrong with being super "wet." There is nothing wrong with not being super "wet." It's just bodies doing stuff. What matters is how you feel. So, add to the list of things we are collectively going to change, this cultural obsession with the idea of "wetness." You should use lube anyway to prevent microtears, so it really doesn't matter.

You

You have just learned a lot, very quickly, about estrogen-based bodies and bodies with vaginas and/or vulvas. As with everything else in this book, I hope it encourages you to do more research on the topics that interest you. I want to leave you with this: You get only this life. You, only you, get to decide how you want to live it. You get only this body. You, only you, should get to decide how you live in that body. Your happiness matters. Your feelings of comfort, ease, and joy in your body matters. Your sexual pleasure matters. Your freedom matters. **You matter.**

This has been some stuff for bodies with vaginas or vulvas.

References

[1] Hoyert, D. L. (2024). *Maternal mortality rates in the United States, 2022.* National Center for Health Statistics, NCHS Health E-Stats. https://stacks.cdc.gov/view/cdc/152992

[2] Gunja, M. Z., Gumas, E. D., & Williams, R. D., II. (2024). *Insights into the U.S. maternal mortality crisis: An international comparison.* Commonwealth Fund. https://doi.org/10.26099/cthn-st75

[3] Junge, C., von Soest, T., Weidner, K., Seidler, A., Eberhard-Gran, M., Garthus-Niegel, S. (2018). Labor pain in women with and without severe fear of childbirth: A population- based, longitudinal study. *Birth,45,* 469-477.
Moghaddam Hosseini, V.M., Nazarzadeh, M. & Jahanfar S. (2018).Interventions for reducing fear of childbirth: a systematic review and meta-analysis of clinical trials. *Women Birth, 31*(4), 254-262.
Goutaudier, N., Bertoli, C., Séjourné, N., & Chabrol, H. (2019). Childbirth as a forthcoming traumatic event: Pretraumatic stress disorder during pregnancy and its psychological correlates. *Journal of Reproductive and Infant Psychology, 37*(1), 44–55.

[4] Thayer, Z. M., Geisel-Zamora, S. A., Uwizeye, G., & Gildner, T. E. (2023). Childbirth fear in the USA during the COVID-19 pandemic: key predictors and associated birth outcomes. *Evolution, Medicine, and Public Health,* 11(1), 101–111.

[5] Thompson, J. (2023, August 22). No one studied menstrual product absorbency realistically until now: A new study reveals the absorbency of pads, tampons and other menstrual products is significantly different than labels suggest. *Scientific American.*

[6] Mayer, E. A. (2011). Gut feelings: The emerging biology of gut–brain communication. *Nature Reviews Neuroscience, 12*(8), 453-466.

[77] Twenty One Pilots. (2018). *Morph.* On **Trench** [Album]. Fueled by Ramen.

[8] Nagoski, E. (2024). Come Together: The Science (and Art!) of Creating Lasting Sexual Connections. Vermilion.

[9] Engel, G. L. (1977). The need for a new medical model: A challenge for biomedicine. *Science, 196*(4286), 129-136.

[10] Please note these are heart attack symptoms common to male bodies. They differ in female bodies. Milner, K. A., Funk, M., Richards, S., Wilmes, R. M., Vaccarino, V., & Krumholz, H. M. (1999). Gender differences in symptom presentation associated with coronary heart disease. *The American Journal of Cardiology, 84*(4), 396-399.

[11] Lopes, M. R., & Araújo da Silveira, E. A. (2021). Expectations and experiences in the childbirth process from the perspective of symbolic interactionism. *Online Brazilian Journal of Nursing, 20*(1).

[12] Luce, A., Cash, M., Hundley, V., Cheyne, H., van Teijlingen, E. R., & Angell, C. (2016). "Is it realistic?" the portrayal of pregnancy and childbirth in the media. *BMC Pregnancy and Childbirth, 16*.

[13] Larkin, P., Begley, C.M. & Devane, D. (2009) Women's experiences of labor and birth: an evolutionary concept analysis. *Midwifery, 25*(2), e49-e59.

[14] The decline of hunting and fishing. Wildlife for All. (2022, November 4). https://wildlifeforall.us/resources/decline-of-hunting-and-fishing/ Centers for Disease Control and Prevention. (2024). U.S. fertility rate drops to another historic low.

[15] Spamer, Melissa (2016) 300-Hour Yoga Teacher Training. Lotus in the Flame. Adapted from Rick Hanson.

[16] Beigi, N. M., Broumandfar, K., Bahadoran, P., & Abedi, H. A. (2010). Women's experience of pain during childbirth. *Iranian journal of nursing and midwifery research, 15*(2), 77–82.

[17] Jones, L. E., Whitburn, L. Y., Davey, M.-A., & Small, R. (2015). Assessment of pain associated with childbirth: Women's perspectives, preferences and solutions. *Midwifery, 31*(7), 708– 712. https://doi.org/10.1016/j.midw.2015.03.012

[18] Whitburn, L. Y., Jones, L. E., Davey, M. A., & Small, R. (2017). The meaning of labour pain: how the social environment and other contextual factors shape women's experiences. *BMC Pregnancy and Childbirth, 17*(1), 157.

[19] Mayo Clinic Staff. (2024). Anorgasmia in women: Symptoms and causes. Mayo Clinic.

20 Kate W. (2023, June 2). 45 Orgasm Statistics in 2024. PleasureBetter.

[21] Khajehei, M., & Doherty, M. (2012). Childbirth in pleasure and ecstasy: A fountain of hormones and chemicals. *International Journal of Childbirth Education, 27*(3), 73–80.

[22] Carrellas, B. (2017). Urban Tantra: Sacred Sex for the Twenty-First Century (2nd ed.). Ten Speed Press.

[23] Karakoyunlu, Ö, Ejder Apay, S., & Gürol, A. (2019). The effect of pain, stress, and cortisol during labor on breastfeeding success. *Developmental Psychobiology, 61*(7), 979-987.

[24] Field, T., Hernandez-Reif, M., Diego, M., Figueiredo, B., Schanberg, S., & Kuhn, C. (2006). Prenatal cortisol, prematurity and low birthweight. *Infant Behavior and Development, 29*(2), 268–275.

[25] Uvnäs-Moberg, K., Ekström-Bergström, A., Buckley, S., Massarotti, C., Pajalic, Z., Luegmair, K., Kotlowska, A., Lengler, L., Olza, I., Grylka-

Baeschlin, S., Leahy-Warren, P., Hadjigeorgiu, E., Villarmea, S., & Dencker, A. (2020). Maternal plasma levels of oxytocin during breastfeeding—a systematic review. *PLOS ONE, 15*(8).

[26] Kobayashi, K., Oyama, S., Kuki, C., Tsugami, Y., Matsunaga, K., Suzuki, T., & Nishimura, T. (2017). Distinct roles of prolactin, epidermal growth factor, and glucocorticoids in β- casein secretion pathway in lactating mammary epithelial cells. *Molecular and Cellular Endocrinology, 440*, 16–24.

[27] Karakoyunlu, Ö, Ejder Apay, S., & Gürol, A. (2019). The effect of pain, stress, and cortisol during labor on breastfeeding success. *Developmental Psychobiology, 61*(7), 979-987.

[28] Dimitraki, M., Tsikouras, P., Manav, B., Gioka, T., Koutlaki, N., Zervoudis, S., & Galazios, G. (2015). Evaluation of the effect of natural and emotional stress of labor on lactation and breast-feeding. *Archives of Gynecology and Obstetrics, 293*(2), 317–328.

[29] Dimitraki, M., Tsikouras, P., Manav, B., Gioka, T., Koutlaki, N., Zervoudis, S., & Galazios, G. (2015). Evaluation of the effect of natural and emotional stress of labor on lactation and breast-feeding. *Archives of Gynecology and Obstetrics, 293*(2), 317–328.

[30] Dawans, B., Vance, M., Iranmanesh, A., Thorner, M., & Veldhuis, J. (1996). Fasting as a metabolic stress paradigm selectively amplifies cortisol secretory burst mass and delays the time of maximal nyctohemeral cortisol concentrations in healthy men. *The Journal of Clinical Endocrinology and Metabolism, 81*(2), 692-9.

[31] Cheng, Y. W., Shaffer, B., Nicholson, J., & Caughey, A. (2009). Second stage of labor and epidural use: A larger effect than previously suggested. *Obstetrics & Gynecology, 123*(2), 527-535.

Hatamleh, R., Ali, R. A., & Elian, A. I. (2019). Epidural analgesia and its effects on maternal and neonatal outcomes: a retrospective comparable study in Northern Jordan. Evidence Based Midwifery, 17(4), 135–142.

[32] Chien, L., & Ko, Y. (2004). Fatigue during pregnancy predicts caesarean deliveries. *Journal of Advanced Nursing, 45*(5), 487-494.

[33] Young, C., Bhattacharya, S., Woolner, A., et al. (2023). Maternal and perinatal outcomes of prolonged second stage of labour: A historical cohort study of over 51,000 women. BMC Pregnancy and Childbirth, 23, 467.

[34] Allen, V. M., Baskett, T. F., O'Connell, C. M., McKeen, D., & Allen, A. C. (2009). Maternal and perinatal outcomes with increasing duration of the second stage of labor. *Obstetrics and Gynecology, 113*(6), 1248–1258.

[35] Blankenship, S., Raghuraman, N., Delhi, A., Woolfolk, C., Wang, Y., Macones, G., & Cahill, A. (2020). Association of abnormal first stage of labor duration and maternal and neonatal morbidity. *American Journal of Obstetrics and Gynecology, 223*(3), 445.e1-445.e15

[36] Sandström, A., Altman, M., Cnattingius, S., Johansson, S., Ahlberg, M., & Stephansson, O. (2017). Durations of second stage of labor and pushing, and adverse neonatal outcomes: a population-based cohort study. *J Perinatol* 37, 236–242.

Wang, L., Wang, H., Jia, L., Qing, W., Li, F., & Zhou, J. (2020). The impact of stage of labor on adverse maternal and neonatal outcomes in multiparous women: a retrospective cohort study. *BMC Pregnancy Childbirth 20*, 596.

[37] Epstein, R., & Lake, A. (Directors). (2008). *The Business of Being Born* [Film]. Barranca Productions.

[38] Riawati, M. S., Budihastuti, U. R., & Prasetya, H. (2021). The effect of prenatal yoga on birth labor duration and pain: A meta analysis. *Journal of Maternal and Child Health, 6*(3), 327–337.

[39] Goutaudier, N., Bertoli, C., Séjourné, N., & Chabrol, H. (2019). Childbirth as a forthcoming traumatic event: Pretraumatic stress disorder during pregnancy and its psychological correlates. *Journal of Reproductive and Infant Psychology, 37*(1), 44–55.

[40] Google Ngram Viewer. (n.d.). *Google Books Ngram Viewer*. Retrieved August 2nd, 2024, from https://books.google.com/ngrams

[41] Brown, B. (2010). The Gifts of Imperfection: Let Go of Who You Think You're Supposed to Be and Embrace Who You Are. Hazelden Publishing.

[42] Huxley, A. (1932). *Brave New World*. Chatto & Windus.

[43] Roosevelt, F. D. (1933, March 4). Inaugural Address.

[44] Ramey-Collier, K., Jackson, M., Malloy, A., McMillan, C., Scraders-Pyatt, A., & Wheeler, S. M. (2023). Doula care: A review of outcomes and impact on birth experience. *Obstetrics and Gynecology Survey, 78*(2), 124-127.

[45] National Partnership for Women & Families. (2023). Why is the C-Section Rate So High?

[46] Sausser, L. (2022, April 14). *High cesarean section rates plague the South as doctors and hospitals profit from surgical deliveries*. USA Today.

[47] Hamilton, B. E., Martin, J. A., & Osterman, M. J. K. (2024). *Births: Provisional Data for 2023* (Report No. 35). National Vital Statistics Reports.

[48] Epstein, R., & Lake, A. (Directors). (2008). *The Business of Being Born* [Film]. Barranca Productions.

[49] Keag OE, Norman JE, Stock SJ (2018) Long-term risks and benefits associated with cesarean delivery for mother, baby, and subsequent pregnancies: Systematic review and meta-analysis. PLoS Med 15(1): e1002494.

Uvnäs-Moberg, K., Ekström-Bergström, A., Buckley, S., Massarotti, C., Pajalic, Z., Luegmair, K., Kotlowska, A., Lengler, L., Olza, I., Grylka-Baeschlin, S., Leahy-Warren, P., Hadjigeorgiu, E., Villarmea, S., &

Dencker, A. (2020). Maternal plasma levels of oxytocin during breastfeeding—a systematic review. *PLOS ONE, 15*(8).

[50] Bourdillon, K., McCausland, T., & Jones, S. (2020). The impact of birth-related injury and pain on breastfeeding outcomes. *British Journal of Midwifery, 28*(1), 52-61.

Grajeda Rubén, & Pérez-Escamilla Rafael. (2002). Stress during labor and delivery is associated with delayed onset of lactation among urban Guatemalan women. *The Journal of Nutrition, 132*(10), 3055–3060.

[51] Hobbs, A. J., Mannion, C. A., McDonald, S. W., Brockway, M., & Tough, S. C. (2016). The impact of caesarean section on breastfeeding initiation, duration and difficulties in the first four months postpartum. *BMC Pregnancy and Childbirth, 16*(1).

[52] Ahamed, F. M., Solkar, S., Stevikova, M., & Moya, B. P. (2023). Link between cesarean section scar defect and secondary infertility: Case reports and review. *JBRA Assisted Reproduction, 27*(1), 134–141.

[53] Chen, H. H., Lai, J. C., Hwang, S. J., Huang, N., Chou, Y. J., & Chien, L. Y. (2017). Understanding the relationship between cesarean birth and stress, anxiety, and depression after childbirth: A nationwide cohort study. *Birth (Berkeley, Calif.), 44*(4), 369–376.

[54] Grisbrook, M.-A., Dewey, D., Cuthbert, C., McDonald, S., Ntanda, H., Giesbrecht, G. F., & Letourneau, N. (2022). Associations among Caesarean section birth, post-traumatic stress, and postpartum depression symptoms. *International Journal of Environmental Research and Public Health, 19*(8), 4900.

[55] *Narcotics for pain during childbirth.* American Pregnancy Association. (2021, December 9).

[56] Lavin, D. (2001). Focal point on breastfeeding: Improving breastfeeding outcomes. *International Journal of Childbirth Education, 16*(3), 27-33.

[57] *Narcotics for pain during childbirth.* American Pregnancy Association. (2021, December 9).

[58] Brimdyr, K., Cadwell, K., Widström, A.M., Svensson, K., & Phillips, R. (2019). The effect of labor medications on normal newborn behavior in the first hour after birth: A prospective cohort study, *Early Human Development, 132*, 30-36.

Riordan, J., Gross, A., Angeron, J., Krumwiede, B., & Melin, J. (2000). The effect of labor pain relief medication on neonatal suckling and breastfeeding duration. *Journal of Human Lactation, 16*(1), 7–12.

[59] Anim-Somuah, M., Smyth, R., Cyna, A., & Cuthbert, A. (2018). Epidural versus non-epidural or no analgesia for pain management in labour. *The Cochrane Database of Systematic Reviews, 5.*

[60] Weiss, R. E. (2024, July 22). *What is a walking epidural?* Parents. https://www.parents.com

[61] Dimitraki, M., Tsikouras, P., Manav, B., Gioka, T., Koutlaki, N., Zervoudis, S., & Galazios, G. (2015). Evaluation of the effect of natural and emotional stress of labor on lactation and breast-feeding. *Archives of Gynecology and Obstetrics, 293*(2), 317–328.

[62] Uvnäs-Moberg, K., Ekström-Bergström, A., Buckley, S., Massarotti, C., Pajalic, Z., Luegmair, K., Kotlowska, A., Lengler, L., Olza, I., Grylka-Baeschlin, S., Leahy-Warren, P., Hadjigeorgiu, E., Villarmea, S., & Dencker, A. (2020). Maternal plasma levels of oxytocin during breastfeeding—a systematic review. *PLOS ONE, 15*(8).
Uvnäs-Moberg, K., & Prime, D. K. (2013). Oxytocin effects in mothers and infants during breastfeeding. *Infant, 9*(6), 201–206.
Walter, M. H., Abele, H., & Plappert, C. F. (2021). The role of oxytocin and the effect of stress during childbirth: Neurobiological Basics and implications for mother and child. *Frontiers in Endocrinology, 12.*

[63] Parise, D. C., Gilman, C., Petrilli, M. A., & Malaspina, D. (2021). Childbirth Pain and Post-Partum Depression: Does Labor Epidural Analgesia Decrease This Risk? *Journal of Pain Research*, 14, 1925–1933.

[64] Anim-Somuah, M., Smyth, R., Cyna, A., & Cuthbert, A. (2018). Epidural versus non-epidural or no analgesia for pain management in labour.. *The Cochrane database of systematic reviews, 5.*

[65] *Nitrous oxide during Labor.* American Pregnancy Association. (2021, December 9).

[66] Mayo Clinic. (n.d.). Fetal heart rate monitoring.
University of Rochester Medical Center. (n.d.). External and internal heart rate monitoring of the fetus.

[67] Mayo Clinic. (n.d.). Intrauterine pressure catheter.

[68] Liang, Y., Li, Y., Huang, C., Li, X., Cai, Q., Peng, J., & Fan, S. (2022). Safety of Internal Electronic Fetal Heart Rate Monitoring During Labor. *Maternal-Fetal Medicine*, 4, 121 - 126.

[69] Frolova, A., Stout, M., Carter, E., Macones, G., Cahill, A., & Raghuraman, N. (2020). Internal fetal and uterine monitoring in obese patients and maternal obstetrical outcomes. *American Journal of Obstetrics & Gynecology MFM*, 3 1, 100282 .

[70] LeWine, H. (2023, June 13). *Oxytocin: The love hormone.* Harvard Health.

[71] Gaudernack, L., Frøslie, K., Michelsen, T., Voldner, N., & Lukasse, M. (2018). De-medicalization of birth by reducing the use of oxytocin for augmentation among first-time mothers – a prospective intervention study. *BMC Pregnancy and Childbirth*, 18.

[72] American College of Obstetricians and Gynecologists. (2019). Induction of labor. ACOG Practice Bulletin, Number 107.

[73] Gaudernack, L., Frøslie, K., Michelsen, T., Voldner, N., & Lukasse, M. (2018). De-medicalization of birth by reducing the use of oxytocin for augmentation among first-time mothers – a prospective intervention study. *BMC Pregnancy and Childbirth*, 18.

[74] Gu, V., Feeley, N., Gold, I., Hayton, B., Robins, S., Mackinnon, A., Samuel, S., Carter, C., & Zelkowitz, P. (2016). Intrapartum Synthetic Oxytocin and Its Effects on Maternal Well-Being at 2 Months Postpartum. *Birth*, 43 1, 28-35.

[75] Achanna, S., & Monga, D. (1994). Outcome of forceps delivery versus vacuum extraction--a review of 200 cases.. *Singapore Medical Journal*, *35*(6), 605-608.

[76] Jawed-Wessel, S. (2016). The lies we tell pregnant women [Video]. TED Conferences. https://www.ted.com/talks/sofia_jawed_wessel_the_lies_we_tell_pregnant_women

[77] Oster, E. (2014). Expecting better: Why the conventional pregnancy wisdom is wrong–and what you really need to know. Penguin Books.

[78] Finucane EM, Murphy DJ, Biesty LM, Gyte GML, Cotter AM, Ryan EM, Boulvain M, Devane D. Membrane sweeping for induction of labour. *Cochrane Database of Systematic Reviews* 2020, Issue 2. Art. No.: CD000451.

[79] Sukumaran, S., & Chandraharan, E. (2021). The historical practice of "Membrane sweep" to initiate labour: Does it have a role in contemporary obstetric practice? *Global Journal of Reproductive Medicine*, *8*(2).

[80] Lothian, J. A. (2014). Healthy Birth Practice #4: Avoid interventions unless they are medically necessary. *The Journal of Perinatal Education*, *23*(4), 198–206.

[81] Sukumaran, S., & Chandraharan, E. (2021). The historical practice of "Membrane sweep" to initiate labour: Does it have a role in contemporary obstetric practice? *Global Journal of Reproductive Medicine*, *8*(2).

[82] Finucane, E. M., Murphy, D. J., Biesty, L. M., Gyte, G. M., Cotter, A. M., Ryan, E. M., Boulvain, M., & Devane, D. (2020). Membrane sweeping for induction of labour. *Cochrane Database of Systematic Reviews*.

[83] Roberts, J., Evans, K., Spiby, H., Evans, C., Pallotti, P., & Eldridge, J. (2020b). Women's information needs, decision-making and experiences of membrane sweeping to promote spontaneous labour. *Midwifery*, *83*, 102626.

[84] Milgram, S. (1963). Behavioral study of obedience. *Journal of Abnormal and Social Psychology*, *67*(4), 371-378.

[85] Chang, Y.-H., & Liao, M.-Y. (2009). The effect of aviation safety education on passenger cabin safety awareness. *Safety Science, 47*(10), 1337-1345.

[86] Gilligan, C. (1982). In a different voice: Psychological theory and women's development. Harvard University Press.

[87] Cho, Mi-Kyoung, and Mi-Young Choi. 2021. Effect of Distraction Intervention for Needle-Related Pain and Distress in Children: A Systematic Review and Meta-Analysis. *International Journal of Environmental Research and Public Health* 18, no. 17: 9159.

[88] Browning, C. (2000). Using music during childbirth. *Birth*, (27)4, 272-276.

[89] Gokyildiz Surucu, S., Ozturk, M., Avcibay Vurgec, B., Alan, S., & Akbas, M. (2018). The effect of music on pain and anxiety of women during labour on First time pregnancy: A study from Turkey. *Complementary Therapies in Clinical Practice, 30*, 96–102.

[90] Guo, H., Que, M., Shen, J., Nie, Q., Chen, Y., Huang, Q., & Jin, A. (2022). Effect of music therapy combined with free position delivery on labor pain and birth outcomes. *Applied Bionics and Biomechanics*, 2022, 1–6.

[91] Chase, Julie. (2021). Wind Willow Sound Class. Wind Willow Sound Health.

[92] Trivedi, G., & Saboo, B. (2019). A Comparative Study of the Impact of Himalayan Singing Bowls and Supine Silence on Stress Index and Heart Rate Variability. *Journal of Behavior Therapy and Mental Health*.

Pesek, A., & Bratina, T. (2016). Gong and its therapeutic meaning. *Musicological Annual, 52*, 137-161.

[93]Salunkhe, J., & Pawale, M. (2020). Effectiveness of back massage on pain relief during first stage of labor in Primi Mothers admitted at a tertiary care center. *Journal of Family Medicine and Primary Care, 9*(12), 5933–5938.

Ranjbaran, M., Khorsandi, M., Matourypour, P., & Shamsi, M. (2017). Effect of massage therapy on labor pain reduction in primiparous women: A systematic review and meta-analysis of randomized controlled clinical trials in Iran. *Iranian Journal of Nursing and Midwifery Research, 22*(4), 257 Türkmen, H., & Oran, N. T. (2021). Massage and heat application on labor pain and comfort: A quasi-randomized controlled experimental study. *Explore (New York, N.Y.), 17*(5), 438–445.

94 Eskandari, F., Mousavi, P., Valiani, M., Ghanbari, S., & Iravani, M. (2022). A comparison of the effect of Swedish massage with and without chamomile oil on labor outcomes and maternal satisfaction of the childbirth process: A randomized controlled trial. *European Journal of Medical Research, 27*(1).

95 Azizi, M., Yousefzadeh, S., Rakhshandeh, H., Behnam, H., & Mirteymouri, M. (2020). The Effect of Back Massage with and without Ginger Oil on the Pain Intensity in the Active Phase of Labor in Primiparous Women. *Journal of Midwifery and Reproductive Health*, 8, 2033-2040.

96 Tabatabaeichehr, M., & Mortazavi, H. (2020). The effectiveness of aromatherapy in the management of Labor Pain and anxiety: A systematic review. *Ethiopian Journal of Health Sciences*, *30*(3).

Kaya, A., Yeşildere Sağlam, H., Karadağ, E., & Gürsoy, E. (2023). The effectiveness of aromatherapy in the management of labor pain: A meta-analysis. *European Journal of Obstetrics & Gynecology and Reproductive Biology: X*, *20*, 100255.

97 Smith, C. A., Collins, C. T., Cyna, A. M., & Crowther, C. A. (2006). Acupuncture for pain management in labour. *Cochrane Database of Systematic Reviews*, (4).

98 Rabl, M., Ahner, R., Bitschnau, M., Zeisler, H., & Husslein, P. (2001). Acupuncture for cervical ripening and induction of labor at term—a randomized controlled trial. *Wiener Klinische Wochenschrift*, *113*(23-24), 942-946.

99 Park, J., Sohn, Y., White, A. R., Lee, H., & Ernst, E. (2014). The safety of acupuncture during pregnancy: a systematic review. *Acupuncture in Medicine*, *32*(3), 257-266.

100 da Costa, N., Silva Martins, E., Pinheiro, A. K. B., Soares, P. R. A. L., de Souza Aquino, P., & Castro, R. C. M. B. (2022). Acupuncture for perceived stress in pregnant women: an intervention study. *Revista da Escola de Enfermagem da U S P*, 56, e20210233.

101 Alimoradi, Z., Kazemi, F., Gorji, M., & Valiani, M. (2020). Effects of ear and body acupressure on labor pain and duration of labor active phase: A randomized controlled trial. *Complementary therapies in medicine*, *51*, 102413.

102 Mohyadin, E., Ghorashi, Z., & Molamomanaei, Z. (2020). The effect of practicing yoga during pregnancy on labor stages length, anxiety and pain: a randomized controlled trial. *Journal of Complementary & Integrative Medicine*, *18*(2), 413-417.

Koyuncu, S. B., & Bülbül, M. (2021). The impact of yoga on fear of childbirth and childbirth self-efficacy among third-trimester pregnants. *Complementary Therapies in Clinical Practice*, *44*, 101438.

Newham, J. J., Wittkowski, A., Hurley, J., Aplin, J. D., & Westwood, M. (2014). Effects of antenatal yoga on maternal anxiety and depression: A randomized controlled trial. *Depression and Anxiety*, *31*(8), 631–640. https://doi.org/10.1002/da.22268

Van der Riet, P., Francis, L., & Rees, A. (2020). Exploring the impacts of mindfulness and yoga upon childbirth outcomes and maternal health: An integrative review. *Scandinavian Journal of Caring Sciences, 34*(3), 552-565.

[103] García-Sesnich, J. N., Flores, M. G., Ríos, M. H., & Aravena, J. G. (2017). Longitudinal and immediate effect of Kundalini Yoga on salivary levels of cortisol and activity of alpha- amylase and its effect on perceived stress. *International Journal of Yoga, 10*(2), 73.

Thirthalli, J., Naveen, G. H., Rao, M. G., Varambally, S., Christopher, R., & Gangadhar, B. N. (2013). Cortisol and antidepressant effects of yoga. *Indian Journal of Psychiatry, 55*(7), 405.

[104] Chuntharapat, S., Petpichetchian, W., & Hatthakit, U. (2008). Yoga during pregnancy: effects on maternal comfort, labor pain, and birth outcomes. *Complementary Therapies in Clinical Practice, 14*(2), 105-115.

Jahdi, F., Sheikhan, F., Haghani, H., Sharifi, B., Ghaseminejad, A., Khodarahmian, M., & Rouhana, N. (2017). Yoga during pregnancy: The effects on labor pain and delivery outcomes (A randomized controlled trial). *Complementary Therapies in Clinical Practice, 27*, 1-4.

Mohyadin, E., Ghorashi, Z., & Molamomanaei, Z. (2020). The effect of practicing yoga during pregnancy on labor stages length, anxiety and pain: a randomized controlled trial. *Journal of Complementary & Integrative Medicine, 18*(2), 413-417.

Riawati, M. S., Budihastuti, U. R., & Prasetya, H. (2021). The effect of prenatal yoga on birth labor duration and pain: A meta analysis. *Journal of Maternal and Child Health, 6*(3), 327–337.

[105] Chuntharapat, S., Petpichetchian, W., & Hatthakit, U. (2008). Yoga during pregnancy: effects on maternal comfort, labor pain, and birth outcomes. *Complementary Therapies in Clinical Practice, 14*(2), 105-115.

Jahdi, F., Sheikhan, F., Haghani, H., Sharifi, B., Ghaseminejad, A., Khodarahmian, M., & Rouhana, N. (2017). Yoga during pregnancy: The effects on labor pain and delivery outcomes (A randomized controlled trial). *Complementary Therapies in Clinical Practice, 27*, 1-4.

Mohyadin, E., Ghorashi, Z., & Molamomanaei, Z. (2020). The effect of practicing yoga during pregnancy on labor stages length, anxiety and pain: a randomized controlled trial. *Journal of Complementary & Integrative Medicine, 18*(2), 413-417

Riawati, M. S., Budihastuti, U. R., & Prasetya, H. (2021). The effect of prenatal yoga on birth labor duration and pain: A meta analysis. *Journal of Maternal and Child Health, 6*(3), 327–337.

Rong, L., Dai, L., & Ouyang, Y. (2020). The effectiveness of prenatal yoga on delivery outcomes: A meta-analysis. *Complementary Therapies in Clinical Practice, 39*, 101157.

Rong, L., Wang, R., Ouyang, Y.-Q., & Redding, S. R. (2021). Efficacy of yoga on physiological and psychological discomforts and delivery outcomes in Chinese primiparas. *Complementary Therapies in Clinical Practice*, *44*, 101434.

Yekefallah, L., Namdar, P., Dehghankar, L., Golestaneh, F., Taheri, S., & Mohammadkhaniha, F. (2021). The effect of yoga on the delivery and neonatal outcomes in nulliparous pregnant women in Iran: A clinical trial study. *BMC Pregnancy and Childbirth, 21*(1), 1- 8.

[106] Jahdi, F., Sheikhan, F., Haghani, H., Sharifi, B., Ghaseminejad, A., Khodarahmian, M., & Rouhana, N. (2017). Yoga during pregnancy: The effects on labor pain and delivery outcomes (A randomized controlled trial). *Complementary Therapies in Clinical Practice, 27*, 1-4.

Rong, L., Dai, L., & Ouyang, Y. (2020). The effectiveness of prenatal yoga on delivery outcomes: A meta-analysis. *Complementary Therapies in Clinical Practice, 39*, 101157.

Rong, L., Wang, R., Ouyang, Y.-Q., & Redding, S. R. (2021). Efficacy of yoga on physiological and psychological discomforts and delivery outcomes in Chinese primiparas. *Complementary Therapies in Clinical Practice*, *44*, 101434.

Yekefallah, L., Namdar, P., Dehghankar, L., Golestaneh, F., Taheri, S., & Mohammadkhaniha, F. (2021). The effect of yoga on the delivery and neonatal outcomes in nulliparous pregnant women in Iran: A clinical trial study. *BMC Pregnancy and Childbirth, 21*(1), 1- 8.

[107] Yekefallah, L., Namdar, P., Dehghankar, L., Golestaneh, F., Taheri, S., & Mohammadkhaniha, F. (2021). The effect of yoga on the delivery and neonatal outcomes in nulliparous pregnant women in Iran: A clinical trial study. *BMC Pregnancy and Childbirth, 21*(1), 1- 8.

[108] Koyuncu, S. B., & Bülbül, M. (2021). The impact of yoga on fear of childbirth and childbirth self-efficacy among third-trimester pregnants. *Complementary Therapies in Clinical Practice, 44*, 101438.

[109] Jahdi, F., Sheikhan, F., Haghani, H., Sharifi, B., Ghaseminejad, A., Khodarahmian, M., & Rouhana, N. (2017). Yoga during pregnancy: The effects on labor pain and delivery outcomes (A randomized controlled trial). *Complementary Therapies in Clinical Practice, 27*, 1-4.

Mohyadin, E., Ghorashi, Z., & Molamomanaei, Z. (2020). The effect of practicing yoga during pregnancy on labor stages length, anxiety and pain: a randomized controlled trial. *Journal of Complementary & Integrative Medicine, 18*(2), 413-417.

[110] Chuntharapat, S., Petpichetchian, W., & Hatthakit, U. (2008). Yoga during pregnancy: effects on maternal comfort, labor pain, and birth outcomes. *Complementary Therapies in Clinical Practice, 14*(2), 105-115.

Jahdi, F., Sheikhan, F., Haghani, H., Sharifi, B., Ghaseminejad, A., Khodarahmian, M., & Rouhana, N. (2017). Yoga during pregnancy: The effects on labor pain and delivery outcomes (A randomized controlled trial). *Complementary Therapies in Clinical Practice, 27*, 1-4.

Mohyadin, E., Ghorashi, Z., & Molamomanaei, Z. (2020). The effect of practicing yoga during pregnancy on labor stages length, anxiety and pain: a randomized controlled trial. *Journal of Complementary & Integrative Medicine, 18*(2), 413-417.

Riawati, M. S., Budihastuti, U. R., & Prasetya, H. (2021). The effect of prenatal yoga on birth labor duration and pain: A meta analysis. *Journal of Maternal and Child Health, 6*(3), 327–337.

Rong, L., Wang, R., Ouyang, Y.-Q., & Redding, S. R. (2021). Efficacy of yoga on physiological and psychological discomforts and delivery outcomes in Chinese primiparas. *Complementary Therapies in Clinical Practice, 44*, 101434.

Yekefallah, L., Namdar, P., Dehghankar, L., Golestaneh, F., Taheri, S., & Mohammadkhaniha, F. (2021). The effect of yoga on the delivery and neonatal outcomes in nulliparous pregnant women in Iran: A clinical trial study. *BMC Pregnancy and Childbirth, 21*(1), 1- 8.

111 Mohyadin, E., Ghorashi, Z., & Molamomanaei, Z. (2020). The effect of practicing yoga during pregnancy on labor stages length, anxiety and pain: a randomized controlled trial. *Journal of Complementary & Integrative Medicine, 18*(2), 413-417.

Riawati, M. S., Budihastuti, U. R., & Prasetya, H. (2021). The effect of prenatal yoga on birth labor duration and pain: A meta analysis. Journal of Maternal and Child Health, 6(3), 327–337.

García-Sesnich, J. N., Flores, M. G., Ríos, M. H., & Aravena, J. G. (2017). Longitudinal and immediate effect of Kundalini Yoga on salivary levels of cortisol and activity of alpha-amylase and its effect on perceived stress. *International Journal of Yoga*, 10(2), 73.

Thirthalli, J., Naveen, G. H., Rao, M. G., Varambally, S., Christopher, R., & Gangadhar, B. N. (2013). Cortisol and antidepressant effects of yoga. Indian Journal of Psychiatry, 55(7), 405.

Rong, L., Dai, L., & Ouyang, Y. (2020). The effectiveness of prenatal yoga on delivery outcomes: A meta-analysis. *Complementary Therapies in Clinical Practice*, 39, 101157.

112 Gavin, N. R., Kogutt, B. K., Fletcher, W., & Szymanski, L. M. (2020). Fetal and maternal responses to yoga in the third-trimester. *The Journal of Maternal-Fetal & Neonatal Medicine, 33*(15), 2623–2627.

113 Polis, R., Gussman, D., & Kuo, Y. (2015). Yoga in pregnancy: an examination of maternal and fetal responses to 26 Yoga Postures. *Obstetrics and Gynecology (New York. 1953), 126*(6), 1237-1241.

[114] Pramanik, T., Pudasaini, B., & Prajapati, R. (2009). Immediate effect of a slow pace breathing exercise Bhramari pranayama on blood pressure and heart rate. *Nepal Medical College Journal, 11*(3), 182-184.

[115] Sengupta, P. (2012). Health impacts of yoga and pranayama: A state-of-the-art review. *International Journal of Preventive Medicine, 3*(7), 444.

[116] Telles, S., Nagarathna, R., & Nagendra, H. R. (1994). Breathing through a particular nostril can alter metabolism and autonomic activities. *Indian Journal of Physiology and Pharmacology, 38*(2), 133-137.

[117] Jerath, R., Edry, J. W., Barnes, V. A., & Jerath, V. (2006). Physiology of long pranayamic breathing: Neural respiratory elements may provide a mechanism that explains how slow deep breathing shifts the autonomic nervous system. *Medical Hypotheses, 67*(3), 566-571

[118] Saoji, A. A., Raghavendra, B. R., & Manjunath, N. K. (2019). Effects of yogic breath regulation: A narrative review of scientific evidence. *Journal of Ayurveda and Integrative Medicine, 10*(1), 50–58.

[119] Sinha, B., Sinha, T. D., & Shankar, G. (2013). Effect of Ujjayi Pranayama on selected physiological variables. *Indian Journal of Traditional Knowledge, 12*(2), 377-381.

[120] Kumar, A., Prasad, A., & Varma, V. K. (2013). Effects of Bhramari Pranayama on Health – A Review. *International Journal of Biomedical Research, 4*(12), 633-638.

[121] Raghuraj, P., & Telles, S. (2008). Immediate effect of specific nostril manipulating yoga breathing practices on autonomic and respiratory variables. *Applied Psychophysiology and Biofeedback, 33*(2), 65–75.

[122] Bhargav, H., Metri, K. G., & Koka, P. S. (2016). Immediate effect of bhramari pranayama on resting cardiovascular parameters in healthy adolescents. *Journal of Clinical and Diagnostic Research: JCDR, 10*(12), CC17.

[123] Rampalliwar, S., Rajak, C., Arjariya, R., Poonia, M., & Bajpai, R. (2013). The effect of bhramari pranayama on pregnant women having cardiovascular hyper-reactivity to cold pressor. *National Journal of Physiology, Pharmacy and Pharmacology, 3*, 137-141.

124 Alimoradi, Z., Kazemi, F., Gorji, M., & Valiani, M. (2020). Effects of ear and body acupressure on labor pain and duration of labor active phase: A randomized controlled trial. *Complementary Therapies in Medicine, 51*, 102413.

Ahmadi, S., Aradmehr, M., & Azhari, S. (2017). Saffron and childbirth; a triple blind clinical trial. *QUID: Investigación, Ciencia y Tecnología, (1)*, 2846-2856.

Yilmaz, E. (2022). Antenatal hypnosis: Does it have an effect on fear of childbirth? *Eurasian Journal of Medical Investigation, 6*(4), 394–400.

[125] Moghaddam Hosseini, V., Nazarzadeh, M. & Jahanfar S. (2018). Interventions for reducing fear of childbirth: a systematic review and meta-analysis of clinical trials. *Women Birth, 31*(4), 254-262.

[126] Goldstein, I., Makhoul, I., Weissman, A., & Drugan, A. (2005). Hemivertebra: Prenatal diagnosis, incidence, and characteristics. *Fetal Diagnosis and Therapy, 20*(2), 121–126.

[127] Simpson A. R. (1908). Birth-Stools in Egypt. *Edinburgh Medical Journal, 1*(3), 198–202.

[128] Smith G. C. (2001). Use of time to event analysis to estimate the normal duration of human pregnancy. *Human Reproduction (Oxford, England), 16*(7), 1497–1500.

[129] Cervical mucus provides a lot of information about fertility before pregnancy. Check out the bonus book in the back of this book to learn more about cervical mucus tracking.

[130] Miller, Y., Armanasco, A., Mccosker, L., & Thompson, R. (2020). Variations in outcomes for women admitted to hospital in early versus active labour: an observational study. *BMC Pregnancy and Childbirth*, 20.

[131] Rota, A., Antolini, L., Colciago, E., Nespoli, A., Borrelli, S., & Fumagalli, S. (2017). Timing of hospital admission in labour: latent versus active phase, mode of birth and intrapartum interventions. A correlational study. *Women and Birth:* Journal of the Australian College of Midwives, 31(4), 313-318.

[132] Evbuomwan, O., & Chowdhury, Y. S. (2023). Physiology, cervical dilation. In StatPearls [Internet]. StatPearls Publishing.

[133] Padiyar, S., Nandakumar, V., Kollikonda, S., Karnati, S., Sangwan, N., & Aly, H. (2024). Maternal and infant microbiome and birth anthropometry. *iScience, 27*(110312).

[134] Bigelow, A. E., & Power, M. (2020). Mother–infant skin-to-skin contact: Short- and long-term effects for mothers and their children born full-term. *Frontiers in Psychology, 11.*

Uvnäs-Moberg, K., Handlin, L., & Petersson, M. (2015). Self-soothing behaviors with particular reference to oxytocin release induced by non-noxious sensory stimulation. *Frontiers in Psychology, 5.*

Vittner, D., McGrath, J., Robinson, J. A., Lawhon, G., Cusson, R., Eisenfeld, L., Walsh, S., Young, E., & Cong, X. (2017). Increase in oxytocin from skin-to-skin contact enhances development of parent–infant relationship. *Biological Research For Nursing, 20*(1), 54– 62.

[135] Lee, J., Parikka, V., Lehtonen, L., & Soukka, H. (2022). Parent-infant skin-to-skin contact reduces the electrical activity of the diaphragm and stabilizes respiratory function in preterm infants. *Pediatric Research, 91*(5), 1163–1167.

[136] Montez, Elizabeth (2022). Foundations of Lactation Center for Indigenous Midwifery.

[137] World Health Organization. (2021, May 26). Kangaroo mother care started immediately after birth critical for saving lives, new research shows.

[138] Bigelow, A. E., & Power, M. (2020). Mother–infant skin-to-skin contact: Short- and long-term effects for mothers and their children born full-term. *Frontiers in Psychology, 11.*

[139] Feldman, R. (2007). Mother-infant synchrony and the development of moral orientation in childhood and adolescence: Direct and indirect mechanisms of developmental continuity. *American Journal of Orthopsychiatry, 77*(4), 582–597.

140 Centers for Disease Control and Prevention. (2021). Depression Among Women.

[141] National Institute of Mental Health. (n.d.). Postpartum Depression Facts.

Pope, C. J., & Mazmanian, D. (2016). Breastfeeding and postpartum depression: An overview and methodological recommendations for future research. *Depression Research and Treatment,* 4765310.

[142] Hutchens, B. F., & Kearney, J. (2020). Risk factors for postpartum depression: An umbrella review. *Journal of Midwifery & Women's Health, 65*(1), 96–108.

[143] Silverman, M. E., Reichenberg, A., Savitz, D. A., Cnattingius, S., Lichtenstein, P., Hultman, C. M., Larsson, H., & Sandin, S. (2017). The risk factors for postpartum depression: A population-based study. *Depression and Anxiety, 34*(2), 178–187.

[144] Chen, H. H., Lai, J. C., Hwang, S. J., Huang, N., Chou, Y. J., & Chien, L. Y. (2017). Understanding the relationship between cesarean birth and stress, anxiety, and depression after childbirth: A nationwide cohort study. *Birth, 44*(4), 369–376.

[145] Grisbrook, M. A., Dewey, D., Cuthbert, C., McDonald, S., Ntanda, H., Giesbrecht, G. F., & Letourneau, N. (2022). Associations among Caesarean Section Birth, Post-Traumatic Stress, and Postpartum Depression Symptoms. *International Journal of Environmental Research and Public Health, 19*(8), 4900.

[146] Chang, S., Chen, K., Lee, C., Shyu, M., Lin, M., & Lin, W. (2016). Relationships between perineal pain and postpartum depressive symptoms: A prospective cohort study. *International Journal of Nursing Studies,* 59, 68-78.

Kwok, S. C., Moo, D., Sia, S. T., Razak, A. S., & Sng, B. L. (2015). Childbirth pain and postpartum depression. *Trends in Anaesthesia and Critical Care, 5*(4), 95–100.

Ilska, M., Banaś, E., Gregor, K., Brandt-Salmeri, A., Ilski, A., & Cnota, W. (2020). Vaginal delivery or caesarean section – Severity of early symptoms of postpartum depression and assessment of pain in Polish women in the early puerperium. *Midwifery, 87,* 102731.

[147] Boudou, M., Teissedre, F., Walburg, V. & Chabrol, H. (2007). Relation entre l'intensité de la douleur de l'accouchement et celle du postpartum blues. *L'Encéphale, 33*(5), 805-810.

Lim, G., LaSorda, K. R., Farrell, L. M., McCarthy, A. M., Facco, F., & Wasan, A. D. (2020). Obstetric pain correlates with postpartum depression symptoms: a pilot prospective observational study. *BMC Pregnancy and Childbirth, 20*(1), 240.

[148] Kountanis, J. A., Vahabzadeh, C., Bauer, S., Muzik, M., Cassidy, R., Aman, C., MacEachern, M., & Bauer, M. E. (2020). Labor epidural analgesia and the risk of postpartum depression: A meta-analysis of observational studies. *Journal of Clinical Anesthesia,* 61, 109658.

[149] Hall, W. A., Hauck, Y. L., Carty, E. M., Hutton, E. K., Fenwick, J., & Stoll, K. (2009). Childbirth fear, anxiety, fatigue, and sleep deprivation in pregnant women. *Journal of Obstetric, Gynecologic & Neonatal Nursing, 38*(5), 567-576.

[150] Eleftheriou, D., Athanasiadou, K. I., Sifnaios, E., & et al. (2024). Sleep disorders during pregnancy: An underestimated risk factor for gestational diabetes mellitus. *Endocrine, 83*(1), 41–50.

[151] Chang, J. J., Pien, G. W., Duntley, S. P., Macones, G. A. (2010). Sleep deprivation during pregnancy and maternal and fetal outcomes: is there a relationship? *Sleep Medicine Reviews, 14*(2), 107-114.

[152] University of Pittsburgh Schools of the Health Sciences. (2013, July 17). Poor sleep in pregnancy can disrupt the immune system and cause birth-related complications. *ScienceDaily.* Retrieved August 4, 2024, from www.sciencedaily.com/releases/2013/07/130717164725.htm

[153] Hyman, C. (2004, December 15). Inadequate sleep in late pregnancy may influence length of labor and type of delivery. *ScienceDaily.* Retrieved July 20, 2024, from https://www.ucsf.edu/news/2004/12/97669/ucsf-study-finds-inadequate-sleep-late-pregnancy-may-influence-length-labor-and

[154] Abadibavil, D., Sharifi, N., Dashti, S., & Fathi Najafi, T. (2021). Effects of yoga in pregnancy on postpartum depression: A systematic review. *Modern Care Journal, 18*(2).

[155] Battle, C. L., Uebelacker, L. A., Magee, S. R., Sutton, K. A., & Miller, I. W. (2015). Potential for prenatal yoga to serve as an intervention to treat depression during pregnancy. *Women's Health Issues, 25*(2), 134–141.

[156] Aparicio, M., Browne, P. D., Hechler, C., Beijers, R., Rodríguez, J. M., de Weerth, C., & Fernández, L. (2020). Human milk cortisol and immune factors over the first three postnatal months: Relations to maternal psychosocial distress. *PLOS ONE, 15*(5).

[157] Pundir, S., Gridneva, Z., Pillai, A., Thorstensen, E. B., Wall, C. R., Geddes, D. T., & Cameron- Smith, D. (2020). Human milk glucocorticoid levels are associated with infant adiposity and head circumference over the first year of life. *Frontiers in Nutrition, 7.*

[158] Ziomkiewicz, A., Babiszewska, M., Apanasewicz, A., Piosek, M., Wychowaniec, P., Cierniak, A., Barbarska, O., Szołtysik, M., Danel, D., & Wichary, S. (2021). Psychosocial stress and cortisol stress reactivity predict breast milk composition. *Scientific Reports, 11*(1).

[159] Karakoyunlu, Ö, Ejder Apay, S., & Gürol, A. (2019). The effect of pain, stress, and cortisol during labor on breastfeeding success. *Developmental Psychobiology, 61*(7), 979-987.

[160] Shiraishi, M., Matsuzaki, M., Kurihara, S., Iwamoto, M., & Shimada, M. (2020). Post-breastfeeding stress response and breastfeeding self-efficacy as modifiable predictors of exclusive breastfeeding at 3 months postpartum: A prospective cohort study. *BMC Pregnancy and Childbirth, 20*(1).

[161] World Health Organization. (2024). Breastfeeding.

[162] Lokossou, G. A., Kouakanou, L., Schumacher, A., & Zenclussen, A. C. (2022). Human breast milk: From food to active immune response with disease protection in infants and mothers. *Frontiers in Immunology, 13.*

[163] Butler, C., Adams, G., Blum, J., Byrne, S., Carpenter, L., Gussy, M., Calache, H., Catmull, D., Reynolds, E., & Dashper, S. (2022). Breastmilk influences development and composition of the oral microbiome. *Journal of Oral Microbiology, 14.*

[164] Sweeney, E., Al-Shehri, S., Cowley, D., Liley, H., Bansal, N., Charles, B., Shaw, P., Duley, J., & Knox, C. (2018). The effect of breastmilk and saliva combinations on the in vitro growth of oral pathogenic and commensal microorganisms. *Scientific Reports, 8.*

[165] Pang, W. W., Tan, P. T., Cai, S., Fok, D., Chua, M. C., Lim, S. B., Shek, L. P., Chan, S., Tan, K. H., Yap, F., Gluckman, P. D., Godfrey, K. M., Meaney, M. J., Broekman, B. F. P., Kramer, M. S., Chong, Y., & Rifkin- Graboi, A. (2019). Nutrients or nursing? Understanding how breast milk feeding affects child cognition. *European Journal of Nutrition, 59*(2), 609-619.

[166] Huang, J., Zhang, Z., Wu, Y., Wang, Y., Wang, J., Zhou, L., Ni, Z., Hao, L., Yang, N., & Yang, X. (2018). Early feeding of larger volumes of formula milk is associated with greater body weight or overweight in later infancy. *Nutrition Journal, 17*(1), 12.

Reynolds, D., Hennessy, E., & Polek, E. (2014). Is breastfeeding in infancy predictive of child mental well-being and protective against obesity at 9 years of age? *Child: Care, Health & Development, 40*(6), 882–890.
[167] Ludvigsson, J., Faresjö, Å., & Faresjö, T. (2021). Breastfeeding and cortisol in hair in children. *International Breastfeeding Journal, 16*(1).
[168] Shiraishi, M., Matsuzaki, M., Kurihara, S., Iwamoto, M., & Shimada, M. (2020). Post-breastfeeding stress response and breastfeeding self-efficacy as modifiable predictors of exclusive breastfeeding at 3 months postpartum: A prospective cohort study. *BMC Pregnancy and Childbirth, 20*(1).
[169] Centers for Disease Control and Prevention. (2023, July 31). *Why it matters.*
[170] Petroaie, A. D., Bolos, A., Slanina, A. M., Petroaie, L., & Cosmescu, A. (2020). The consequences of the postpartum depression on breastfeeding. *Bulletin of Integrative Psychiatry, 26*(1),69+.
Pope, C. J., & Mazmanian, D. (2016). Breastfeeding and postpartum depression: An overview
and methodological recommendations for future research. *Depression Research and Treatment,* 4765310.
[171] Dias, C. C., & Figueiredo, B. (2015). Breastfeeding and depression: A systematic review of the literature. *Journal of Affective Disorders, 171,* 142-154.
Figueiredo, B., Canário, C., & Field, T. (2014). Breastfeeding is negatively affected by prenatal depression and reduces postpartum depression. *Psychological Medicine, 44*(5), 927-936.
Hamdan, A., & Tamim, H. (2012). The relationship between postpartum depression and breastfeeding. *The International Journal of Psychiatry in Medicine, 43*(3), 243–259.
Mercan, Y., & Selcuk, K. T. (2021). Association between postpartum depression level, social support level and breastfeeding attitude and breastfeeding self-efficacy in early postpartum women. *PLoS ONE, 16*(4).
Mikšić, Š., Uglešić, B., Jakab, J., Holik, D., Milostić Srb, A., & Degmecić, D. (2020). Positive effect of breastfeeding on child development, anxiety, and postpartum depression. *International Journal of Environmental Research and Public Health, 17*(8), 2725.
[172] Jobst, A., Krause, D., Maiwald, C., Härtl, K., Myint, A., Kästner, R., Obermeier, M., Padberg, F., Brücklmeier, B., Weidinger, E., Kieper, S., Schwarz, M., Zill, P., & Müller, N. (2016). Oxytocin course over pregnancy and postpartum period and the association with postpartum depressive symptoms. *Archives of Women's Mental Health,* 19, 571-579.

[173] Dief, A. E., Sivukhina, E. V., & Jirikowski, G. F. (2018). Oxytocin and stress response. *Open Journal of Endocrine and Metabolic Diseases, 08*(03), 93–104.

[174] Tsai, T.-Y., Tseng, H.-H., Chi, M. H., Chang, H. H., Wu, C.-K., Yang, Y. K., & Chen, P. S. (2019). The interaction of oxytocin and social support, loneliness, and cortisol level in major depression. *Clinical Psychopharmacology and Neuroscience, 17*(4), 487–494.

Uvnäs-Moberg, K., Handlin, L., & Petersson, M. (2015). Self-soothing behaviors with particular reference to oxytocin release induced by non-noxious sensory stimulation. *Frontiers in Psychology, 5.*

[175] Hinde, K. (2016). *What we don't know about mother's milk.* Katie Hinde: What we don't know about mother's milk. https://www.ted.com/talks/katie_hinde_what_we_don_t_know_about_mother_s_milk?language=en (3:29)

[176] Andresen, E. C., Hjelkrem, A. R., Bakken, A. K., & Andersen, L. F. (2022). Environmental impact of feeding with infant formula in comparison with breastfeeding. *International Journal of Environmental Research and Public Health, 19*(11), 6397.

[177] Paris, M. (2022, July 15). Analysis | why the baby formula shortage continues in the US. The Washington Post.

[178] Smith, J.P. (2019). A commentary on the carbon footprint of milk formula: harms to planetary health and policy implications. *International Breastfeed Journal 14(49).*

[179] Joffe, N., Webster, F., & Shenker, N. (2019). Support for breastfeeding is an environmental imperative. *British Medical Journal (Online), 367.*

[180] Andresen, E. C., Hjelkrem, A. R., Bakken, A. K., & Andersen, L. F. (2022). Environmental impact of feeding with infant formula in comparison with breastfeeding. *International Journal of Environmental Research and Public Health, 19*(11), 6397.

[181] Joffe, N., Webster, F., & Shenker, N. (2019). Support for breastfeeding is an environmental imperative. *British Medical Journal (Online), 367.*

[182] Dadhich, J. P., Smith, J. P., Iellamo, A., & Suleiman, A. (2021). Climate change and infant nutrition: Estimates of greenhouse gas emissions from Milk Formula sold in selected Asia Pacific countries. *Journal of Human Lactation, 37*(2), 314–322.

[183] Dadhich, J. P., Smith, J. P., Iellamo, A., & Suleiman, A. (2021). Climate change and infant nutrition: Estimates of greenhouse gas emissions from Milk Formula sold in selected Asia Pacific countries. *Journal of Human Lactation, 37*(2), 314–322.

European Food Safety Authority. (2013, October 25). *'Growing-up' formula: No additional value to a balanced diet, says EFSA.* European Food Safety Authority.

Pomeranz, J. L., Romo Palafox, M. J., & Harris, J. L. (2018). Toddler drinks, formulas, and milks: Labeling practices and policy implications. *Preventive Medicine, 109*, 11–16.

[184] National Aeronautics and Space Administration. (2022, September 14). *The effects of climate change.* Global Climate Change.

[185] World Health Organization. (2023, August 9). *Infant feeding for the prevention of mother-to-child transmission of HIV.*

[186] Chantry, C. J., Dewey, K. G., Peerson, J. M., Wagner, E. A., & Nommsen-Rivers, L. A. (2014). In-hospital formula use increases early breastfeeding cessation among first-time mothers intending to exclusively breastfeed. *The Journal of Pediatrics, 164*(6).

Pérez-Escamilla, R., Segura-Millán, S., Canahuati, J., & Allen, H. (1996). Prelacteal feeds are negatively associated with breast-feeding outcomes in Honduras. *The Journal of Nutrition, 126*(11), 2765–2773.

[187] Flaherman, V. J., Cabana, M. D., McCulloch, C. E., & Paul, I. M. (2019). Effect of early limited formula on breastfeeding duration in the first year of life. *JAMA Pediatrics, 173*(8), 729.

[188] Grajeda Rubén, & Pérez-Escamilla Rafael. (2002). Stress during labor and delivery is associated with delayed onset of lactation among urban Guatemalan women. *The Journal of Nutrition, 132*(10), 3055–3060.

[189] Montez, Elizabeth (2022). Foundations of Lactation Center for Indigenous Midwifery.

[190] Widström, A.-M., Brimdyr, K., Svensson, K., Cadwell, K., & Nissen, E. (2020). A plausible pathway of imprinted behaviors: Skin-to-skin actions of the newborn immediately after birth follow the order of fetal development and intrauterine training of movements. *Medical Hypotheses, 134*, 109432.

[191] Chen, D. C., Nommsen-Rivers, L., Dewey, K. G., & Lönnerdal, B. (1998). Stress during labor and delivery and early lactation performance. *The American Journal of Clinical Nutrition, 68*(2), 335–344.

Dewey, K. G. (2001). Maternal and fetal stress are associated with impaired lactogenesis in humans. *The Journal of Nutrition, 131*(11).

[192] Karakoyunlu, Ö, Ejder Apay, S., & Gürol, A. (2019). The effect of pain, stress, and cortisol during labor on breastfeeding success. *Developmental Psychobiology, 61*(7), 979-987.

[193] Nakamura, Y., Walker, B. R., & Ikuta, T. (2016). Systematic review and meta-analysis reveals acutely elevated plasma cortisol following fasting but not less severe calorie restriction. *Stress, 19*(2), 151–157.

[194] Hatamleh, R., Ali, R. A., & Elian, A. I. (2019). Epidural analgesia and its effects on maternal and neonatal outcomes: a retrospective comparable study in Northern Jordan. *Evidence Based Midwifery, 17*(4), 135–142.

[195] Brimdyr, K., Cadwell, K., Widström, A. M., Svensson, K., Neumann, M., Hart, E. A., Harrington, S., & Phillips, R. (2015). The association between common labor drugs and suckling when skin-to-skin during the first hour after birth. *Birth, 42*(4), 319–328.

Riordan, J., Gross, A., Angeron, J., Krumwiede, B., & Melin, J. (2000). The effect of labor pain relief medication on neonatal suckling and breastfeeding duration. *Journal of Human Lactation, 16*(1), 7–12.

[196] Lavin, D. (2001). Focal point on breastfeeding: Improving breastfeeding outcomes. *International Journal of Childbirth Education, 16*(3), 27-33.

[197] Uvnäs-Moberg, K., Ekström-Bergström, A., Buckley, S., Massarotti, C., Pajalic, Z., Luegmair, K., Kotlowska, A., Lengler, L., Olza, I., Grylka-Baeschlin, S., Leahy-Warren, P., Hadjigeorgiu, E., Villarmea, S., & Dencker, A. (2020). Maternal plasma levels of oxytocin during breastfeeding—a systematic review. *PLOS ONE, 15*(8).

Uvnäs-Moberg, K., & Prime, D. K. (2013). Oxytocin effects in mothers and infants during breastfeeding. *Infant, 9*(6), 201–206.

Walter, M. H., Abele, H., & Plappert, C. F. (2021). The role of oxytocin and the effect of stress during childbirth: Neurobiological Basics and implications for mother and child. *Frontiers in Endocrinology, 12.*

[198] Andrew, M. S., Selvaratnam, R. J., Davies-Tuck, M., Howland, K., & Davey, M.-A. (2022). The association between intrapartum interventions and immediate and ongoing breastfeeding outcomes: an Australian retrospective population-based cohort study. *International Breastfeeding Journal, 17*(1), 1–10.

[199] Hobbs, A. J., Mannion, C. A., McDonald, S. W., Brockway, M., & Tough, S. C. (2016). The impact of caesarean section on breastfeeding initiation, duration and difficulties in the first four months postpartum. *BMC Pregnancy and Childbirth, 16*(1).

Gomes, M., Trocado, V., Carlos-Alves, M., Arteiro, D., & Pinheiro, P. (2018). Intrapartum synthetic oxytocin and breastfeeding: a retrospective cohort study. *The Journal of the Institute of Obstetrics and Gynaecology, 38*(6), 745–749.

[200] Bourdillon, K., McCausland, T., & Jones, S. (2020). The impact of birth-related injury and pain on breastfeeding outcomes. *British Journal of Midwifery, 28*(1), 52-61.

[201] Karakoyunlu, Ö, Ejder Apay, S., & Gürol, A. (2019). The effect of pain, stress, and cortisol during labor on breastfeeding success. *Developmental Psychobiology, 61*(7), 979-987.

[202] Breastfeeding during pregnancy. HSE.ie. (2022, August 20).

[203] Breastfeeding while pregnant. American Pregnancy Association. (2023, November 25).

[204] Ballesta-Castillejos, A., Gomez-Salgado, J., Rodriguez-Almagro, J., et al. (2020). Relationship between maternal body mass index with the onset of breastfeeding and its associated problems: an online survey. *International Breastfeed Journal 15*(55).

[205] Brown, A., Rance, J., & Warren, L. (2015). Body image concerns during pregnancy are associated with a shorter breastfeeding duration. *Midwifery, 31*(1), 80–89.

[206] Swanson, V., Keely, A., & Denison, F. C. (2017). Does body image influence the relationship between body weight and breastfeeding maintenance in new mothers? *British Journal of Health Psychology, 22*(3), 557–576.

[207] Jawed-Wessel, S. (2016). The lies we tell pregnant women [Video]. TED Conferences. https://www.ted.com/talks/sofia_jawed_wessel_the_lies_we_tell_pregnant_women

[208] American Psychological Association, Task Force on the Sexualization of Girls. (2007). Report of the APA Task Force on the Sexualization of Girls. American Psychological Association.

[209] Ballesta-Castillejos, A., Gomez-Salgado, J., Rodriguez-Almagro, J., et al. (2020). Relationship between maternal body mass index with the onset of breastfeeding and its associated problems: an online survey. *International Breastfeed Journal 15*(55).

[210] Groleau, D., Pizarro, K. W., Molino, L., Gray-Donald, K., & Semenic, S. (2017). Empowering women to breastfeed: Does the Baby Friendly Initiative make a difference? *Maternal & Child Nutrition, 13*(4).

[211] Rodgers, R. F., O'Flynn, J. L., Bourdeau, A., & Zimmerman, E. (2018). A biopsychosocial model of body image, disordered eating, and breastfeeding among postpartum women. *Appetite, 126*, 163–168.

[212] Weis, N. (Director), & Allain, S. (Producer). (2015). *Milk* [Film]. Filmblanc.

[213] American Psychological Association. (n.d.). Food advertising and children's health.

[214] Bartick, M., & Reinhold, A. (2010). The burden of suboptimal breastfeeding in the United States: a pediatric cost analysis. *Pediatrics, 125*(5), e1048-e1056.

U.S. Breastfeeding Committee. (2019). Breastfeeding saves dollars and makes sense.

[215] Centers for Disease Control and Prevention. (2024a). *Breastfeeding report card.*

[216] Centers for Disease Control and Prevention. (2022b). *Adult Obesity Facts.*

Huang, J., Zhang, Z., Wu, Y., Wang, Y., Wang, J., Zhou, L., Ni, Z., Hao, L., Yang, N., & Yang, X. (2018). Early feeding of larger volumes of formula milk is associated with greater body weight or overweight in later infancy. *Nutrition Journal, 17*(1), 12.

Reynolds, D., Hennessy, E., & Polek, E. (2014). Is breastfeeding in infancy predictive of child mental well-being and protective against obesity at 9 years of age? *Child: Care, Health & Development, 40*(6), 882–890.

Wood, C. T., Witt, W. P., Skinner, A. C., Yin, H. S., Rothman, R. L., Sanders, L. M., Delamater, A. M., Flower, K. B., Kay, M. C., & Perrin, E. M. (2021). Effects of breastfeeding, formula feeding, and complementary feeding on rapid weight gain in the first year of life. Academic Pediatrics, 21(2), 288–296.

Wu, Y., Lye, S., Dennis, C.-L., & Briollais, L. (2020). Exclusive breastfeeding can attenuate body-mass-index increase among genetically susceptible children: A longitudinal study from the ALSPAC cohort. *PLoS Genetics, 16*(6), 1–14.

[217] Cawley, J., Biener, A., Meyerhoefer, C., Ding, Y., Zvenyach, T., Smolarz, B. G., & Ramasamy, A. (2021). Direct medical costs of obesity in the United States and the most populous states. *Journal of Managed Care & Specialty Pharmacy, 27*(3), 354–366.

[218] National Cancer Institute. (2021, July). *Financial burden of cancer care.* Financial Burden of Cancer Care.

[219] Luca, D. L., Margiotta, C., Staatz, C., Garlow, E., Christensen, A., & Zivin, K. (2020). Financial toll of untreated perinatal mood and anxiety disorders among 2017 births in the United States. *American Journal of Public Health, 110*(6), 888–896.

[220] Boyd, C. (2012). The Nestlé Infant Formula Controversy and a Strange Web of Subsequent Business Scandals. *Journal of Business Ethics, 106*(3), 283–293.

[221] Weis, N. (Director), & Allain, S. (Producer). (2015). *Milk* [Film]. Filmblanc.

[222] Lennon, K. (2019). "Feminist Perspectives on the Body", The Stanford Encyclopedia of Philosophy (Fall 2019 Edition), Edward N. Zalta (ed.), https://plato.stanford.edu/archives/fall2019/entries/feminist-body

[223] Gallagher, A., Kring, D., & Whitley, T. (2020). Effects of Yoga on anxiety and depression for high risk mothers on hospital bedrest. Complementary Therapies in Clinical Practice, 38.

[224] Ariel-Donges, A. H., Gordon, E. L., Bauman, V., & Perri, M. G. (2019). Does Yoga help college-aged women with body-image dissatisfaction feel better about their bodies? *Sex Roles: A Journal of Research, 80*(1–2), 41.

[225] Schnell, A. (2020, March 23). Breastfeeding without giving birth. La Leche League International.
World Health Organization. (2023, August 9). Donor human milk for low-birth-weight infants. World Health Organization.
[226] World Health Organization. (2023, August 9). Donor human milk for low-birth-weight infants. World Health Organization.
[227] Pratchett, T. (2004). *A hat full of sky*. Doubleday.
[228] Montell, Amanda. Word Slut: A Feminist Guide to Taking Back the English Language. Harper Wave, 2019.
[229] Wilcox, A. J., Dunson, D., & Baird, D. D. (2000). The timing of the "fertile window" in the menstrual cycle: day specific estimates from a prospective study. *BMJ (Clinical research ed.)*, 321(7271), 1259–1262.